Daredevil at the Wheel

DAREDEVIL AT THE WHEEL
The Climb and Crash of Joan LaCosta

TONY ST. CLAIR

FORWARD BY AIME ALLEY CARD

Essex, Connecticut

An imprint of The Globe Pequot Publishing Group, Inc.
64 South Main Street
Essex, CT 06426
www.globepequot.com

Distributed by NATIONAL BOOK NETWORK

British Library Cataloguing in Publication Information available

Library of Congress Cataloging-in-Publication Data available

ISBN 9781493087464 (cloth : alk. paper) | ISBN 9781493087471 (epub)

∞™ The paper used in this publication meets the minimum requirements of American National Standard for Information Sciences—Permanence of Paper for Printed Library Materials, ANSI/ NISO Z39.48-1992.

For Kate, my North Star

Contents

FOREWORD

Coming of age in the 1980s, I was left a little wild, as many in my generation were, due more to a sort of benign neglect than to any lack of boundaries. I could barely reach the wheel the first time my dad let me sit on his lap in the driver's seat, steering my way up the street while his feet controlled the pedals of our family Wagoneer, the kind with the woody panels.

I was 16 when I finally got my driver's license and my first taste of independence. Windows down, radio turned up, a foot a little too heavy on the gas, I zoomed around Nashville. The possibilities were endless.

That sense of freedom along with an imagination born from countless long and unstructured days created a fascination with stories that thrill and entertain. The most compelling stories of my youth were of the inspirational sports variety, like *The Natural*, *A League of Her Own*, and *The Karate Kid*—the underdog that defies expectations, never taking no for an answer, and the ever-winning combination of breathtaking action and so much heart.

As I have grown, I have discovered that truth is in fact stranger than fiction, and for every made-up story, there are 100 true stories just waiting to be uncovered. Tony St. Clair has found one of these stories, about long-forgotten race car driver Joan LaCosta—a woman who lived life to the hilt and deserves her time back in the spotlight.

St. Clair sets the scene with a slick promoter who fabricated a story meant to pack stadiums with the kind of spectators drawn to notoriously reckless drivers swerving and swishing their tin can cars around a muddy track. The stakes were amped up even further when Joan LaCosta, the new darling of the track, promised to take on the male drivers. Wild and wily, the young thrill seeker created a spectacle that the Roaring Twenties of North America couldn't get enough of. St. Clair deftly captures the scene on the page, describing the way the sand and salt pricked the face of Joan LaCosta as her body and car flew across Daytona Beach at speeds never before believed possible by anyone, much less by a wisp of a woman.

Women in sports are gaining more attention in this cultural moment but have always wanted to participate, many having to fight to gain entry, sometimes accepting the role of the spectacle simply for the opportunity to compete. Joan LaCosta's ever-evolving identity began with a spirit that carried through her life—the spirit of a restless soul chasing excitement and opportunity and refusing to be caged by societal expectations.

Writing a deeply researched nonfiction narrative about overlooked historical figures is a passion and a privilege. The hours, days, months, and years of tireless research, digging through obscure archives and sifting through decades of information for relevant context to bring these figures to life, takes a relentless drive and an unflinching belief that untold stories matter in the world. I spent my time immersed with women racing by foot and Tony St. Clair with women racing by car, but both our books show women refusing to be held back and determined to prove beyond a shadow of a doubt exactly what they were capable of—and it was extraordinary.

For many of us, sports of any form are as essential a part of our human experience as the air we breathe, and the legends that form around the heroes on field, turf, or track can endure well beyond their lifetimes. The glory those competitors are chasing can also be fleeting, which in the racing world compelled the drivers toward more and more dangerous attempts to break the next record and amaze the next audience. The drivers were keenly aware that their livelihoods depended on filling the stadiums and putting on a show, causing an escalating series of stunts that often ended in tragedy.

It took a certain kind of person to zoom around the track at breakneck speed inside an open-roof, bare-boned automobile and set land speed records across hard-packed sand behind a flaming engine. The stakes could not be higher, and as St. Clair shows us, Joan LaCosta seemed to thrive within that risk.

Framed by the high-rolling world of cutting-edge sporting, speak-easies, and Hollywood, with the looming sense of the coming collapse both on and off the racetrack, Tony St. Clair gives us an inside look at the early world of racing and a woman who was regularly competing with and clocking times that were better than the boys.

Jump in and enjoy the ride!

Aime Alley Card
Author of *The Tigerbelles: Olympic Legends from Tennessee State*

CHAPTER ONE

The Fastest Woman in the World

At noon on Thursday, October 3, 1929, at the lakefront Chicago Beach Hotel, a woman knocked at the door of Apartment 802. It was her second visit to the apartment. The day before, she had screwed up her courage just enough to make it to the eighth floor, but her nerve had deserted her after she hesitantly knocked on the door, and she had fled in a panic. This time, there was no turning back.

The hotel was a landmark resort and residential building in the prestigious Hyde Park area in the southern part of the city. The amenities were lavish, with 600 elegantly appointed rooms, all with an unobstructed view of Lake Michigan. There was a 400-foot front veranda, featuring tip-top service from one of the finest restaurants in the city. It had a ballroom for dancing and events, a radio station transmitter, a house orchestra, and a convertible tennis court/ice skating rink. The Chicago Beach Hotel was widely recognized as one of the top resorts in the world.

It was a beautiful seasonal destination, but by this time of year, the cool autumn air and the crisp breeze off Lake Michigan had emptied the hotel beach of vacationers and given notice that summer was officially over. The empty hallways, lack of cigarette smoke, and open dinner reservations hurtled the hotel into its chilly slow season.

The country was entering a similar season; it just didn't know it yet. People were still dancing, still popping champagne corks. Filmmakers continued to release movies filled with optimism and joy. *On with the Show!*, the first all-color full-length talkie, heralded the start of the lavish

Technicolor movie musical era. It reinforced the public consensus that the country was still in an upward arc.

But in August, the warnings of an oncoming recession whispered in small towns and large cities and across the Great Plains. Auto and house sales declined, as did steel production. Easy credit had inflated personal debt, which was reaching dangerous levels. In September, the stock market hit a record high that it would not see again for 25 years. Later that month, the London Stock Exchange collapsed, and 24 million pounds of value was wiped out. American investors started to lose confidence in foreign investments.

By the end of October, it would all come crashing down at home.

The knock at the door surprised Mrs. Rebecca Bobbe. Guests usually rang from the downstairs desk that they were arriving or at least gave some prior notice, and Mrs. Bobbe didn't recall ordering any service from the dining hall. Her husband, Joseph, wasn't at home. Draped in $20,000 of jewelry in anticipation of dinner service in a few hours, she went to the door and cautiously opened it.

In front of her stood a slim, haggard-looking young woman in a light-tan overcoat with a turned-up collar. A sporty hat covered her chestnut hair. She held what appeared to be a small pistol in one hand and a chloroformed cotton rag in the other.

"Don't scream or make a noise and you'll be safe,"[1] the trembling woman said.

Mrs. Bobbe could see the assailant was desperate, but somehow, the shaking hands and pained eyes of the thin woman didn't evoke danger. Bobbe resisted.

The two women struggled. The robber lashed out, fighting with a surprising fury, and with a wild blow she blackened Mrs. Bobbe's eye. Bobbe's maid heard the shouts and rushed to the entranceway from the other room. All three struggled to the floor, and Mrs. Bobbe and her maid were able to restrain the attacker. Other residents passing by in the hallway saw the commotion and raised the alarm, and hotel security quickly apprehended the now-docile thief. Her aggression melted away immediately.

When the police arrived, they sized up the assailant. She was slight in frame, but her arms were strong and tight, like boat ropes; they seemed out of place on the petite woman. Her flashing eyes weren't flat and hard like one might imagine a career criminal's; they were soft shimmering, bright-gray pools, like polished gunmetal. She was taken downtown to the police station, booked into custody, and held in lieu of $25,000 bail.

The woman carried no identification but eventually volunteered to the police that she had been in Chicago for only the past three days after leaving Toronto. Her name was Josephine Rust, of Alabama. Her husband, Thomas, a Canadian bootlegger racketeer, had forced her to commit the robbery. With her plaintive eyes and soft Southern accent, the police quickly grew sympathetic to her, dubbing her "the sweet girl graduate of the rackets." Sargent Egan of the Chicago Police admitted, "She's one of the nicest girls I ever saw . . . and a slick one."[2]

This unlikely yarn from the slick-talking Southern girl about being bamboozled by a Canadian ne'er-do-well only fueled the lead detective's skepticism. After two and a half days of continuous questioning and the constant evaporation of the multiple stories that poured out from the "poised, song-voiced"[3] suspect, the truth finally came out. The now-sobbing woman in the detective's office wasn't the victim of a feared booze kingpin, browbeaten into committing an armed holdup. She wasn't even Josephine Rust.

Her name was Joan LaCosta, and she was the most famous female race car driver in the country.

* * *

Before LaCosta became a nationwide racing celebrity, she was born Marion Carver in Kentucky on May 11, 1901. Her parents, William and Nora Carver, raised Marion and her younger sister, Jeanette Helen, in Paducah, a transportation hub at the confluence of the Ohio and Tennessee rivers, not far from the Mississippi. She never lost the soft lilt of her Southern upbringing. Marion was the name her father had wanted to give his first son (the boy he never had) and instead gave it to his first daughter, keeping the typically male spelling. The masculine moniker

Figure 1.1. Joan LaCosta posing behind the wheel.
ATLANTA JOURNAL. IMAGE ENHANCED FOR CLARITY BY ADELIS SEGUNDO BRICEÑO.

suited her well. She grew up as a rough-and-tumble tomboy who learned to drive the family car at age 12 and rode motorcycles in her teens.

As a child, she would walk by the Nashville, Chattanooga and St. Louis Railway train cars as they swayed on the tracks, slowly creeping through town, hauling loads of coal to the boats that carried that coal to the rest of the country. Children would pick up rocks and toss them on a passing open car heaped with the black ore, sending the smooth pebbles from quiet Kentucky to the big cities up north.

William Carver was a stonecutter and a hardworking laborer, noted for his taciturn expression and conservative attitude. His sober personality matched his profession as a careful and successful carver of marble and granite memorials. In December 1901, six months after Marion's birth, he put a paid announcement in the local *Paducah News-Democrat* newspaper advertising the opening of his "New Marble Shop"[4] on

1308 Trimble Street, conveniently located just three blocks from the Oak Grove Cemetery. Marion grew up walking through that graveyard, staring at the beautiful engraved headstones of folks from her town (some of those memorials carved by her father), reading the "born" and "died" bookends of the lives of the small-town Kentuckians. So many of the stones simply read, "Loving Daughter, and Loved Mother," an entire life in a few words.

The summers in Kentucky were muggy and hot. Mornings brought a misty haze that floated over the strawberry fields, and the heated afternoons warmed the Ohio River. Marion swam in the slow waters that wound along Paducah and walked barefoot to and from the beach, singing along with the cicadas. That green-eyed chorus of bugs emerged in June, waking from their slumber and crawling from their loamy beds for a few weeks of summer exultation, thrumming the air, males croaking for a mate, searching to pair off with another dewy partner. They then laid their brood in the soft earth for another year, tucked in with the oak and maple tree roots.

The first crisp crack of the September autumn air was a farewell to the cicada. The Ohio River shrank to its seasonal ebb, the fescue grass came alive again, and the quiet Kentucky fall signaled the start of the school year for Marion. Her daily attention now leaned to books, music, and silent pictures.

The movie theaters were an exciting new portal for the child's imagination. In 1910, there were more than 7,000 theaters across the country, around 500 in Chicago alone. The Wallace Theater and Casino was the favorite spot in Paducah to see the latest films. The movies were still crude, with rudimentary special effects, and featured far more gaudy action scenes than plot twists. But the impact of the screen was stupendous. The new moving picture medium closed down vaudeville venues faster than the automobile killed the horse and buggy. And almost every week, a new actor or actress graced the entertainment pages of the papers.

Marion saw the public rise of Lillian Gish, Charlie Chaplin, Gloria Swanson, and Rudolph Valentino, each one a singular star in the film firmament. And one night in January 1910, after the theaters had closed for the evening, she saw an actual wonder of the skies.

Halley's Comet was expected to return to view that spring. The legendary comet was the first one discovered to have a predictable orbit, visiting this world approximately every 76 years. In early 1910, astronomers saw the comet heading toward Earth and announced that a spectacular night show was due to arrive in May.

In an amazing coincidence, in January 1910, a different, mystery comet appeared in the Southern sky. It was first visible in Paducah on Sunday evening, right after dusk on January 24 and for several days after that. It was extremely bright from some viewpoints in the world, possibly the brightest comet of the century. Many hastily assumed it was Halley's Comet.

Instead, it was one of those exceedingly rare, long-orbit visitors that had last been seen in the night sky 9,200 years ago, when the walls of Jericho were crumbling, and that no human alive would see again. There were famous recurring comets like Halley's, and then there were these fantastic, once-in-every-several-millennia occurrences like this one, the spectacular "Great Daylight Comet."[5]

Some believe that heavenly bodies have influence over people's destinies. In 1910, the year of the comet, Marion's father made the momentous decision to leave Kentucky, hoping to make a better and more prosperous life for his family. Paducah was a beautiful small town, but the opportunities of a bigger city and a larger customer pool made financial sense. In 1911, he chose Tennessee. William Carver became a partner in the Memphis Marble & Granite Works and built up the business rapidly.

His no-nonsense attitude carried over from his work to his homelife. He bought a house on Bullington Avenue, a rough middle-class neighborhood with its share of colorful characters. The churchgoing Mr. Carver never backed down in the face of anyone breaking the Lord's Commandments, and Marion witnessed her father in action often.

In one instance, on a muggy Saturday night in July 1913, the Carver family was bedding down to sleep when 22-year-old Ruth King staggered down the street that ran in front of their home. She was loudly complaining about her three-day-old marriage to a local man by the name of T. J. Kelly and drowning out the creek frogs with her screaming epithets. Carver was incensed. He stormed outside and confronted her,

Figure 1.2. The Great Daylight Comet of 1910, pictured from the Lowell Observatory on January 28 in Flagstaff, Arizona.

LOWELL OBSERVATORY.

then went to the police station and filed a complaint. She was apprehended the next day on the warrant. Her policeman husband and a local saloon owner paid her bail, but unfortunately, it didn't quiet her or the neighborhood for long.

After years of similar adventures, including one that involved Carver and three other men chasing down and apprehending a couple of armed robbers near the Calvary Cemetery, the family moved and built a house at 1748 Glenview Place in a more upscale neighborhood.

Mr. Carver's increasing financial success provided young Marion the opportunities to showcase her creative potential. She loved music and took private piano lessons at a small Memphis studio run by Lillian Fraser Payne.

On Thursday, June 6, at 8:00 in the evening, Marion stood offstage at Houck's Concert Hall, staring at the audience with her friend Opal Bender. Miss Payne addressed the crowd (made up mostly of parents and friends) and announced the names of the first two pianists to take the stage. Marion and Opal looked at each other nervously; both were leading off the recital. As the lights dimmed, the pair stepped to the dais and took their seats at the piano. With a nod from the instructor, Marion, who was playing first chair, launched into a rousing rendition of "Charge of the Uhlans."

The atmosphere was electric. Being the center of attention was a natural environment for Marion, and she came alive when every eye in the house was focused on her and her talent. It was an auspicious debut for the young Kentucky transplant. There were a few more musical interludes from other students, then it was Marion's turn again. She rushed to get back onstage for her second performance, this time playing a solo piece by Paul Wachs, "In the Swing." It was here in the spotlight that the dark features of young Marion became fully illuminated. After that moment, for the rest of her life, she would switch into "performance mode" whenever she was in a public setting, and she showed no fear, no hesitation. As long as she was perched center stage, she was magnetic.

Marion's outer confidence belied the nervous child inside. She wouldn't back down from a scrap, but she was more than a little afraid of thunderstorms and mice. Tornados weren't rare around the Memphis area, and a particularly violent series of twisters tore through the South in early June 1916, killing more than 100 people, two-thirds of them in neighboring Arkansas. Images of destruction and grief plastered the papers. Marion never forgot about the loss and devastation so close to home.

But the possibility of danger didn't curb her predilection for excitement. She quickly evolved into a teenage version of *The Perils of Pauline*.

The Perils of Pauline was a 20-part serial that played on nearly every movie screen in the country in 1914. It was the iconic cliff-hanger series, and each chapter highlighted another death-defying episode that put Pauline (actress Pearl White) in palm-sweating danger. Whether she was under attack by "Indians," submarines, airplanes, or counterfeiters, she somehow always managed to escape by mere inches thanks to her heretofore hidden talents of piloting, swimming, or fighting.

In episode 15, Pauline tackles the new world of race car driving. The opening scene shows Pauline at home, sitting in a comfortable living room chair, when a note arrives. She eagerly tears open the envelope, revealing an invitation to a racing engagement sponsored by the International Motor Car Association. Despite the scoffing of the men of the house, Pauline and her copilot take on the evil nemesis, named Ferrari (years before the real-life Ferrari became a racing legend).

Avoiding the metal tacks scattered across the racetrack and overcoming the dirty tactics of Ferrari, Pauline finally triumphs, driving first across the finish line and promising to give her winnings to the underprivileged, thanks to the IMCA race sponsors.

Marion was the target audience for these thrillers. She was driving cars and riding motorcycles around the dirt roads of Memphis as a teen in 1914, and she was always pushing for more excitement, more danger.

This passion for racing was stoked by the Tri-State Fair held in Memphis. In 1914, an ambitious young promoter by the name of J. Alex Sloan approached the secretary of the fair, Frank Fuller, and pitched an idea. Sloan was putting together a circuit of dirt racetracks for automobiles across the country, and he thought Memphis was a perfect fit. The planning board was eventually swayed, and a one-day event was scheduled. The response was so positive that the fair committee made it an annual event. The next year in 1915, the October 4 and 5 races were trumpeted throughout the Tennessee media, with the *Commercial Appeal* printing the press notes from the promoter Sloan in its September 26 edition:

> Secretary Frank Fuller of the Tri-State Fair has set aside Monday and Tuesday, October 4 and 5, as automobile race days and has secured the entries of Louis Disbrow, Eddie Hearne, Bill Endicott, Tommy Milton, Joe Bianchi, George Clark, Louie LeCocq, Howard Kizer, Sig Haugdahl and other stars of the gasoline competition game. . . . A special match race for an additional purse of $1,000 has been arranged by Secretary Fuller between Mrs. Elfrieda Mais, champion woman driver of the United States, and Miss Bunny Thornton, Europe's premiere woman auto race pilot.

A certain fourteen-year-old tomboy with a passion for speed was getting one of the best presents of her life, and it cost only a 10-cent ticket.

Around that time, a barnstorming pilot had come through the area, and Marion yearned for a ride in the two-seater plane. She watched the plane swirl and swoop several hundred feet above the Memphis dirt, and she told herself that one day, it would be her up there flying, swinging through the low white clouds. It inspired her to join a birdhouse-making class at Memphis Vocational School, and she was pictured in the local paper proudly holding her creation.

While attending Vocational, she fell in love with a financially well-off young man, Percy Huddleston, who had graduated from Oakland Avenue school a few years earlier, and she became pregnant. They married when Marion was just 16.

Marion drove the family car at 12, played piano for audiences at 14, and built birdhouses at 15, an almost idyllic life of a teenager. But she dropped out of school with a baby a year later, and when her teen hijinks gave way to parenthood, she saw her epitaph being carved.

The young couple gave their daughter the same masculine moniker that the mother wore with pride. Born on June 23, 1917, her parents named her Marion June (her daughter went by her middle name June all of her life). The youngster was nearly a carbon copy of her mother, taking on both her looks and her impulsive temperament.

Figure 1.3. Marion Carver (fifth from the left) pictured with her class in the *Commercial Appeal* on May 7, 1916.

COMMERCIAL APPEAL. IMAGE ENHANCED FOR CLARITY BY ADELIS SEGUNDO BRICEÑO.

She loved and cherished June with all of her heart, but Marion was the rebellious daughter of a taciturn stonecutter, and she fought hard against the stereotypical role of a young mother in the Deep South. Even a move farther north with Percy to the bustling city of Hammond, Indiana, a hub for auto and train manufacturing, wasn't enough of a lifestyle change for Marion. The excitement of big-city life pulled at her. She stood in her yard, looking at the clouds floating by every day on their way to somewhere else, and she anguished.

She tried to stay home, be the dutiful wife and mother, and cook and mend. She loathed the household tasks that her younger sister Helen seemed to love. She resisted the constant yearning for adventure and restrained herself daily. Until one day she couldn't. At 19, Marion divorced Percy and took up with her husband's former car mechanic, a swaggering hot rod driver named Walter Martins. He wasn't handsome, but he brightened his craggy, rough looks with a cocky grin. He was the son of German immigrants, and he was single-minded, tough, and charismatic. Like Marion, he had big ambitions, bigger than Tennessee could fulfill. They fell for each other hard and tied the knot in Memphis on the most romantic day possible, February 14, St. Valentine's Day, 1921.

Walter knew that he had better automotive employment opportunities in Chicago, where the big racetracks and car factories were. He had worked there the previous year, so he and Marion moved to the big city. Her family and her ex-husband agreed to keep four-year-old June with them in Memphis, perhaps assuming Marion might change her mind and return home at any time or maybe bring her daughter up to Chicago when she and Walter were finally settled in.

With kisses and promises, Marion and Walter packed up the Ford and headed to the Midwest and left June back home with her grandparents and Percy (who relocated back to Memphis).

Chicago was an exciting and growing metropolis that attracted artists, musicians, and other creators from around the country. There were nearly 3 million people living in the area when the pair arrived, and the vitality of the city was an irresistible lure for the young couple fresh from Tennessee. Walter Martins immediately gravitated toward the racing world. He had a natural knack for the dusty, red clay tracks, and it was only a few years before he gained fame as a skilled driver on the dirt courses.

Marion had less success finding her way. Having few technical skills but more than her fair share of charisma and musical talent, she became a model and dancer. "Modeling" in 1921 was sometimes posing for an artist, being a burlesque performer, or acting out seminude "tasteful" art tableaux onstage. One of the longest-running revues in Chicago in the 1920s was called "Artists and Models"[6] and featured comely women re-creating famous nude paintings and sculptures onstage.

Marion had many advantages in the entertainment industry. She was a singer and could dance and play the piano. She was often described by others as beautiful. One witness said of her, "She is slight and well-formed, and beautiful of face. . . . She talks with the soft accent of a southerner . . . she has bobbed hair, and dark eyes and small face; fine features, a strong chin and high cheekbones."[7]

In 1922, while walking by the lake with some friends from Northwestern University, Joan spied a barnstorming pilot giving rides for what seemed like an exorbitant price: $25 for 15 minutes.

Her friends tried valiantly to dissuade her from going up, telling her of the dangers and the condition of the rickety old Jenny plane. Marion wouldn't be deterred. She begged them to join her. They shook their heads, and Marion crawled into the plane by herself.

The feeling was unlike anything she'd experienced. The whistling of the warm air vibrated through her bones, and the powerful surge of adrenaline that afternoon forever colored her personality. She felt like a bird, free and floating and untethered to Earth. The only sensation that rivaled it was when she was 17, handling the wild bucking of a Model T Ford tearing along Pigeon Roost Road in the late summer evening, the soft orange light filtering through the Memphis dust. She couldn't wait to tell Walter.

He wasn't encouraging.

Walter Martins began racing regularly at the Roby Speedway, built in 1920 in Hammond. It's the only city in Indiana that borders Chicago. The one-mile oval was built parallel to State Line Road, and the track's backstretch ran about 100 feet east of the Illinois–Indiana border.

It was home to some of the most exciting drivers in the country, racing legends like Wilbur Shaw and Dutch Baumann. And after thousands of dollars of upgrades, it became faster, more deadly, and, paradoxically, more popular. It recorded its first death early in its history when Rance Olds flipped his car over into a ditch during a qualifying lap. Even more people bought tickets when the news hit the papers. It was this phenomenon of huge crowds of fans being drawn in by the carnage and danger that soon caught the attention of several promoters who then decided to try their hand in selling this fast-rising sport.

The tracks were as crude as the sport was. There were no car crumple zones and antilock brake systems—just the reflexes and steely nerve of men who gambled their lives for a few hundred bucks a month. The race cars were small, one-seaters, with no doors and little else to keep you in the seat in case of a collision. The steering wheel was huge, 17 inches, because power steering didn't exist, and the bigger the wheel, the more turning leverage was available. It took strong arms and an iron grip to hang on to the smooth, unpadded wheel as the car shook and groaned around the corners at speed. The steering wheels were made of wood, often maple or walnut, that would require driving gloves for grip (and to prevent splinters). Tommy Milton had the bottom third of the wheel cut off in his H.C.S. Miller Special roadster because the cockpit was so tight that he had trouble getting in and out.

In the rain, the wooden wheels were slick and cold, and in the heat, they were sticky and hot, and you also had to control the speed of the car with a hand accelerator lever inside the spokes. The instrument gauges were rudimentary: oil pressure, a speedometer, and a 4,000-rpm tachometer. The smell of varnish and fuel wafting from the engine and leaking

Figure 1.4. Tommy Milton in his racing whites shows off his custom half steering wheel in the *Boston Globe* of Boston, Massachusetts, on May 31, 1923.
BOSTON GLOBE. IMAGE ENHANCED FOR CLARITY BY ADELIS SEGUNDO BRICEÑO.

through the wooden firewall at the front of the car reminded the driver at all times of their exposure to death. There was no such thing as a fireproof suit, and racing goggles wouldn't keep a stone pitched up from the race car in front of them from shattering the lens or their eyes.

Tommy Milton, one of the pioneer legends of the sport and first two-time winner of the Indianapolis 500, gave one of the best descriptions of the experience of running on the small backwoods tracks in an interview with the *Fort Wayne Sentinel* of Indiana on March 6, 1920:

> At first I wondered how on earth any driver could drive at full speed on a dirt track. It seemed impossible. The dirt and gravel fly like hail, and the dust cloud is so thick sometimes that it's like driving in the thickest, densest fog you ever saw. You can't see anything but a flash of the fence now and then, and you have to take the turns by intuition more than by sight. But after a while you develop a sort of sixth sense of location, and tear through everything as if the track was clear.[8]

One of the greatest drivers ever, Milton averaged one accident per year on the race circuit during his career. He also made it plain, in his own words, what his worst nightmare was when it came to driving because it happened to him:

Figure 1.5. Early 1920s Ford Frontenac racing model, pictured in the 1925 Chevrolet Brothers Frontenac Speed Catalog.
1925 CHEVROLET BROTHERS FRONTENAC SPEED CATALOG.

[I was in] a 200 lap race. At 190 laps I had a three lap lead and was going nicely when my gasoline feed pipe broke. It was a copper pipe—we use flexible tubing now—and it crystallized and broke, although I had annealed it several times. There was air pressure enough in the tank to force that gasoline out at the rate of five gallons a minute. I knew there was a tremendous burst of flame right on me. The hollow body of the car acted like a flue, the wind pressure driving the fire through it and back on me. I was going over 100 miles an hour. A burning car is the worst thing that can happen to a racing driver. There's no escape. You can't jump out at that speed, and you can't stop, and a few seconds in that blaze will burn you to a crisp. For an instant I was literally in a hell of fire, caught and being done to a turn. Then a thought flashed through my mind that if the car was only going backward the flame would blow away from me. I was in an agony to escape the fire, and I'll always believe my action then was the quickest and best of my life. Probably in ninety-nine emergencies out of a hundred I wouldn't think as quickly or as clearly again. You know how a car will skid and turn around on a wet street if you turn the front wheels and put on the brakes at the same time. It will skid the same way anywhere if it's going fast enough, or turn over. Your touring car there would turn over, but a Duesenberg racer is built low and is hard to upset. I stamped on the brake, and reached through the fire and yanked the steering wheel, and she skidded and swung, and in an instant there I was with the car rolling down the track backward and the fire blowing away from me. But I was terribly burned. My legs were under the body and got the worst burning. Nine weeks in a hospital and a lot of skin grafting after that, and I was out of racing for the rest of the season. . . . I'm driving the same Duesenberg car in my races now—that is, most of it. The fire melted the body.[9]

Fire and smoke, dust and gravel, injury and death. Racing wasn't for the weak or the fearful. It took a special kind of courage and, perhaps, naivete to get behind the wheel with only a thin shell of steel to protect you from the flames and the wrecks and to drive faster than the speedometer numbers could display. In the early 1920s, very few men had the nerve to risk their lives in such a deadly sport for just a little cash, but now a handful of brave women were ready for the same chance at glory or death.

In the early part of the century, young men would hang out at local garages trading tips on hopping up their engines, set up match races between each other, and learn to drive their stripped-down Fords and Chevrolets at top speeds on rudimentary tracks and courses. Marion could get behind the wheel of the family sedan as a teen, but young women were discouraged from taking the same risks (and getting the same thrills) as the young men.

The best women drivers had the advantage of being part of the industry before they started racing on their own. Joan LaCosta, Elfrieda Mais, and Mrs. O. G. Temme were all married to race car veterans. When Joan went to the Hammond Racetrack to watch Walter tear around the course, she memorized the lines he took into the bends, the position he took when he was following or leading in the race, and the differences that the acceleration made when the track was dry or muddy.

When they drove the Ford home after the races, Marion would pepper Walter with questions. Where did you hold the hand accelerator on the curves? What oil pressure should the engine be at? What do you do when the brakes lock up?

Walter didn't like it. And he wouldn't let Marion touch his number 13 Ford. If she wanted to get on the track, it wasn't going to be in his pride and joy. Marion could only watch as her husband raced around the Roby track, imagining herself behind the wheel.

* * *

During the summer of 1923, the auto sport movie *Racing Hearts* debuted in theaters throughout the country. Agnes Ayres, the lead actress, was a local girl originally from Illinois (she attended Austin High School) who got her start as a movie extra at the old Essanay Studios in Chicago. She moved to Hollywood and made a huge splash in the Rudolph Valentino movie *The Sheik*. That blockbuster launched her into a series of films that highlighted her cultivated persona of spunky bravado. She was critically lauded for doing the actual driving in *Racing Hearts*, including a heart-stopping scene when her car lost control and crashed into some hay bales lining the track. It was rumored that Agnes had a quickie secret marriage to one of the stunt drivers in the film, Jerry Wunderlich, a two-time Indianapolis 500 participant, a "show-mance" that appeared to have dissolved quickly after the movie premiered.

Agnes Ayres made a well-publicized visit to her mother in Anna, Illinois, in late May 1923, and a picture and write-up about the hometown heroine made it into the *Chicago Tribune*. It's almost a certainty that Marion Martins would have seen the movie and heard about the visit given her obvious interest in getting behind the race car wheel herself.

The movie is in the canon of lost films and is remembered today only from its clippings and press materials. It received good reviews and played in several theaters in Chicago in 1923. The publicity pictures for the film were remarkably prescient in portraying the look that was adopted by the real-life driver from Memphis, with gloved hands on the wheel, goggles at the ready, eyeliner and lipstick artfully applied.

Figure 1.6. Agnes Ayres in a promotional photograph for the 1923 film *Racing Hearts*.
PARAMOUNT PICTURES.

But it was *Bluff*, the 1924 Ayres film, that may have had the most cinematic influence on a young Marion. The movie unspooled with a boilerplate secret identity plot, the kind of story that has thrilled audiences for ages. It told the tale of a simple country girl named Betty, who, down on her luck and desperate for funds to take care of her brother who was recovering from an automobile accident, takes on the persona of a foreign celebrity named Nina Lorning, who, just by sheer coincidence, Betty strongly resembles.

Of course, her trick seems to work swimmingly well until it predictably (and dramatically) unravels. But through the intervention of a handsome straitlaced lawyer, all is rectified, and Betty finds love and her own true self along the way. The ultimate takeaway of this cinematic scheme is "fake it till you make it," and in the 1920s celebrity culture, that was often the path that was used as a career road map to fame.

CHAPTER TWO

J. Alex Sloan

ON JUNE 20, 1923, THE OFFICIALS OF THE NORTH SHORE POLO TRACK placed ads in the *Chicago Tribune* to announce their inaugural auto race event, scheduled for Wednesday, July 4. Their venue in northern Chicago was a reconfiguration of a half-mile horse racetrack located at Lincoln Avenue and Peterson Road. The grandstands were built to hold 6,000 people, and there was nearby parking to accommodate 1,000 cars.

The first few racing shows were the usual all-male affairs, with notable drivers like George Beck, Barney Oldfield, and Curly Young participating. A handful of events were held that summer: the July 4 opener, then on July 29, August 4, and August 19.

George Beck pulled double duty as both a headline racer and the manager of the track. The matches were exciting, with a great mix of well-known professionals and local talent, and the crowds were consistently large in size and enthusiasm. Oliver G. Temme, president of the United Race Drivers Association, mentioned in his later years that dirt track racing had leaped into its own in Chicago in 1923.

There was one man who had been ahead of the promotional curve for years in the auto racing world and ready to change the sport of racing and the life of Marion Martins.

John Alexander Sloan, who went by Alex, was a beefy, lantern-jawed Pittsburgh native, born in 1880, who attended and played football at Ohio Wesleyan University. After college, he became a sportswriter in Minnesota, then moved to Los Angeles in 1905 and wrote for the *Los Angeles Times*. Sloan felt that his talents were wasted, with his imagination restricted to a few print column inches a day. His real skill was promotion, both for himself and for his clients. He claimed to have been a world-record holder in several swim distances, played in the first collegiate basketball game, and participated in the 1900 Olympics in track and field. None of it was true, but he proclaimed it so confidently and convincingly that it became part of his lifelong bio.

When his employment options in newspaper writing seemed most stagnant, he hitched his promotional wagon to the legendary race car star Barney Oldfield. Sloan left the *Los Angeles Times* newspaper company in the spring of 1912 and headed off to promote racing with his handpicked team, which included Louis Disbrow, Leon Duray, and Fred Horey (Sloan's brother-in-law). His star drivers needed racetracks to showcase their stardom, and that's where Alex Sloan shined. In 1915, he moved to Chicago and formed the International Motor Contest Association (IMCA). The name is remarkably similar to the imaginary International Motor Car Association highlighted in the *Perils of Pauline* serials that came out the year before. The savvy Sloan had to have congratulated himself at his business acumen by using the popular films as free publicity.

Throughout the South, the Midwest, and Canada, county and state fairs accommodated horse racing tracks, which were easy to adapt for car racing. They were already built to hold large viewing grandstands, so the tracks welcomed up to several hundred guests. Other popular fair attractions brought in big crowds and introduced those patrons to this new form of entertainment. Sloan constantly prospected these far-flung fairs and tracks, cajoling the local mayors and state governors into financial partnerships with his grand plans of an international race circuit. He told them how important their county fair was going to be in his upcoming schedule and how thrilled their constituents and customers would be in seeing greats like Barney Oldfield, Ralph DePalma, Louis Disbrow, and other legends of the sport fly around the track of their hometown fairgrounds.

Of course, Indiana didn't want Wisconsin to have all the glory, and Wisconsin wouldn't let Minnesota be the hub of this glorious circuit, so in just a few years, there were 137 of these tracks, from Florida to Ottawa, all under the auspices of Alex Sloan.

Figure 2.1. J. Alexander Sloan (right) with Barney Oldfield (left).
INDIANAPOLIS MOTOR SPEEDWAY.

In the beginning, the big attractions at the shows was red-meat carnival fare like auto polo, where the old jalopies had roll cages welded on and mallet-wielding drivers tried to knock a ball across the opponents' goal lines. There were "powder-puff" races that featured the novelty of housewives in flowered hats (and sometimes men dressed as women) driving in lazy loops around the track, and naturally, there was "real" racing, with second-tier names and former legends revving up the crowds with a visual spectacle of dirt clouds and wheel-spun gravel.

It was a nice formula in the beginning, a steady audience-pleaser menu, but nothing that would top the sports pages of a big-town paper 100 miles over. But eventually, as the machines grew more powerful and faster, the piles of crumpled driver bodies stacked up, and the spectacular crash photos splashed across the local papers began to circulate around the country via the national wire services. The general public started to take notice of this deadly sport, and the crowds grew.

Alex Sloan knew almost all of the racers on the dirt track circuit, and many had joined his IMCA. One of those was the German-born Johnny Mais, a journeyman driver who finished at the back of the pack in the 1915 Indianapolis 500. Mais was a good mechanic who was an expert in souping up Dodge engines, and he was married to Elfrieda, who happened to be a very talented driver herself.

Elfrieda Mais was a regular on the Sloan circuit, so it was a given that he would push to feature her in the inaugural women's race in his adopted city of Chicago. With her competing on the track, it ensured that this event was going to be considered a real professional race and not a beauty contest on wheels.

Elfrieda Mais was born in Indianapolis, Indiana, in 1892, the daughter of German immigrants. She helped her husband learn to speak and understand English, and he showed her the ins and outs of taking corners at high speeds on dirt racetracks. Alex Sloan quickly figured out the publicity possibilities of a "woman daredevil"[1] storyline and signed her up. It wasn't long before he began to whip up intriguing background stories about her for his promotional purposes.

An excerpt from the *Wichita Beacon* on Wednesday, June 28, 1916, painted a fanciful portrait of the fearless driver (with the help of Sloan's creative press release):

Famous Woman Auto Racer to Drive in Wichita Races

The only woman auto racer in the world—Miss Elfrieda Mais—will drive her $10,000 "Mais Special" in an exhibition race against time on the West Side Speedway on July 4.

After dickering for a week, Tim Hurst, manager of the races, finally persuaded the woman "daredevil" to come to Wichita for the Fourth of July show. This morning he received a telegram from her manager stating she had accepted the date and was preparing to come to Wichita immediately.

Miss Mais and Mrs. Cuneo, wife of a New York banker, are the only female drivers who ever obtained licenses from the International Motor Contest Association to race. Mrs. Cuneo quit the track a year ago following several defeats at the hands of Miss Mais, leaving the field open to her. She now is the licensed "speed queen" of the I.M.C.A. surrounded by more than a hundred "kings." In the last year, she has hung up some pretty fast records that even the best of the men drivers have failed to lower. Her races, however, are not competitive, only exhibitions being granted to her by the clannish auto race association managers.

Miss Mais lives in Indianapolis. She is barely past the girlish stage, 24, and pretty. At 18, she forsook a social life to "go up in the air" in a biplane and the thrills lured her away. She became a "bird woman," becoming a professional several years ago and giving exhibitions all over the country. When she quit flying for the motor car three years ago, she declared the air game was too tame for her due, it is said, to so many women flyers appearing in public.

"So much competition," she was quoted as saying, "drove me out. Too many women fliers took away the dangers, so I sent to the motor car."

Miss Mais will drive a machine built especially for her at a cost of $10,000 and will attempt to lower the Kansas records for various distances. Mr. Hurst has hung up purses of $100 for each broken state record.[2]

Figure 2.2. Elfrieda Mais pictured in the *Wichita Beacon* of Wichita, Kansas, on June 28, 1916.

WICHITA BEACON.

Note the passing of the "fastest woman" baton from Joan Cuneo to Mais. It wasn't easy to establish the bona fides of an unknown racer to local fans, and before the advent of widespread media, the surest way to become known was to hitch your name to an already established legend. Joan Cuneo was a well-known racing pioneer and the highest-profile female personality in the field, so newspaper reports stating that Mais beat her in races was a de rigueur maneuver for the next "Speed Queen" (whether she actually did was irrelevant; fact-checking the arcana of race results from as close as the neighboring state wasn't standard practice in the early days of competition coverage).

Shy and quiet, Elfrieda Mais did her talking on the racetrack. She was a very good, very consistent racer who competed in tandem with the men in her life. In the beginning, she shared race cars with her first husband, the well-known auto racer Johnny Mais. They managed racetracks together, and she drove his custom-prepared hopped-up cars at the dirt track shows after the men had run their events.

In 1923, the promotion of a World Champion Female Racer was still a novel and lucrative attraction, and Canada, with its rural and far-flung population centers, was the perfect testing grounds for Alex Sloan's moneymaking ideas. Auto Polo was still a crowd-pleaser, as was the barnstorming contingent of dirt track luminaries like Disbrow and DePalma, but the attention span of the crowds was always a scarce and valuable commodity that needed constant nurturing. Novelty and controversy were the shortcuts to quick money, but Sloan had a long-term plan. He knew that bringing more women into the sport would bring more interest—and more money into his pocket. He just had to find the right athlete.

There had been women racetrack drivers before, all the way back to the early teens on the Alex Sloan circuit, but this was different. Back then, there were single female drivers who were part of publicity stunts or occasionally featured in woman-against-woman exhibitions. Those early events in the rural fairgrounds felt like circus acts. These Chicago events were going to be real, multi-contestant races, and the women were deadly serious about winning and driving as fast as possible to do it. They weren't going to be just a quick powder-puff parade of models driving in sundresses.

In the early fall of 1923, the *Chicago Tribune* printed an unusual announcement that several women would be racing autos on September 30 at the North Shore Polo Track. This had Sloan's fingerprints all over it. Grabbing the most attention was the headlining attraction, Elfrieda Mais, Sloan's ace driver. Also on the bill was Mrs. O. G. Temme, who was the wife of IMCA official Oliver Temme (the guiding force behind the development of the track). A handful of unknown drivers filled out the card.

Scheduled as entrants at the North Shore track women's event on September 30, 1923, besides Mais were May Smylie, Elinor Loftus, Erma Hirth, Teresa M. Putz, Margaret Zimmerman, Ruth Hambel, Mrs. B. C. Brautigan, and Mrs. Temme. Also mentioned prominently in the press was the exotically named Simmone Soudan.

So striking was the young Simmone that she is pictured prominently along with the better-known Mrs. Temme in the publicity shots for the race. Her smile is a mile wide, and her eyes show her overwhelming excitement. And why wouldn't she be excited? She was the center of attention in front of thousands of people, competing in a "man's sport."

Her combination of sparkly looks and physical charisma made a huge impression on the promoter Alex Sloan, and he saw how readily the papers, even the big ones like the *Chicago Tribune*, would happily splash a picture of a pretty woman in a fast car across their sports page, and he used that to his advantage. He learned that his spicy puff pieces on women racers in show after show would often displace the predictable drumroll lineup in local papers of the "women's interest" segments, like lists of trendy recipes, dressmaking tips, and nature poetry. Most of the serious newspaper stories in 1923 concerning women would revolve around celebrity or crime.

Interviews with Gloria Swanson competed with dramatic stories of "fallen women." On the day of this race, September 30, 1923, for example, the readers of the *Chicago Tribune* had been treated to the front-page story of Senorita Marguerita Buerque, née Peggy Burke, who had posed as a Spanish beauty to repeatedly lure men into waiting taxis where an

FAIR SPEED DEMONS IN AUTO RACE

MRS. OLIVER G. TEMME. **MISS SIMMONE SOUDAN.**

Two of the women auto race drivers who will compete this afternoon in the races at the North Shore dirt track. Both Miss Soudan and Mrs. Temme are well known in women's auto racing circles and have enviable records. The women will race in a ten mile event and the winner will be pitted against the victor among the men in a special twenty-five mile match race.

Figure 2.3. Mrs. Oliver G. Temme and Miss Simmone Soudan pictured in the *Chicago Tribune* of Chicago, Illinois, on September 30, 1923.

CHICAGO TRIBUNE. IMAGE ENHANCED FOR CLARITY BY ADELIS SEGUNDO BRICEÑO.

accomplice pretending to be a cabdriver assaulted them and relieved them of their valuables. Another method Marguerita perfected was to seduce lonely gentlemen into promises of marriage to clean out their life savings and then disappear before the promised nuptials. Salacious stories about dangerous women, especially beauties like Peggy (who was described as having a "Mona Lisa smile"[3]), were consistent newspaper sellers in the 1920s.

The logical next step in many newspaper publishers' plans to attract subscribers was to feature women who were doing dangerous but legal activities. It was the cue for publicity-hungry promoters to push women into the most death-defying stunts that their imaginations could muster. It gave rise to the "female daredevil," the young women who could be seen dancing the Charleston on the wings of planes, dodging trains in movie serial shorts, and drinking straight whiskey in underground speakeasies in the big cities. The national newspapers splashed plenty of pictures on their front pages of these sirens, who dared to do everything their stuntmen boyfriends did, and publishers sold thousands of copies reporting it.

That September Sunday was overcast and dry. Chicago had had a streak of unusually warm weather the previous week, and it was just starting to make the turn to fall's cooler temperatures. Elfrieda Mais ran a special exhibition against the track record that afternoon, a turn in the spotlight befitting a world champion. Erma Hirth, a local racer, pulled out a win in the other women's main match, but it was Elfrieda whom the crowd came to see.

The setting was intoxicating. Ten thousand fans packed the bleachers, and the grandstand echoed with full-throated cheers. Danger waited around every bend of the track, and the smell of oil and gasoline wafted and eddied along the bleachers. There were half a dozen other racers alongside Simmone and Elfrieda who were doing what was rarely witnessed (and often frowned on); they were competing head-to-head against other brave women. While Erma, May Smylie, Elinor Loftus, Teresa M. Putz, Margaret Zimmerman, Ruth Hambel, and the other names in the event have faded into history, Elfrieda Mais and a hungry young novice were about to begin their personal rivalry.

Mais was as straight as an arrow, dependable, and respected for her excellent driving ability. She was well-liked in the sport, and she had a tremendous amount of talent and courage. But sometimes that isn't enough. Elfreida wasn't as charismatic as some of the other female racers, and that aspect of her personality probably kept her from receiving the same sort of fawning press articles that were to be attached to Simmone Soudan and others. But her solid skills on the dirt tracks ensured her continuing headlining status on the state fair circuit, and it's why she was the headliner that hazy September afternoon in Chicago.

This only all-women's match in 1923 was a thrilling and portentous way to close out the racing season in Chicago.

Somewhere at this track, on this day, Marion sat in the stands and imagined that it was her turn to get behind the wheel of a hot rod Ford

Figure 2.4. Chicago's North Shore track pictured in the *Chicago Tribune* on October 1, 1923.
CHICAGO TRIBUNE.

and tear around this oval, listening as the cheers of the crowd blended into the roar of the engines. It wasn't a far-fetched dream. Hers was the kind of image that could sell tickets; she was a gray-eyed beauty with a blazing smile and an air of casual bravery. She was irresistible. Although Marion didn't run in this inaugural race, she watched with the fans, and in her mind, the plans were being laid.

* * *

In 1924, the year after that sensational debut of the women drivers, the North Shore track heralded its season opener by announcing a huge roster of participants for its six races, including the scheduling of a special head-to-head women's match for its opening season event on Sunday, May 18. The headlining men's races were trumpeted in the papers to be the track's biggest gathering of top-notch talent yet, with 38 drivers signed up. Among the entrants were Harry Root (a winner at the Hawthorne track the week before), Frank Nichols, Sam Davis, and Cliff Woodbury. They were just some of the heavy hitters that attracted the sizable crowd of 6,000 paying fans.

That women drivers were even on the bill in this inaugural event of the season spoke volumes. Promoter Alex Sloan had discovered that the combination of women and danger struck a chord with the public, and he was quick to exploit it. He also decided that it was time to add a hometown angle to the mix by matching the consensus female champion racer with a teenage challenger from Chicago.

On the men's side, dirt track prodigy Curly Young took home the top male driver honors. He ripped through the pack to win the 10-mile race, then followed that up with a third-place finish in the next event, a 15-miler. Curly was also a fierce regular at the Roby track, competing alongside Joan's husband, Walter Martins, and he had a reputation as one of the toughest drivers on that racetrack.

Once again, Elfrieda Mais was the top female attraction of the event, and she received most of the advance press write-ups. She was advertised as appearing in a two-and-a-half-mile match race against Jane Stanage, a local 19-year-old driver who picked up the gauntlet to take on Mais one-on-one. Stanage was featured in a small column in the Sunday issue of the *Chicago Tribune* on May 18. It was topped with her picture, and the article accompanying it mentioned that she "told speedway officials she could drive anything with four wheels and a fast motor and would meet Miss Mais at any distance and under any conditions."[4] But it was Elfrieda Mais who had her big picture printed on the last page of the paper the day after the race.

On that hot, partly cloudy Sunday afternoon, it appeared there was a nascent rivalry beginning here, with both Mais and the young Stanage willing to go wheel to wheel against each other on this muddy track, both driving to win, both "driving like men," as it might have been described back then. Mais won the five-lap exhibition match as expected, but it was a fun, dusty drive from both. Jane Stanage was an incendiary driver, taking chances to make up for her lack of experience. She was dangerous but lucky.

The May 30 Memorial Day event was shaping up to be another exciting showcase, this time for the male racers alone, with the familiar names of Curly Young and George Beck heading the bill. Sloan was still figuring out the right combination of women drivers to put together and left them off this show, but he laid the groundwork by promising a full slate of female drivers for the next big event over the Independence Day weekend.

GAS!

JANE STANAGE.
Chicago girl who will endeavor
to win the woman's national dirt
track auto title in a match race at
the North Shore track today.

Figure 2.5. Jane Stanage pictured in the *Chicago Tribune* on May 18, 1924.
CHICAGO TRIBUNE.

More than 12,000 attendees jammed into the newly expanded bleachers on Memorial Day Weekend as Young managed another impressive victory in the 50-mile race in his trusty Ford "99." He then switched to a Ford Frontenac and took the five-mile consolation race as well. It was quite a day for the "Kid," as Young was nicknamed. The show was a massive success, as word was spread that female racers were going to be included more often in the race season. The stands today were filled with hard-core racing fans and the casually curious alike. Fliers were passed out to thousands. The teaser advertisements on the inclusion of women battling it out in the July 4 show proved integral to its success.

The June 15 event at the North Shore track showed the other reason these spectacles were such a draw: the danger. During the early runs, the wet weather had turned the track into a soggy mess, and veteran George Beck crashed so badly in his "Zepp Special" in the morning time trials that the entire slate was canceled. Beck suffered a broken leg and a broken rib, and he was rushed to the hospital. It put a damper on the weekend, but the resulting dramatic coverage in the press ensured that the Independence Day races the next month would have an overflowing and bloodthirsty crowd.

Six female drivers were highlighted on the bill. That "feminine" angle was what was leading the pre-event story publicity in the big hometown papers.

With Curly Young, Cliff Woodbury, George Beck (at least his famous car if not him), and 34 other male drivers competing, all of whom were quickly becoming local favorites, the Independence Day weekend races were going to be barn burners. But it was the female drivers, not all of the men, who were individually named in the press releases. There was Miss Marie Larson in a Frontenac Ford, Jane Stanage in a Rajo Ford, Ruth Hamel in a Nelson Brothers Special, May Smylie in a Lyons Motor Special, and Helen Piot in a Frontenac, and the last one listed was 23-year-old Mrs. Walter Martin. She was scheduled to drive a Romo Special, and she was the only one designated as married. The print story was fairly accurate, but the actual name of "Mrs. Martin" was Marion Martins, from Memphis, Tennessee.

J. Alex Sloan

WOMEN TO DRIVE CARS IN RACES AT NORTH SHORE

Star women drivers will feature the program at the North Shore Polo club speedway race meet, Lincoln and Peterson avenues, on July 4, 5 and 6. Two of the women will drive in the Frontenacs used by " Fuzzy " Davidson and Cliff Woodbury, and the third will pilot George Beck's " Zepp " special.

Five mile races will be staged by these women on Saturday, July 5, and Sunday, July 6. Two match races will be held on the Fourth. One will bring together " Fuzzy " Davidson and Cliff Woodbury, the other will be between Curley Young and Esthan Wenneston.

Figure 2.6. Article appearing in the *Chicago Tribune* on June 26, 1924.
CHICAGO TRIBUNE.

Alex Sloan had tasted the success of the inaugural women's races and wanted more. The special matches drew big crowds and sold thousands of tickets, but he was still having problems putting together the right group. Simmone Soudan wasn't available, and neither was the other high-profile driver, Elfrieda Mais. There was one unfamiliar woman who inquired about racing. Sloan knew of her husband, who was making waves in a rival racing organization.

35

Mrs. Martins was gutsy enough to ask for a chance to risk her life, and since her husband was a tough competitor, maybe some of his talent rubbed off. And it didn't hurt that she had striking looks, with piercing eyes and a beaming smile.

Did she have a car to drive? Well, no, her husband was using it most of the weekends, but she'd drive anything; perhaps she could borrow a race car?

Sloan balked. That was a pretty tall order. Most of the competitors either had their own rigs or used their partners' cars, but Walter Martins had made it very clear to Marion that he was the only racer in the family, and that was that.

Sloan did have a driver in his stable, Cliff Henderson, who had a modified light Ford that he called the "Romo Special." It wasn't a heavy racer, like, say, a Duesenberg, which would be tough for a novice to handle. Just maybe, if Sloan promised to cover any damage that might happen to it, he could talk Henderson into sharing it for the weekend. There was something about this woman that convinced Sloan that she wasn't afraid to handle a car with speed and power.

He made the deal. But if things went south, she'd never get another shot.

It wasn't unusual in those early days of auto racing for the wives of drivers to pick up some tricks and inside knowledge needed to handle rough dirt tracks. Martins, Elfrieda Mais, Mrs. O. G. Temme, and a few others eventually became even as well known as their husbands both for the novelty of their gender and for their driving skills.

From the beginning, Marion exuded the magnetism that put her in the lede of newspaper articles. Nearly always described in print as "pretty,"[5] "petite,"[6] and "dainty,"[7] she was the perfect combination of the feminine ideal and exotic daredevil, and it's no surprise that in the coverage of the races, she quickly supplanted the staid and less charismatic Elfrieda Mais. And she replaced the suddenly absent Simmone Soudan in the newspaper stories as well.

Alex had a keen eye for talent. If there was anyone who could spot a winning draw, it was the wily promoter. Tragically, Sloan had lost a possible great young driver before.

In the late 1910s and early 1920s, he was a promoter and provider of race cars to a young daredevil of a driver by the name of Jimmie Costa. Costa was dubbed "The Italian Champion from Turin, Italy,"[8] even though he was born and raised in Kansas. His father had been born in Italy, but there's no evidence Jimmie had ever set foot there.

He raced on Sloan's circuit from 1911 through early 1922, becoming more and more skilled and successful, winning often as his career progressed, until he was involved in an airplane accident on March 31, 1922, in Macon, Georgia. He was a passenger in an overcrowded small plane that clipped a smokestack guy wire and plummeted to the ground in flames

Sloan was crushed. He had lent the young driver many of his own cars to race in, and Costa was showing real promise as a dirt track pilot, but the dangerous sport of car racing was being overtaken by a newer and even more dangerous avocation, airplane flying, and Jimmie was the latest noteworthy victim.

Alex Sloan was also still healing from an immense loss in his own life just a few years before. On February 3, 1919, his wife, Maydean, was involved in a terrible accident. The couple had recently purchased a home in Evanston, Illinois, and Maydean was tending to household chores, which involved cleaning the lace curtains.

It was a popular home remedy to use gasoline as a stain remover, and though she was careful to keep her work at a distance from any flames, her vigorous rubbing of the fluid on the material set off a friction spark. The curtains exploded in an instant, and her house dress caught fire. As she screamed and fought the flames, her three-year-old daughter, Melissa Jane, picked up the phone and yelled for help. Neighbors on the party line heard the screams, and they called the police and fire department. Mrs. Sloan was rushed to the hospital, but after struggling valiantly for two months to survive, she ultimately succumbed to her injuries in mid-April.

The papers described her as "a woman of rare beauty and personal charm."[9] Although she had occasionally helped her husband out for special promotional events, she was primarily a devoted mother to their children, Melissa, Naomi, and John. She was 37.

He threw himself into work, which kept him on the road and away from home and the painful memories, and he concentrated on finding a potential talent that he could nurture, protect, and make into a star.

Alex Sloan never remarried.

* * *

The 1924 Independence Day events in Chicago featured 50 miles of racing. There were two 10-mile eliminations, a 15-mile "Straw Hat Derby" (an event where the drivers attempt to win a race while keeping their hats on, no chinstraps allowed), a five-mile consolation match, and two five-mile head-to-head races, one between "Fuzzy" Davidson and Cliff Woodbury and the other between Curly Young and Esthan Wenneston. As they drew closer to the race, the women weren't mentioned as often in the puff pieces leading up to the matches.

The promoters learned that all that was needed was just a simple notice that women were racing, and the stands would fill up. The advertising buildup focused on the men because the women's races were such a guaranteed draw that the promoters wanted to shore up the front side of the bill. That was the reason the women racers were last on the docket; they were the headliners. Much like how the main attraction always closes the show, the organizers knew the women's finale would keep the folks in their seats, buying souvenirs and concessions until the end of the night. The men capitalized on the women's star power to raise their own profiles because the crowds were bigger and they stayed for the whole event.

A local movie theater used the popularity of the matches to publicize an engagement of the newly released automobile flick *Racing Luck*. In the film, Monty Banks plays an old-world Italian boy who emigrated to the new country of the United States to find his fortune, and along the way, he falls in love with the fair Rosina.

However, Monty runs afoul of a local gang leader who is also enraptured with Rosina, so the criminal and the gang prevent our hero from finding employment. In a last-ditch effort to earn some money, Monty is mistakenly assumed to be a great Italian driver by another automotive concern who drafts him into the big race. At stake? Five thousand dollars (about the cost of a home), enough to make his dreams with Rosina a reality.

Does he win? Of course.

The costar of the film, who played the foreign-flavored ingenue Rosina, was Helen Ferguson, a Chicago girl who had left home at 16 to try her luck in the movies. Fired twice for her lack of ability, she continued to pursue her dream. Eventually, she made more than 50 films. Helen was a prime example of an average Midwestern girl from average means morphing into a charismatic cinematic siren for public consumption. It

Figure 2.7. Advertisement for the film *Racing Luck* in the *Chicago Tribune* on June 29, 1924.

CHICAGO TRIBUNE.

was a template that the Southern-born Marion would follow to a tee, and the Independence Day weekend would be her opening act.

There was still one last pretender to the throne. Featured driver Jane Stanage looked poised to be a future champion. She was a woman in her late teens who displayed the same sort of bravado that emanated from Marion, but she was younger, cockier even, and there was an air of recklessness around her.

According to the Minneapolis, Minnesota, *Star Tribune* write-up on Saturday, July 5, before the races,

> Miss Jane Stanage, daring young woman automobile racing pilot, had a narrow escape from death Friday when her car, going at high speed, crashed into a fence and overturned twice during a spin at the North Shore Polo club speedway. Miss Stanage made a sudden swerve of her car to avoid a collision with another racing machine. She escaped with a few cuts and bruises and announced she would compete in the dirt track races which open the speedway here this afternoon. She was making her final practice test when the accident occurred.[10]

Fortunately, the crash resulted in just some light bruises. But the image of a wild teenager drew a lot of ink, and there was anticipation that the upcoming race season would be a coming-out party for the young Queen of Speed.

Chapter Three

Marion Martins's Independence Day

AT 2:30 IN THE AFTERNOON ON SATURDAY JULY 5, 1924, THE EVENT
began. There were three races each day for the men at five-, 10-, and
15-mile distances and a five-mile race on both Saturday and Sunday for
the women. The men's races went off without a hitch, almost as if they
were scripted for a Hollywood movie. Cliff Woodbury added to his streak
of wins, and George Beck, who had finally recovered from his serious
injuries, returned to form. Beck pushed the pace in his Zepp Special most
of the match, showing that his handshake with Death wasn't going to
slow him down. The oddly cool weather that Independence Day weekend helped keep the dust and sun glare to a minimum, making for ideal
driving conditions.

It didn't seem to help the women racers, however. May Smylie ran a
practice lap in front of the crowd and came within a whisker of flipping
her car over. She took the far end turn at too high a speed, slid in the
soft dirt, spun around, and went up on two wheels, nearly rolling her
ride. Smylie managed to right the vehicle at the last second, likely saving
her life.

When the starter's flag was dropped for the actual race, Vera Schoel
lasted less than a lap in her Ford before crashing off the course. Again,
the driver walked away unscathed. Two competitors and two wild accidents, and the race hadn't even hit the halfway point. While the other
drivers seemed to be a bit cowed by the loose dirt track and the violent
wrecks they'd seen, Marion Martins rode the Romo Special like it was a
Thoroughbred and took the lead immediately. She kept increasing that

lead, lap after lap, finally winning by a third of the length of the track over May Smylie. In the post-race coverage of the five-mile women's event, there wasn't any mention of Jane Stanage. The coverage was about the previously unknown and plain-named Mrs. Walter Martin, who won going away in record time, 4:22 over the race distance, setting a women's course record. The win delivered her the Husk O'Hara Trophy (Husk O'Hara and the Peacock Strutters were a popular dance band in the Chicago area).

The July 6 races were filled with even more drama. The weather was moderate, in the upper sixties, once again providing excellent track conditions. The cool air kept the dust down on the course, helping the drivers run at top speeds. On too many dry, hot days, the lead driver would be the only one who could see the course, and the others behind had to follow the brown clouds and hope for the best. On this Sunday, the men once again started things off as the opening acts in their trio of races. George Beck swapped places with Cliff Woodbury on the winner's podium in the longest event (Woodbury's broken axle mid-race had kept him from the victory). That same race featured Al Waters taking a spin behind the wheel of the legendary Barney Oldfield "Golden Egg" race car. Waters took the car and the course too lightly and slammed the shimmering gold-painted coupe into a fence, tearing out a good 80 feet of timber.

Marion Martins was almost involved in a similar accident. She coolly dodged a near collision in her race with Vera Schoel. Schoel had lost control of her auto *again*, scraping along the grandstand fence and giving the spectators in the bleachers a close-up thrill. Martins swept past her to the inside rail and won the race by an even bigger margin than the first match, almost lapping the fading wunderkind Stanage, with the crash-prone Schoel coming in third. The fans were getting a show they hadn't expected from the women drivers, and they were loving it. Marion drove "with the assurance of an expert,"[1] one city paper wrote. She had entered two five-mile races and won both. She added to her silver cup collection by snagging the Nelson Brothers Trophy. It was the keystone moment in her career, cementing her love for this new and dangerous sport, and it assured her that she was also very *very* good at it.

Marion's steely eyes and cocky devilish smile unnerved many of her track rivals. She had a win-at-all-costs attitude that made her intimidating in competition, and it seemed to onlookers as if she should be racing the professional men drivers, not just the once-a-year female dilettantes. She drove fast and a bit dangerously. She took losing personally.

Marion's sudden success put a strain on her marriage. In one weekend, the incredible natural talent of Mrs. Martin overshadowed years of Walter Martins's efforts to make his own reputation, and Walter wasn't handling it well. It was rare for a woman to steal the sports spotlight from their spouse. Marion told a reporter that "when she had taken up racing automobiles, her avocation led to an estrangement between her and her husband, which resulted in her second divorce."[2]

She told a reporter later, "Marriage doesn't interfere with some careers, but some careers interfere with marriage. I think one reason so many marriages of theatrical people end in tragedy and the divorce court is simply the nature of the stage career itself. You can't expect a marriage to be entirely successful and stable when the husband is off on one circuit and the wife playing in New York, or vice versa."[3]

She was asked about marrying again in the future, and Marion shook her head. "Not this minute, but I like to have all these things thought out, so when the ideal man comes along, I'll know."[4]

From this point on, Marion would be billed as "Miss" Martins in the press and posters. No longer married, she could now travel the country alone to take part in different racing events for months at a time, and no one could tell her no. She was great at driving, the fans responded wildly to her outsize personality, and Alex Sloan was excited to promote her. Marion had achieved freedom, and with freedom came more achievement and more pressure.

Most of the northern auto tracks were closed over the winter, which meant that the racing season of the North Shore track began on May 10, 1925, the day before Marion's twenty-fourth birthday. Among the drivers in the all-men opening meet that year were Cliff Woodbury, Al Waters, Herbert Christopher, Bugs Allen, and George Beck. It was a seasoned slate, and the crowd got their money's worth as the aggressive, wheel-to-wheel racing by the veterans resulted in some spectacular spills.

The first accident took place during practice when James Barnett flipped his car at the north corner, and during the races, John Smithson tore out a chunk of the fence with his Western Special roadster in the 10-mile event, and in the 30-lap match, G. A. Hardy overturned just as he entered the early curve. Smithson and Hardy walked away, but Barnett wasn't as lucky, and he was taken to the hospital. The speed and power of the cars in the 1920s was increasing faster than the safety advances, and more and more drivers were ending up hurt or killed.

On June 7, next door to Chicago at the Indiana Roby racetrack, Harry Heinly flipped his car and was pinned beneath the cowl, which stored the fuel. Gasoline soaked his racing togs, and one spark would have meant an excruciating death. Luckily, he walked away. Gus Schrader then took Cliff Woodbury's borrowed Peugeot into a ditch, but he also avoided injury. Another driver wasn't as fortunate.

The *Chicago Tribune* ran the story the next day on page 21. "Chance Kinsley of Indianapolis was killed while making his time trial previous to the races. Kinsley was piloting a new car which had too much speed for him. He went into the first turn too fast, lost control of his car. and was crushed when his car rolled over three times."[5] Tragedies like this one were becoming so common that they were generally relegated to the end of the Sports section.

On May 31, 1925, at an event at the Plainfield Racetrack in Joliet, Illinois, eight cars out of a starting field of 20 crashed. On that same day at that same track, after witnessing those horrific pileups, Marion Martins crawled into the same type of roadster and defeated male driver Emil Buck in a special five-mile race. She had seen the chaos and crashes earlier in the day, but she was undeterred. Alex Sloan, the event's promoter, was impressed by Marion's professionalism and courage and, after seeing even more potential in his new attraction, began to push for her to run in higher-profile events.

The next big show on the North Shore calendar was June 14, and it was Marion's coming-out event. Sloan had signed her to a multi-race contract, and he provided a nice publicity shot for the Sunday *Chicago Tribune* with a thumbnail bio beneath. Marion was beaming in the picture, anticipating her busy upcoming schedule.

Miss Marion Martin, champion woman race driver of Illinois, will meet the winner of the elimination tests at the North Shore speedway, Lincoln avenue and Peterson road, this afternoon. Miss Martin has not only defeated all women rivals for speedway honors but has also scored victories over speedy men drivers.

Figure 3.1. Marion Martin pictured in the *Chicago Tribune* on June 14, 1925.
CHICAGO TRIBUNE. IMAGE ENHANCED FOR CLARITY BY ADELIS SEGUNDO BRICEÑO.

In that June event at North Shore, Marion Martins was billed as facing Phil Schaefer in a head-to-head match. The legendary Elfrieda Mais had previously taken on all comers, but they were almost always women opponents. Marion was eager to show her skills against the top local drivers with no regard for gender. Sloan helped to get her that exposure by feeding the papers fantastic stories that they eagerly printed, most of which contained more than a few exaggerations. He created the public fantasy that Marion was routinely taking on and beating the best male racers in races all over the country. That wasn't the case, at least not yet.

On the day of the race, Marion was matched against hometown favorite Curly Young instead of Schaefer. The papers didn't print a reason for the substitution, but Young was a very good young driver. Curly Young was also a peer of Walter Martins on the dirt circuit and would have been reluctant to purposely lose to another man, let alone the wife of a competitor in that day and age. There's no doubt that he had a pre-match meeting with his boss, Mr. Sloan, and agreed to make the race competitive. Marion was excited to run against a good, tough driver who would be a true measuring stick of her own skill level.

Despite the threatening weather that had been stormy and had muddied the track the day before, a huge crowd cheered her on as the two pilots ran neck and neck around the track five times. As they approached the finish, Curly pulled ahead by just half a car length and took home the win. It was a dangerous exhibition on a wet course, and Marion Martins impressed the reporters at trackside who wrote, "Miss Martin proved to be a daring driver, cutting the turns with as much skill as the men."[6] The bravura driving on the sloppy course also impressed Alex Sloan, and he decided to introduce Marion to his other circuits.

Prior to the 1924 Independence Day weekend, Marion Martins wasn't even a footnote in the story of women's auto racing. But now, a year later, she *was* the story. Just as her star was rising, however, the track that made her reputation was winding down. On November 4, 1924, the *Chicago Tribune* had reported that the North Shore Polo Club property was being sold to developers for $540,000, and that meant the writing was on the wall for the North Shore Racing organization. They were shutting operations down after the 1925 season. This would be the swan song of the track that had birthed at least a dozen good male drivers and one legendary woman.

Sloan promoted races for a fairgrounds racetrack network that ran from Mississippi to Canada, with dozens of tracks under his influence. With Chicago's North Shore track closing down, the summer up north was going to be a more financially lucrative time. Sloan could book more dates in Alberta and Saskatchewan to fill the new holes in the racing calendar. He was a master at ginning up excitement and anticipation for his events anywhere they took place, and Canada would now receive the promotional attention that was once showered on Chicago.

In the provinces, Sloan had a promotional blank canvas. The local papers knew only what Sloan told them. Marion Martins was the best semi-fictional subject he'd had to work with in years, and he relished the potential of creating instant fame for her and reaping lucrative ticket sales for him. She was now inspiring some of his most florid promo writing.

It was a 16-hour train ride from Illinois to Regina, Saskatchewan, on the Chicago & Northwestern Railroad, and to the average big-city dweller, it must have felt like traveling to a different world.

Compared to Chicago, which boasted 3 million people, Regina's population was tiny, with roughly 37,000 citizens. The combined population of the *entire* province where Regina was located was barely a third of that of the Second City. It did boast a panorama of open plains and wide, rolling vistas that stood in sharp contrast to the Chicago high-rise architecture. The scenery that Marion saw speeding past the Pullman car windows on her long ride north was beautiful, vast, and wild. During the long trip, Marion and Alex worked on the nuances of the fictional character that Marion would inhabit. Also on the train were the other drivers, with their Fords and Briscoes loaded onto a separate car. It was two days of eating and drinking, hashing out the schedule, and sharing racing war stories between the men and two women. Marion was traveling with Elfrieda Mais, who was a veteran on the Canadian circuit, and Marion was soaking up all the advice that she could get from Mais.

Marion and Alex settled on her fictional racing character. She would be a celebrated English record holder and European champion, ready to take on the continental champions and impress on the locals the superiority of foreign drivers.

Marion Martins was new, but that meant that she could be painted in any sort of biographical portraiture, including that of an international record holder. She would be a European star making her first appearance in Canada in front of the lucky crowds right there in the Saskatchewan province, taking on perennial favorite Elfrieda Mais.

"The English Daredevil" versus "The American Champ" storyline was catnip for the fans, and the pre-event tickets sold fast.

On July 2, 1925, the Saskatchewan *Leader-Post* newspaper announced the lineup for the Dominion Day celebration at the Regina Fairgrounds. Besides listing the familiar names of John DePalma, Bob Wallace, and Emory Collins, the interview article focused on the arrival of Marion Martins:

> Miss Marion Martin, daring English pilot and holder of the Brooklands [England] racing record, is probably the only space-eater entered that was really pleased over the rain. Miss Martin said that her mount, that she has labeled "Betsy Tom" always stores up a lot of energy after a postponed race, and she has never been beaten in a match held after the regular time. Miss Elfreida Mais, champion lady race driver of the world, who is matched in a special event against Miss Martin, will probably have a few kicks at the throttle to say about that.[7]

Sloan attracted the entertainment-hungry locals through newspaper press releases that his stable of "international stars" would be appearing at their small hometown fairgrounds and racing against the local boys. The small Canada market couldn't lure the big vaudeville legends like Al Jolson to come to Regina, but they could get "American Racing Champion Elfrieda Mais,"[8] and the townspeople would show up in droves to cheer the celebrity on.

The fans already knew and loved Mais. She had been a star on this northern track circuit for several years, and she was still the main female attraction here. She performed admirably and drove well, but there was just *too little* drama with Elfrieda and therefore little in the way of headlines. Elfrieda Mais was too humble and too clean-cut, and the sight of a solitary woman driving by herself in circles just wasn't the draw it once was. The 1925 season was one in which Mais would no longer be the sole marquee woman racer north of the border.

The Dominion Day races were rained out and rescheduled for the following evening. It had the effect of priming the pump of interest, as the newspaper feature had pronounced that Martins was undefeated after a rainout, so her reputation was now on the line.

Four thousand people showed up for the match on July 2, with 2,900 of them outside the gate with an obstructed view of the track. These fans were more than happy to trade a distant view of the action for the savings of an admission ticket.

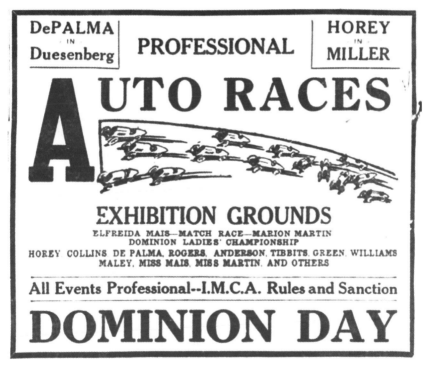

Figure 3.2. Advertisement for the Dominion Day Auto Races appearing in the *Leader-Post* of Regina, Saskatchewan, Canada, on June 30, 1925.

LEADER POST

49

After a few men's events, the women contestants were announced, and they paraded side by side in front of the grandstand, steering their race cars onto the wet dirt track. The crowd hushed and waited for the flag to drop.

They were off!

The race was a wild one. It was a muddy, loose track, and the two women seemed to be competing for more than just the entertainment of the crowd; this was serious racing for bragging rights, a battle for supremacy.

Both Miss Martin and Miss Mais drove dangerously, fighting desperately for the win. Each time one pulled ahead of the other, a mud shower thrown up by the hard rubber tires drenched their competitor. Had it been two men going head-to-head like this, they would have been applauded for their bravery, but instead, the women received backhanded compliments from the newspapers on their battle.

"Women are notoriously reckless drivers, and this pair were no exception. Miss Mais, driving a Mercedes, was outmaneuvered by the French girl who was at the wheel of a Fronty-Ford. They skidded their mile in a quick time of one minute and a fraction over eleven seconds. It was a nice exhibition of wheel-work and nerve,"[9] the *Leader-Post* reported. They also admitted that the race had given the crowd "a real thrill."[10] Marion crossed the finish line first, backing up her bravado about never losing in the rain, and Canada's racetracks now had a white-hot rivalry for the summer.

The men's results were almost an afterthought in the same article. In just one race, Marion had been transformed in the papers from "English Brooklands record holder"[11] to French champion.

On July 6, the *Calgary Herald* announced the arrival of Alex Sloan of Chicago, who showed up before the racers to see the events. He needed the extra time to count the gate receipts because his new star attraction was gathering a tremendous amount of publicity momentum, and he was selling a lot of tickets. The July 8 *Herald* headline about the races that coming weekend were straight to the point: "Marion Martin Challenges Lady Auto Racing Champion,"[12] and Elfrieda Mais was bumped down below the fold.

It's clear that the personal magnetism of her "foreign" opponent was driving the coverage, and it must have stung Mais because their next race had a much different feel than the first.

The local Alberta papers did their part and primed the pump for the July 11 event, lauding Miss Martins's stellar racing record in Chicago, trumpeting her defeat of Curly Young at the North Shore track (the opposite was actually the truth) and peddling the idea that "she has the greatest following of any driver."[13] That line *may* have been true. Sloan was busy feeding the press all the myths he could compose, and the papers were all too happy to print them. It sold papers, and it was a great buildup for the rematch.

The other Calgary Stampede festivities at Victoria Park that Saturday were just warm-ups for the big track events. Twenty-one thousand attendees bought tickets for the bucking horses and steer-riding contests, but at the end of the day, after a series of races featuring the men, the one auto match everyone was waiting for would close the show.

Elfrieda Mais hedged her bets for the rematch. No longer driving the bigger and slower Mercedes, Mais was at the wheel of a quick Briscoe. It was the same car that had finished a close second in an earlier race that afternoon with Emory Collins piloting it, finishing just behind Fred Horey, who was driving the feared Miller Special.

Marion drove the Frontenac Ford again. She fell four car lengths behind when a terrible mechanical failure occurred at a critical spot in the race. The left rear wheel of her Ford came loose, spun off the rim, and ricocheted against the outer fence. Coming into the corner curve and on the verge of disaster, her tail end dragged crazily through the fine dirt. Marion remained calm. She kept as tight a grip on her nerves as she did on the wheel. The steering wheel yanked viciously in her grasp and tore her right glove off, taking with it some skin from the back of her hand. Quick to react, she somehow managed to maintain control, and no one else was hurt. She lost the race but won the hearts of the fans.

The reporters on the scene swooned over the European with the cool demeanor, who had looked death in the eye and didn't flinch. Once more, the post-race headlines were all about Miss Martins. The rivalry intensified. The Edmonton fans, next up on the schedule, were champing at the bit, anticipating their own local appearance of the daredevil duo, and the *Edmonton Journal* spun out a lengthy feature on the upcoming racing event. The chief male contestant, Fred Horey, was profiled first, and then the article closed with a description of the match between European champion Martins and the "Champion Lady Race Driver of the World,"[14] Mais. The story said that the organizers were contemplating setting up the event as a time trial with the purpose of breaking the track record, but after two nose-to-nose matches, both Marion and Elfrieda were taking the races too seriously for trials and exhibitions.

On Monday, July 13, 1925, Marion Martins and her Ford stormed into the Edmonton Fairgrounds. She pulled double duty for the event. Her first go-round was in the match race against Elfrieda. Mais, in the quick Briscoe race car, developed early engine trouble and was forced to pull up lame to the side in the first lap. Marion showed no mercy and floored it, tearing around the track by herself, with the screaming crowd spurring her on.

She "showed plenty of racing courage" and "never loafed a second on her journey,"[15] said the local paper. And she was just warming up. In the second-to-the-last match of the night, she took on Al Cotey in a three-lap run. Al was one of the top dirt track drivers in the world, nearly always finishing in the money in the men's matches. He was running in his Elcar, and Marion was once again in a Fronty Ford. Al chivalrously ceded her the inside track line for most of the race, and Marion made the most of it. She put the pedal down and opened up a lead immediately, pulling ahead in the first curve and increasing it on the first backstretch. Cotey poured it on in the second lap, closing the gap, but the third lap was all Martins, and she won comfortably. Her time was a full second faster than in the Mais match.

When Alex Sloan saw how smoothly Marion drove against the men, he immediately sent out a new press release, along with a picture of the charming champ for good measure, announcing that on the following Saturday, July 18, at the Edmonton track, Marion would match her skill against not one but *three* men: Bob Wallace, Red Maley, and Emory Collins.

This was unheard of. Never before had a woman raced three top male professionals on a track in Canada. The injury and fatality rate in this young sport was sobering, and Marion was now driving the same dangerous tracks at the same speed as the experienced and aggressive older drivers.

A win might have been too much to expect against three of the savviest drivers on the circuit, but Bob Wallace had engine trouble and dropped out after the first lap. That left her battling Maley and Collins. Emory Collins (with that fast Briscoe) jumped out in front and drove with one eye on the track and the other on Marion. His Briscoe stirred up a dry, dusty dirt cloud that made the curves twice as difficult for the two following cars, and Collins used it to his utmost advantage to keep his number one seeding. He had been near the top in most of the previous races in this Canadian tour, and he wasn't about to give an edge to a rookie driver, man or woman. But Martins came in second, clawing ahead of Maley at the finish line.

From here on out, Marion's races against men would be much more common than her matches against women. Sloan saw that Marion could hold her own against any of the male drivers in his stable, and that made her an even more valuable part of the team.

The next two months were a whirlwind for her. She was achieving quick and public success in one of the least likely fields of opportunity for women in 1925. She was getting adulation from the crowds and fame that she never could have anticipated just a few years before when she was a young woman living in Memphis. She was seeing places and doing things she never would have otherwise.

Martins was delighted by everything new, even the old-fashioned hansom carriages that carried the tourists around Montreal. The *Montreal Star* newspaper remarked on this in one of its race features on August 21. "When the young lady driver arrived in Montreal today she expressed her delight in seeing the old-fashioned cabs here for the convenience of getting around the city, as she does not feel at ease driving in a taxi, no matter how slow it is proceeding. On the track it is a different story, however, with herself at the wheel."[16]

The 1925 season in northeastern Canada was a short schedule, just a few events, and then Marion Martins would be done and headed south. One noticeable change in her billing at this time was the reference to her

in the papers as "Mademoiselle Martens,"[17] her Quebec-friendly saluta-
tion. Her chief competitor in Montreal was Louis Disbrow. Disbrow was
a legend in the sport, and Marion followed his lead on the track and off.
Just like Disbrow's own adaptation of the "Frenchman" moniker for him
made sense because of the largely Francophile crowds up north, Marion
also embraced and adopted a fictional French identity for herself, starting
with her series of races with Disbrow.

Figure 3.3 Advertisement for Delorimier Park Auto Races announcing the appear-
ance of Mademoiselle Martens, appearing in the *Gazette* of Montreal, Quebec,
Canada, on August 20, 1925.
GAZETTE.

Louis Disbrow did his part in selling the events. He spoke at length with the *Montreal Gazette* on August 20, spinning out a warning to anyone who thought there the dangers were exaggerated:

Automobile racing is the profession adopted by two classes of men. Those who value their necks and mix brains with gasoline, and those who are not afraid nor hear any warning signs when they are at the wheel of a juggernaut. I have not sufficient fingers to enumerate the stout-hearted, but foolish drivers of the latter type who are no longer with us. But, on a single hand I can count the number of fellows who have been able to cheat the scythe wielder, year after year just by using a little judgment when they are piloting the man-killing gasoline chariots around the death-inviting turns of a modern speedway.[18]

Instead of building fear, the newspaper warnings of possible death on the racetrack had heightened public interest. In front of a raucous crowd at the Central Canada Exhibition in Ottawa on Saturday, August 22, Marion took a lap around the course in a borrowed Bugatti at a bit of a slower pace than normal. It was the first time in this car, so she didn't take any chances, and there wasn't anyone else on the track to bring out her competitive nature. She was prepping herself for the Louis Disbrow matches.

On Sunday afternoon, August 23, at Delorimier Park in Montreal, Marion aired out the Fronty Ford for a quick masterclass of speed, tearing around the track at almost 60 miles per hour. Marion and Louis then thrilled the fans in Montreal with an exhibition run together around the converted horse track for the huge crowd. It was understood by all that this was a friendly pairing, two teammates airing out their mounts in a two-lap show. There isn't even a mention of a winner; this was Louis and her having fun and Marion picking up some more tricks from the veteran.

The largest fair crowds in half a decade, 8,000 strong, showed up at the Ottawa Fairgrounds the following week, Saturday, August 29, to see the heralded Miss Martins flaunt her skill. The book on her now was that her experience as the French champion would cause consternation for all of the male drivers on the circuit.

Martins never disappointed in the thrills department. Halfway through the first lap against two male opponents in Ottawa, her car caught fire. Thanks to her calm nerves and smooth steering, she escaped the flames while fanning the adulation of the crowd.

It wasn't just pure talent that made her succeed; no one else worked harder. In the middle of the Montreal–Ottawa–Toronto tour, she took a detour to Detroit, Michigan, for the state fair, did an exhibition, and then headed to Rochester, New York, for a racing event at the Dewey Avenue Track, performing at all three distant venues in the space of two weeks.

Promoter Alex Sloan was on a roll. He was sending out press releases at a rapid clip, embroidering the background of his star attraction with more and more fanciful descriptions, painting her as a Joan of Arc for women's equality. He sent a bio to the Rochester, New York, *Democrat and Chronicle*, printed on the day of her dramatic Ottawa race:

> Mlle. Martens is a petite French maid who is declared to handle a racing car over the beach courses, the board tracks and the dirt speedways in a manner which has aroused the jealousy of the daredevils of the roaring road. Not since the early days of the auto racing sport when Mrs. Joan Newton Cuneo, wife of a New York Banker, participated in the famed Glidden Tour and on the dirt tracks against the most daring and skillful experts of the opposite sex has a woman entered the sport with ability to match ability and gameness with the male stars. That is, not until the clever little Martens girl appeared on the scene in this country.[19]

Sloan then sent another piece to the Rochester paper to be printed two days later:

> The entry of Mlle. Marion Martens, petite French girl, champion woman driver of the world, has created great enthusiasm among the women speed fans of Rochester. Certain it is that the daring little girl will have the support of every woman who attends the races. Her ability to handle the fast French Renault racing car over the Dewey Avenue track in actual comparison with the greatest male drivers in the game, should prove most gratifying to a host of women who drive their own

cars in excellent fashion but are always on defensive on the account of the criticism born of prejudice from men who are not willing to admit that women can ever become good automobile drivers.[20]

In a couple of paragraphs, Alex Sloan had made Marion's racing against men a referendum of women drivers while simultaneously comparing her to the most famous female driver ever, Joan Cuneo. His portrayal of Marion as a dainty foreign girl competing head-to-head against grizzled male veterans made the races "can't miss" events.

* * *

On one of her many side trips, Marion dipped down to Detroit for a quick appearance with Louis Disbrow at the state fair. She set another women's track speed record but not without a price. On a match race, she lost control of the car, a rare event, and ended up taking out several feet of fence and damaging her ribs. She took no time off to recuperate, hopping on a train to New York for the Labor Day event.

On September 7, in Rochester, thick black clouds rolled in from the Atlantic, dumping an ocean's worth of water onto the track. With torrential rain turning the course into a mud slog, some drivers withdrew, including the legendary Sig Haugdahl, who wasn't keen on risking a possible wreck of his famous Wisconsin Special for a low-key event. Haugdahl had run the monster-sized racer on Daytona Beach in 1922 and set an unofficial speed record of 180 miles per hour, and it was more suited for dry straightaways, not twisty bogs.

In the driving rain, a dirt track isn't a course for speed; it's an endurance test. You can't see the proper line for the bends because one mud pit looks like another. With the open cockpits and no roofs to protect them, they were completely exposed to the elements. The drivers felt every splash and every clump of mud in their teeth and their eyes. It was miserable. Marion loved racing in the rain, but she hated thunder and lightning.

No one would have said a word if she took her ball and went home, but Martins got behind the wheel of a misfiring Peugeot in the storm. There she was, flying through the muck and gravel, hanging on for dear life, with broken ribs, in some of the most dangerous driving situations possible. She limped around the track at half speed, with the flooded car stopping often and being pulled to the side by mechanics to get it going again.

Louis Disbrow and Puddy Hoffman took it on themselves to entertain the drenched audience by staging a spontaneous match race while the pit mechanics tried repeatedly to fix Marion's backfiring car. The racecourse actually developed a small pond along the inside rail that required workmen to dig a small ditch to drain, but these vile conditions were just an afterthought to Disbrow. He had won and placed in two earlier matches that day, and he finished this third race covered from head to toe in globs of mud. Marion, soldiering on through the sheets of rain in her own open-topped and malfunctioning vehicle, grew in stature as a driver in Disbrow's eyes. Marion clearly wasn't just a pretty ornament for newspaper ads; she was a tough, ambitious competitor. Getting a legend's respect was a bonus.

* * *

Marion was ready to make a break with her past. She was at the point where she didn't want to be associated with her ex-husband or to be accused of riding the coattails of his success in the racing arena. It was time to break away from her married identity, and on October 3, she made one last visit to hometown Memphis as Marion Martens. It was her last appearance as a driver under that name.

She had fond memories of the state fair as a child. In 1915, almost 10 years ago to the day, when she had seen Elfrieda Mais race Bunny Thornton, the U.S. champion versus the European champion, and now Marion wore both of those champion titles.

The race day was set for Saturday, October 3, by Frank Fuller, who was still the secretary of the fair and also an employee of the IMCA, and Marion was running in two contests. She would attempt to set a track record for women in a one-lap exhibition, then she would close the show, one slot before the race finals, in a head-to-head match against Al Cotey.

She did set the speed record as expected, but lost a close nip-and-tuck battle with Cotey. Al always fought like the devil to beat Marion, and he had to use every bit of his veteran's skill and ability to eke out the win.

And that was the end of "Marion Martins." From winning two out of three races in Chicago in July 1924, she rose through the ranks of dirt track drivers to become one of the main draws on the entire racing circuit, earning herself and Alex Sloan a lot of publicity and a lot of money. But Sloan and Marion were cooking up bigger plans.

On October 7, 1925, the *Atlanta Constitution* announced that there was to be a special attraction at the Lakewood Track during the South eastern Fair later that month. In addition to the previously publicized Louis Disbrow, the world champion "Mlle. Joan LeCosta"[21] was going to attempt to break her world record in the mile (Marion always pronounced Joan as "Jo-Ann"[22]). Marion Carver had become Marion Martins by marriage and now Joan LeCosta (soon to be spelled LaCosta) by committing herself to the spotlight.

This event at the racetrack in Atlanta would be her first driving appearance since her duel in the rain with Louis Disbrow in September.

From complete obscurity to the main attraction of the circuit, that was the magic of Alex Sloan. She hadn't appeared under this name anywhere in the country, and here she was at the top of the bill, with the *Atlanta Constitution* calling her "the real attraction in the day's program"[23] in its October 7 edition. And she was.

Unfortunately, in her maiden voyage with her new name, Joan LaCosta, Mother Nature intervened. Heavy rains came down Saturday, and the races were called off. But it was just a blip in Joan's bookings. She was scheduled for both the Mississippi State Fair and the Alabama State Fair in Birmingham days later, and now the papers were running her picture along with the stories about the races.

According to the *Birmingham News*, she was a track and course record holder in France, Belgium, and England and was looking to set another in Alabama. The Mississippi paper the *Clarion-Ledger* made note of her "laurels won on many racetracks"[24] in its headline posted over their article about Joan.

The stories also mentioned that Joan was receiving telegraph wires to determine if she was interested in a match race with any of the male drivers, including Louis Disbrow. It was a clever feeler planted in a very public way, setting up Joan as the recipient of the stunt and not the instigator. It was a way of promoting her as a champion instead of an upstart challenger, and it worked.

Louis Disbrow played along. He had seen that same grit and determination before in another female racer: Joan Newton Cuneo. Disbrow had helped her to set women's speed records back in the 1910s. But there was a key difference between the two women. Cuneo had plenty to return to after her racing exploits; she was wealthy, well known, and the toast of society. Joan LaCosta had nothing. She was a twice-divorced single mother, running from a restrictive childhood, chasing ravenous ambition, and probably still trying to impress her parents back in Memphis. This one thing, racing, was what she was proud of, and she was better at it than almost any other woman alive.

In the lead-up to the Mississippi event, there is no published acrimony between the two, no snide remarks published in the papers about women and racing. Disbrow had seen it all, and he was probably secretly pleased that Joan was using the same first-name moniker as his old friend Joan. And he knew LaCosta was talented, that she wasn't just a gewgaw to draw in the gawkers. She was good, and she was fearless.

The October 22, 1925, Mississippi State Fair event was getting a grand buildup. Besides the star "European woman champ" Joan, promoter Alex Sloan had booked a top-notch roster of male professionals, including Fred Horey, Louis Disbrow, Johnny Waters, Al Cotey, Ray Lampkin, and more. This was the same team that was headed two days later to Alabama for that state's fair races. This close-knit group was like a family, so naturally they had conflicts and fights, but every time the drivers walked out to their cars and heard the cheers of thousands of men, women, and children in the grandstands, their hearts beat faster, and the sun felt warmer on their faces. The people in the stands paid their 50 cents so that they would remember this day as long as they lived, and the drivers knew they had to make these shows memorable.

In Jackson, Mississippi, the conditions were perfect. It was dry, so the track was hard, and Joan LaCosta flew around the course at "a mile a minute,"[25] thrilling the crowd and again topping the headlines about the races in the local papers, including one from the *Clarion-Ledger*.

In Alabama, on October 24, she had the same impressive result, clocking an "official" time of 1:04 to equal the record. It was an incredible achievement given that it had rained hard on Friday, so LaCosta had to use a completely different skill set to be competitive. Even though Saturday was drier early in the day, it rained again before her run, making her record time even more impressive.

Quite often, the "official" winning race times at these shows were more dependent on the size of the crowds than the actual stopwatch. Today, there were 30,000 paying customers in the stands, and though the track was a muddy mess and a series of horse races earlier in the day had torn it up even more, a record-tying time was announced after LaCosta had slid and slopped her way around the course and over the finish line. The weather was so inclement Saturday evening that the popular

MILE A MINUTE PACE MADE
BY YOUTHFUL WOMAN PILOT
GREAT CROWD CHEERS RACERS

Woman Champion Drives a Mile in Minute, Six Seconds, Which is Four Second Faster Than the Average Time Made by Male Drivers in Regular Races

Figure 3.4. Headline in the *Clarion-Ledger* of Jackson, Mississippi, on October 23, 1925.
CLARION-LEDGER.

postshow fireworks display was canceled, so witnessing a "world record" was a nice consolation prize for the soaking-wet crowd.

Joan LaCosta and her supporting acts were so popular that the fans demanded another round of racing for the next year, and it was a request that state fair president Mr. Brown gave serious consideration to. The main attraction was a woman who was perceived by the public as a dainty, pretty lady outside of the racing world and who then transformed into a determined, focused driver at the harness of a high power of a Frontenac Ford on event day. The regular fair attendees were used to watching the best of the best on the dirt track, but Joan LaCosta was someone extraordinary. Right there, in their town, racing the top male drivers head-to-head, was the fastest woman in the world. She had arms like steel cables, a lead foot on the gas, and tremendous courage.

There were a few stray instances where her old name was trotted out. On November 8, in Waco, Texas, "Marion Martens" made an appearance without the standard accompanying fanfare of her being the European champion. In these smaller rural venues, just the novelty of watching a good woman driver face off against the men was enough to sell out tickets.

In the big-city shows, Joan was consistently at the top of the billing at almost every event, which meant that she got paid at the top of the scale and had the biggest font on the promotional posters. Did the other, more experienced drivers like Ray Lampkin care that Joan was getting the lion's share of attention? Possibly, but they also realized that if more fans came out to see Joan, it also meant that more fans would see them. That increase in exposure translated to more money and more bookings for everyone. If any resentment existed, it was snuffed out by the obvious benefit of racing before the biggest crowds most of these drivers had ever seen.

The return to the Alabama Fairgrounds was a perfect example. Because of the sheer enthusiasm and size of the crowds at the October event, the state fairgrounds track added two more encore dates on November 10 and 11 for the Sloan team headed by Joan LaCosta.

Alex Sloan wasn't content with just repeating the same old shows; he wanted to raise the stakes and maybe get a few more bucks in his pocket

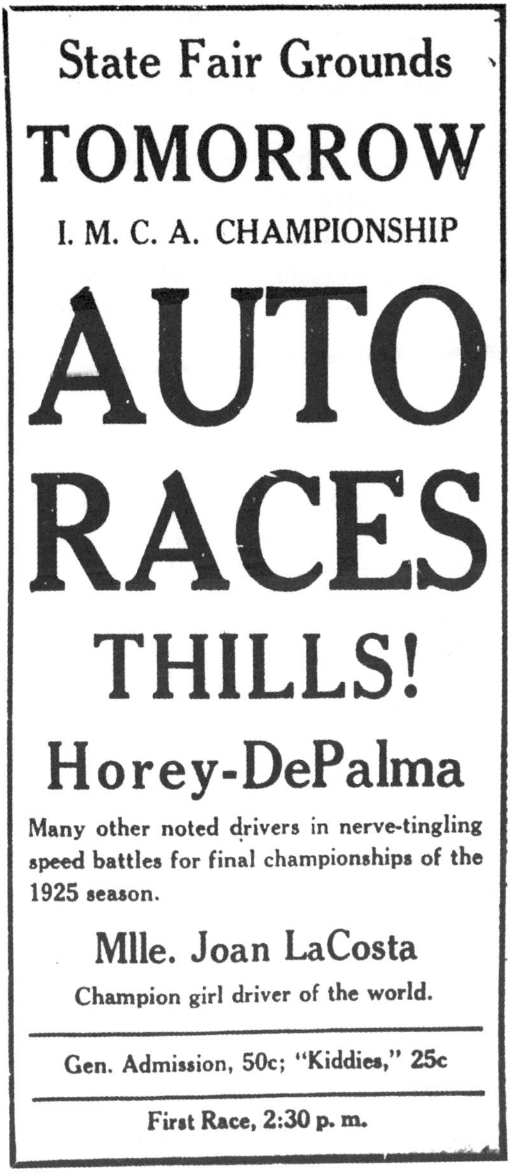

Figure 3.5. Advertisement for Auto Races at the Alabama State Fair Grounds appearing in the *Birmingham News* of Birmingham, Alabama, on November 10, 1925.

BIRMINGHAM NEWS.

as well. In a flash of inspiration, he conjured up a brilliant promotional controversy that would prove to have long legs over the next year.

Sloan fed local newspapers stories that Joan LaCosta wanted to race against the men and had her send official requests to the national governing body. Those requests (which were actually ghostwritten by Sloan himself) were denied via a spate of angry telegrams from the IMCA. This caused an outraged backlash from the female race fans of Birmingham, according to the papers. But unbeknownst to the paper's subscribers, Alex Sloan not only promoted these same races but also was the head of IMCA, the racing association that made the rules. Sloan was telegraphing himself for permission for Joan to race the men's champ, and then he was ceremoniously denying that request in public, but in reality, *it was in response to himself.*

It was brilliant marketing. Joan appeared disappointed in public, but she was in on the plot as well. She knew her time would eventually come; it just took a little time for the crust to cook.

Part of the long-term plan was leaked in the pre-race publicity for Birmingham. It was mentioned in an article that Joan had returned from Daytona Beach, where she was preparing her car for a new speed record, and this time it wasn't just Sloan hyperbole. She would be making the trip back to Daytona Beach later in April for just that reason.

Joan's appearances in those last two days of exhibition racing in Alabama were scheduled for the middle of the race card, illustrating the collective star power that was gathered for this show. She attempted to break her own previous record by completing two laps in just over a minute. She came close, tying her best mark at 1:04 on November 10, but the next day in Birmingham was wet and cold, and Joan had trouble keeping her line. She skidded her speedy Frontenac Ford in the south corner of the track and finished five seconds slower than her previous run the month before at 1:09. It was still a commendable effort, though, and enough of a performance to please the grandstand crowd of 5,000.

The 1925 general race season ended, and Mrs. Walter Martins had transformed into Joan LaCosta. It wasn't the last name she would answer to, but it would be the one she would be remembered by.

CHAPTER FOUR

The Record Book

THE YEAR 1926 WAS A MOMENTOUS ONE FOR FEMALE ATHLETES. THE most famous in the world was Suzanne Lenglen, a charismatic, fashionable French tennis player who was young, bold, and brash and at the top of the game. She was cocky, wore scandalous outfits, and didn't kowtow to men or authority. Her only weaknesses appeared when she lost matches and, in turn, her temper, which was a rare sight.

It was an exciting time for sportswomen and their promoters, and Alex Sloan wasn't the type to let the publicity parade pass him by. It was the early beginnings of purely amateur female athletes transitioning into professional celebrities, and never again would the top women competitors in any sport receive only small honorariums for winning events. Sponsorships and prize money were escalating as the women's public popularity rose. There was more and more money and fame to be exploited.

Sloan was a master at creating and then riding the crest of the latest fad, and he was conjuring up a masterpiece.

December, January, and February were the quiet months in the racing calendar. In Miami, the Daytona Beach and other Deep South racetracks were still being constructed, and the other venues up north and around the country were mothballed for the winter season. During this lull, being idle meant losing money, so in this slow season, Alex Sloan brainstormed new publicity stunts to keep the attention on his entertainment business.

Daytona's white sand beach along the ocean's waterline beckoned. It was remarkably suited for speed. The beach was hard and smooth,

500 feet wide, with long straightaway stretches. In 1922, Sig Haugdahl had set the world speed record there, hitting 180 miles per hour in his Wisconsin Special.

He had moved down to South Florida permanently and still owned that legendary race car, a sliver-shaped monster of a machine. Sig was also part of the Alex Sloan stable, and he was well aware of Sloan's instincts for drama and stories. When he was approached by Sloan about the use of his fabled Special and whom it was for, Sig quickly agreed and made sure it was mechanically ready for action, then turned the keys over. He trusted only one woman to pilot this giant speedster: Joan LaCosta.

Joan looked right at home behind the wheel. She fit snugly into the cockpit, tucked in behind the miniature windscreen, her head just barely peeking up above the dash. Her corded arms were plenty powerful enough to wrestle with the wooden steering wheel, and speed didn't scare her; it thrilled her. It was a throwback to the memory of her adventurous Chicago days when she went whistling through the clouds in a creaky, canvas-winged airplane.

On April 2, Joan LaCosta announced to the press that she was going to be making a run at the world speed record for women. She was going to be using the Sig Haugdahl Wisconsin Special, the car that already held the overall record, and she was going to accomplish it at the same venue where Haugdahl had set the record: Daytona Beach. Advising her in the attempt would be famous racer and ace mechanic Ray Lampkin and legendary driver Louis Disbrow.

Disbrow was happy to help. He was impressed that Joan had the courage to strap herself into a land rocket that could fly along the beach at over 100 miles per hour with no fire suit, no roll cage, and no three-point safety harness system in place to save her in case of an accident. All she had was a leather helmet, a shield mask to deflect the abrasive salt air whipping past her face, her driving overalls, and 100 pounds of pure courage. Louis admired her grit.

In the Jackson, Mississippi, *Clarion-Ledger* newspaper from May 23, 1926, a picture showcased the group when they were together on Daytona Beach.

Figure 4.1. Sig Haugdahl at the wheel of his Wisconsin Special at Daytona Beach, Florida, on April 7, 1922.
ARKIV.

Joan LaCosta wore her protective face mask, and the high ocean waves provided a backdrop for her and her close friend Oscar Anderson. Wedging himself into the shot is Alex Sloan as the flagman, his former football lineman physique and jutting jaw giving him away. Crew chief Ray Lampkin (who would later own the Wisconsin Special) is at the wheel in the shot with Sloan. Ray was there to make sure Joan's mechanical steed was in record-breaking shape. Not pictured was Sig Haugdahl, who went over the course daily and offered Joan tips on handling the vehicle at speed.

LaCosta had a very powerful weapon at her disposal in Louis Disbrow. He was her driving mentor who gave her his hard-earned advice and pushed her to improve. No one knew more about different driving conditions than Disbrow. By 1926, he had been racing 30 years on hundreds of tracks, and there wasn't anything related to racing he hadn't experienced. In addition, he was a top-notch mechanic, having owned

Figure 4.2. Joan LaCosta in the Wisconsin Special, photographed for Wide World Photo on April 25, 1926, and appearing in the *Minneapolis Journal* of Minneapolis, Minnesota, on May 2, 1926.
WIDE WORLD PHOTO.

a couple of custom car build shops that created racing machines out of parts and pieces. He would help make sure the Wisconsin Special was in top form. Joan was ecstatic.

A publicity photo taken to be sent over the wires to all the major newspapers in the country shows LaCosta at the wheel and a young girl about her daughter June's age (she would have been nine years old) perched on the rear of the speedster. Her smile betrays no fear of any possible danger ahead. It was a postcard-pretty scene, a lark at the beach.

AUTO SPEED MERCHANTS COMING

Figure 4.3. Oscar "Swede" Anderson, Joan LaCosta, and Alex Sloan pictured in the *Clarion-Ledger* on April 25, 1926.
CLARION-LEDGER.

On Wednesday, April 14, 1926, Joan's day started early, with a full-speed practice run at 6:00 in the morning. Joan took off confidently, the speedster silhouetted against the light gray, hazy sky. The gentle ocean waves lapped rhythmically beside her. The salt air was brisk and cool, with temperatures in the mid-sixties. The sand was smooth and hard, and the wheels glided along the beach almost effortlessly, but as she guided the steering wheel, she sensed something was not quite right.

The engine was sounding different than usual, straining with the acceleration. Seconds later, her gas tank exploded in flames, sending up a

Figure 4.4. Joan LaCosta in the Wisconsin Special, with a child who may be her daughter, June, pictured in the *Illustrated London News* of London, England, on April 16, 1927.
ILLUSTRATED LONDON NEWS.

wall of fire in front of her face. She had been in tricky situations before and experienced her share of spinouts and fence crashes on the dirt tracks, but this was frighteningly new to her. Immediately, she felt her arms and neck searing from the heat.

She relied on her instincts and the lessons instilled in her. Louis Disbrow's instructions for handling an emergency had been hammered into her brain. If you can't stop or if the vehicle's mechanics go haywire, then go into the water, he had told her. The surf will slow you, protect you. Don't be afraid of crashing the car; just make sure you're protected.

With his voice in her head, at over 100 miles per hour, Joan yanked the wheel toward the waves. It did the trick, slowing the roadster down and giving Joan the chance to leap from the burning wreck.

Figure 4.5. Joan LaCosta jumping into the Daytona surf on April 14, 1926, pictured in the *New York Herald Tribune* of New York, New York, on May 2, 1926.
NEW YORK HERALD TRIBUNE.

Figure 4.6. Joan LaCosta jumping from her flaming Wisconsin Special on April 14, 1926.
CARADISIAC.

According to the April 15 edition of the *Birmingham News*, she collapsed unconscious on the beach and was revived by onlookers. The thrilling pictures were wired to newspapers around the world.

That was the *official* story. The most dramatic parts of this account were true: Joan had a very close call, and she received some nasty burns from the accident. But there were no newspaper photographers around to witness the early morning practice run, so one of the most incredible moments in speed history was almost lost to the press.

Alex Sloan, always the showman, made sure that there was a "recording" of Joan's now-legendary leap from the burning Wisconsin Special. There was even a behind-the-scenes report in a local paper about his efforts:

WRECK REENACTED AS CAMERAS CLICK
Joan LaCosta Repeats Near Tragedy on Beach for Moving Pictures.

Mlle. Joan LaCosta, world's champion girl driver, proved her daring nerve and spirit yesterday by reenacting for the movies her narrow escape from death Wednesday when her Wisconsin Special burst into flames as she was streaking down in practice for world record trials.

The scenes of the machine burning in the ocean and her rescue will furnish the "big punch" of a moving picture which will probably be released under the title of "The Queen of Speed," and will include other episodes of her work on Daytona Beach while attempting to shatter all feminine speed records.

Thrilling hundreds of Floridans [*sic*] and visitors who stopped traffic on the beach between Clarendon approach and Ormand with their automobiles, Mlle. LaCosta drove the big white machine out into the ocean while fire spurted into the air and flames lashed back at her.

Exactly as during the real experience of Wednesday, she leaped from the machine in shallow water, slid for a ways on the rough beach and was rescued by a mechanic with cameras grinding on the nearby sand. Her tumble into the water was less disastrous than on Wednesday, although she was bruised by the force of the fall. She proved her mettle, however, by staying in the flaming car until the director shouted "jump," endangering her life for the second time. After her realistic leap into the water, she lay on the beach with the waves washing over her until she was carried out soaked from head to foot.

Motion pictures will be taken of her official beach trials and of other experiences on the beach, and the "shots" will be worked into a continuity to be written by one of the best known film writers.[1]

But that wasn't the only version of the event. The *Bridgeport Telegram* of April 30, 1926, had another yarn waiting for its readers:

WOMAN DRIVER OF RACING CAR HAS TEST OF NERVE
Joan LaCosta Brings Speeding Auto to Quick Stop When Flames Spread.

While long-headed psychologists are debating the probable causes for the modern feminine pursuit of thrills and the evident attempt to throw off the age-old inhibitions of womanhood, young women are figuratively winning their spurs in some of the most death-defying activities in the field of sports. An outstanding example in this new phase of the feminine chase of the elusive "kick" to be had from life, is Mlle. Joan LaCosta, speedstress, whose experiences as the driver of racing automobiles have already afforded her enough thrills to last one ordinary person a lifetime. But Mlle. LaCosta, who is young, charming and chic, as well as French, keeps right at it.

The female of the species may or may not be more deadly than the male, as Mr. Kipling would have it, but certainly she would appear to be fully as daring. She is now going in for aviation, speed boat racing, motorcycle contests and automobile racing at a rate which would appear to prove that the old-fashioned woman whose place was the home and nowhere else has been relegated to the limbo of lost things, together with long feminine tresses, dodo eggs and that late lamented attribute, girlish modesty and the blush. Gin, jazz and "necking" provided diversion for young womanhood in the period which seems to have just ended, and the frank discussion of sex gave the dear girls a vicarious thrill. Now, psychologists say, young women find themselves desperate for something to lift them from the sordidness of humdrum existence, and they have turned to intensive activity in sports. It is a fact that young women are emerging in rapidly increasing numbers as the victors in activities hitherto reserved for the so-called dominant and aggressive male. She is overtaking her lord and master in contests of speed, nerve and endurance, and she appears to be finding great pleasure and exhilaration in this new field.

The woman golfer and tennis champion has become a fixture in modern life, and the woman aviator has long been a staple of the rotogravure sections of the newspapers. But the woman driver of a racing automobile is a comparatively new thing and it will require time for most of us to realize that she is a competitor in the field with Barney Oldfield, Dario Resta, Ralph DePalma, and the other dare-devil drivers of high speed motorcars.

Mlle. LaCosta was driving her racing car on Daytona Beach, Florida, at the rate of 130 miles an hour in her attempt to break all records previously hung up by women racing drivers, when the gas feed line broke on her underslung speed car and the automobile caught fire. She demonstrated her quick-thinking ability and resourcefulness by bringing the flaming automobile to a quick stop and leaping to safety.

She received a few slight burns, which were treated by a physician, but she made no complaint except to regret the loss of her "ba-bee," the car which she came to know and to caress with the fondness of a lover. Witnesses of the accident congratulated her, but she waved them aside as she smiled deprecatingly and said "Eet ees nozzing."

Most of those who saw the young French woman's narrow escape a terrible death amid the flames and wreckage of her racing car thought the incident would serve to definitely discourage her from again attempting to drive at such high speed. But Mlle. LaCosta only smiled and announced that her determination to smash all previous records was merely strengthened by her failure on this occasion through an unfortunate happening.

So, instead of this nerve-racking experience causing her to become discouraged, as it would have done to thousands, nay, millions of other women, the pretty young French woman drove another car three days later and attained the astonishing speed of 138 miles an hour on the Daytona Beach speedway before a large crowd who marveled at her remarkable ability in the adept handling of such a fast-moving car. She hung up a record as a woman driver that will remain for sometime as a target for other young women similarly inclined to shoot at. But she is not satisfied, and believes she will soon be able to drive a car at the rate of 150 miles an hour or more.[2]

On June 17, 1936, Alex Sloan sat down with an interviewer from the *Des Moines Register* and told his version—and probably the one closest to the truth—of what actually happened that day:

> I took Joan LaCosta, a woman driver, and a good one, down to Florida to set a woman's record on a beach course. The trial was at 6 o'clock in the morning and when the car caught fire and Joan had to run it into the ocean to douse the flames, there were no photographers around. The camera boys showed up later and wanted pictures, so I told the boys I'd have her do it over again.
>
> But the car was so badly damaged it wouldn't run. We towed it about 60 miles an hour, cut it loose and Joan ran it into the ocean for the pictures. Racing togs made her look like a man, so I had her wear a frilly, feminine outfit. She came out of the water looking like the Wreck of the Hesperus.
>
> Just then another photographer came up, sore because he hadn't gotten a photo. But Joan wouldn't do it again unless she wore a bathing suit. She put one on, we towed the car again and pictures were snapped as the auto went into the water.[3]

Looking closely, a black cable was visible at the bottom right of the photo, pulling the car as she jumped from the opposite side of the Special.

How is it that the beat reporter's account and Sloan's crazy story could possibly be true? The biggest clue is that there are more than a few pictures of this singular event, and they're all different. Not different angles or different points in the action, but the car itself is at a different spot, and (this is the crucial proof), in the photo run by the *Atlanta Constitution* (which were always given the best stories about LaCosta by Sloan), *she's wearing a bathing suit* and a bathing cap, the least useful piece of equipment to wear at 100 miles per hour in a world record speed attempt, riding inside a ton of hot steel.

This was how publicity worked then and the way it often works today. If the reality doesn't fit the narrative, change the reality. So for

Joan Makes Daring Leap

Figure 4.7. Joan LaCosta jumping into the Daytona surf on April 14, 1926, pictured in the *Clarion-Ledger* on May 25, 1926.
CLARION-LEDGER.

nearly 100 years, readers saw the pictures of the nerveless Joan LaCosta plunging into the ocean, seconds ahead of incineration, all in pursuit of immortality and to forever etch her name in the record book. Mission accomplished. Although the car was heavily damaged, it was repairable, and the publicity of Sig's car being featured in most newspapers across the country was worth it to him. The car would be up and running again in a few months.

And what was Joan's final word on the subject?

"Wait till they rebuild that car, I'll run the wheels off of it!"[4] she told the *Journal Times* of Racine, Wisconsin.

A 1926 archive photo from the Berlin wire service Skandinaviske Berliner Korrespondez has the actual international press release with a thumbnail description of the event pasted to the back of the print. It seems to confirm some of the main facts that Sloan revealed in his interview:

A Lesson in the Curriculum of World's Records

[Dayto]na Beach, Fla.—Mlle. Joan LaCosta, plucky French girl speedstress [b]roke three world's automobile straightaway records for the kilometer, half [mile] and mile on the Ormond-Daytona Beach Speedway here recently, left no stone [untur]ned in her effort to make 138 miles per hour. After being forced to drive [her b]urning car into the ocean on her first attempt, in which she was nearly [drown]ed due to heavy clothing, she donned a bathing suit and practiced leaping [from] a racing car that was towed.

[Photo] shows Mlle. LaCosta leaping from a car driven into the ocean supposedly [on fire], to save herself from burns and possible drowning.[5]

After crashing the Wisconsin Special, LaCosta switched to Ray Lampkin's Miller Special, and in it, she established the initial fastest runs of 136 or more miles per hour. A few days later, she broke that record, speeding over the course at 138 miles per hour. The official times at

Figure 4.8. Joan LaCosta jumping into the Daytona surf on April 14, 1926, photographed by P. V. Rasmussen for Skandinaviske Berliner Korrespondent

P V RASMUSSEN,

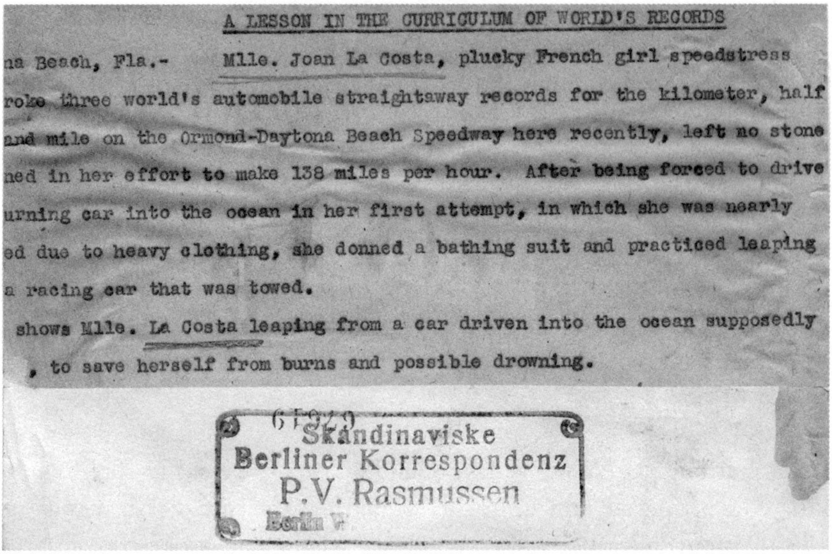

A LESSON IN THE CURRICULUM OF WORLD'S RECORDS

na Beach, Fla.-   Mlle. Joan La Costa, plucky French girl speedstress
roke three world's automobile straightaway records for the kilometer, half
and mile on the Ormond-Daytona Beach Speedway here recently, left no stone
ned in her effort to make 138 miles per hour. After being forced to drive
urning car into the ocean in her first attempt, in which she was nearly
ed due to heavy clothing, she donned a bathing suit and practiced leaping
a racing car that was towed.

   shows Mlle. La Costa leaping from a car driven into the ocean supposedly
, to save herself from burns and possible drowning.

Skandinaviske
Berliner Korrespondenz
P.V. Rasmussen
Berlin W

Figure 4.9. Label pasted to the back of the photo of Joan LaCosta jumping into the Daytona surf on April 14, 1926.
P. V. RASMUSSEN.

Daytona were noted by IMCA official A. R. Corey, who listed three passes with times of a mile in 26.27 seconds, a half mile in 13.10 seconds, and a kilometer in 16.30 seconds, which converted to rates of 136.98, 137.40, and 138 miles per hour, respectively. And the publicity pictures showed the comely Joan driving in the Miller Special in her bathing suit.

The verifications of the 145-mile-per-hour Jacksonville runs on April 23 appear to have been less than stringent. The *Atlanta Constitution*, which was the Sloan mouthpiece, mentioned the Jacksonville speeds at 145.14 miles per hour a mere two days after they supposedly happened, with no mention of pictures or official timings. The later papers would list times of 12.4 seconds for the half mile and 24.8 seconds for the mile. There were no mentions of multiple passes, which is a standard procedure to produce an average (like the three-run results she had produced the week previously).

Is it possible that she increased the speed mark by that much from her Daytona attempts yet no one was there to take pictures, release official

Figure 4.10. Joan LaCosta in her bathing suit behind the wheel, pictured in the *Times* of Munster, Indiana, on August 7, 1926.
TIMES. IMAGE ENHANCED FOR CLARITY BY ADELIS SEGUNDO BRICEÑO.

times, or write scintillating copy about "the race against the record" for release to the papers? Perhaps. Or did a skilled promoter like Sloan talk privately with Joan and suggest, "You know what? 145 miles an hour is a catchier number than 138. Let's go with that."

In any case, that was the number that stuck. It was 180 miles per hour for Sig Haugdahl and 145 for Joan LaCosta, "fastest girl in the world."[6] The number would be trotted out from Texas to Florida over the next year, and Joan suddenly had a tagline next to her name that would sell tickets even without the promotional puffery of "European Champion" or being the U.S. dirt track record holder. She was the fastest woman alive, period, and 1926 was going to be her year.

The famous beach accident had no apparent effect on Joan's psyche. She survived intact, raced many more times, and came out unscathed save for a scar on her right hand that served as a lifelong souvenir.

"I never lost my head for a second," she later recounted, "but I was scared. Calmly scared, because I knew I was trapped, and yet I never failed to know what to do. And in some way I managed to get out."[7]

Her competitive fire was stoked, and she was champing at the bit to get on the dirt tracks again. Fortunately for her and the IMCA, the high season for racing was approaching quickly.

CHAPTER FIVE

Love on the Track

MAY 12, 1926 WAS THE DAY OF THE BIG TRACK SHOW AT THE MONT-gomery Motor Classic in Alabama, a benefit race for the city's public playgrounds. This track had been a good-luck charm for Joan LaCosta. She had set records here and won over the fans, and the locale was close to her Southern roots, with her family and child just a few hours' drive away. And now there was Oscar.

Oscar Anderson, who usually went by "Swede" in the racing world, was a son of Stockholm who came to the United States to race and earned a bad-boy reputation as a professional. Anderson was a man of few words, earning the nickname "the quiet Norseman."[1] The Scandinavian was a hard worker who preferred Mercedes race cars, and he obtained his green card when he married a woman from Michigan. On the track, he was more prone to crashing his race car than the other drivers were, and he also had a temper to go with his strong good looks. He had real talent that was mixed with recklessness and determination.

Joan fell for him, hard.

Anderson was working with her in Daytona, Florida, at the time LaCosta was running her speed trials. There were a few track races in the area, and after those events concluded, Oscar and Ray Lampkin split a train freight car along with Joan to transport all of their vehicles from Florida to Alabama. It was a celebratory trip, with Joan and Oscar making racing history together, and she grew close to the bad boy from the far North. It was problematic. Oscar was married, but Joan still harbored dreams of being with him

Figure 5.1. Oscar "Swede" Anderson pictured in the *Clarion-Ledger* on May 26, 1926.
CLARION-LEDGER. IMAGE ENHANCED FOR CLARITY BY ADELIS SEGUNDO BRICEÑO.

Swede Anderson was making a name for himself as well. He got a spin in the spotlight when promoter Alex Sloan recounted to the paper a heroic story about Anderson saving a young woman's life.

According to the May 9 edition of that Sloan-fed promotional machine, the *Atlanta Constitution*, Anderson was making some practice runs on Daytona Beach on April 17 (around the time that Joan was attacking the speed records there) when he was flagged down by a frantic woman running along the surf. Her friend, Helen Weingarden, was in distress about half a mile offshore. She was having difficulty swimming in the strong ocean current and was on the verge of slipping underneath the water.

Swede (with the help of another onlooker, Mr. Richards) swam out with a raft and used it to drag Helen to safety. She was rushed to the hospital, and thanks to the quick actions of the rugged Nordic race car driver, she pulled through and was released after a few days.

Joan had suffered through two unfortunate marriages, and now she was working every week, wheel to wheel, with a handsome daredevil who was being hailed as a hero. Joan would later coyly describe her situation in an interview where she states her love with between-the-lines trepidation. She told Fred Tuerek, the sports editor for the *Peoria Star*, that she planned to marry Oscar in December 1926, retire from competitive driving, and become a silent partner in the racing business. Those marriage plans weren't publicly mentioned again.

Joan LaCosta, along with her record-breaking Miller Special, arrived in Montgomery, Alabama, on May 4. The press heralded her feat of beating the woman's speed record, which was previously held by a "Dagmar Sarkowski of Russia"[2] (more imaginary fluff from the fertile imagination of Alex Sloan). She was feted by the city and even given a spot of honor on a parade float in the Alabama Historical Pageant.

Louis Disbrow was entered in the local race event along with Bobby Green (who was a child actor in Hollywood before being bitten by the racing bug) plus a few other good drivers and, of course, Oscar "Swede" Anderson.

The Birmingham event was proclaimed "the greatest dirt track racing program ever held in Alabama"[3] by the *Weekly Herald*. Scheduled as a full day's worth of top-notch live entertainment, it was the opening event on the IMCA National Points circuit schedule, to be followed by the May 15 races just outside of Atlanta in Lakewood, Florida. The drivers would leave for the Atlanta show immediately after the Birmingham race.

Joan, as usual, was press-ganged into doing extra publicity chores for each event she was scheduled for. The current controversy drummed up for the Speed Queen was a fictitious rivalry with the legend Louis Disbrow.

Disbrow was crowing to the papers his displeasure of being on the same racecourse as LaCosta. He told the *Atlanta Constitution* on May 4 that "racing is a men's game" and that "he refuses to start unless officials cancel the entry of Mlle. Joan LaCosta,"[4] adding,

> Women have no business on a race track—it's a man's game. And besides, I've seen about all the women drivers who have amounted to much and I've never yet seen one who could actually handle a machine the way it ought to be handled.
>
> It takes bone and muscle to handle a machine when it's hitting the terrific pace necessary on the straightaways of a mile dirt track, especially if she is going after world records on the track.
>
> I have seen Mlle. LaCosta many times, but never seen her drive except in practice and I'll say she looks too small and feminine to handle a machine in the pinches. There have been a lot of bad wrecks on the Lakewood track and if there are to be any more I don't want to be entered in any races the same day. As for driving against the girl, I wouldn't think of it.[5]

The columnist added that Disbrow had disregarded "the fact that records disclose only three men have driven faster than Mlle. LaCosta—and Disbrow is not one of the three."[6]

This was more fluff from the mind of the master publicist Alex Sloan. Rivalries and controversies, including fake ones, sold tickets. Alex, Joan, and especially Disbrow were all in on the charade. Louis was a good friend of Joan's ever since their intense side-by-side racing schedule in Canada, and back in 1910, he had been one of the few men willing to step up and be Joan Newton Cuneo's right-hand man and mechanic while she was breaking the gender barrier. Being the wily veteran of the racing scene, he instinctively knew how to drum up interest by playing the public antagonist, and he did it well.

The May 6 sports section of the *Atlanta Constitution* newspaper printed another volley in this war of the sexes:

> When they met to discuss the pointed question of whether to accept the entry of Louis Disbrow and automatically bar Mlle. Joan LaCosta,

world's champion girl driver, race officials of Lakewood park track filed the entry of Ray Lampkin, successor to Sig Haugdahl as dirt track champion of the world and one of the most daring throttle stompers who ever tore down a race track fence. Lampkin's unexpected entry for the May 15 speed battles at Lakewood elated officials, who declared they now have a line on the best field of racing stars ever to start in the south.

No decision was reached by the officials on Disbrow's ultimatum that if his entry is accepted, that of Mlle. LaCosta must be canceled. In the present status, Mlle. LaCosta is entered and has given the fans assurance that she will attempt to smash world dirt track records for women when she gets her Miller Special loose on the speedy Lakewood oval. While she cannot hope to come near her beach straightaway record of 145.14 miles an hour, she is confident that she will wheel her machine around the course faster than any woman has ever navigated a mile.

Since Disbrow is a great favorite with Georgia fans, the racing board decided to wire him, asking that he rescind his decision and come to Atlanta for a shot at the prize money. In the 20 and more years that he has been racing, Disbrow has started in Atlanta many times and also has battled over road race and track courses in other cities of the state.

If the entries of Mlle. LaCosta, Disbrow and Lampkin are assured, the Lakewood meet would boast a constellation of racing stars never beaten by any American track and never equaled in the long history of racing in Dixie. Mlle. LaCosta is the sensation of present-day racing; Disbrow, because of his age and experience, is always a feared and daring pilot, and Lampkin promises to be an even greater favorite than Haugdahl was in his greatest days.[7]

That same issue also mentioned LaCosta's reply to Disbrow:

DISBROW JEALOUS, IS REPLY OF GIRL RACING DRIVER

"Of course I am anxious to start at Atlanta May 15," Mlle. LaCosta wired Secretary Oscar Mills of Lakewood today. "I don't want any drivers who would be drawing cards eliminated because of my entry, but Mr. Disbrow ought to be ashamed of himself for saying he would not start if I did. I think he is jealous of the publicity I have received and of the fact that my beach straightaway time was faster than any he ever made, even with the old Blitzen Benz."[8]

On May 7, Joan was transported from Alabama to Atlanta to "defend her rights and insist that her entry not be canceled"[9] for the Florida show.

Joan had some influential heavyweights in her corner, including Mrs. Althea Alexander, who was a Georgia Democratic committee-woman, and Miss Susie Wailes, president of the Woman's division of the Chamber of Commerce. According to the May 8 edition of the *Atlanta Constitution*, delegations of women "phoned, and wrote the racing board in no uncertain terms, that LaCosta's entry be recognized and that here-after women drivers be given the same recognition as men."[10]

The racing board of Lakewood Track, consisting of Arthur Brook, president; Oscar Mills, secretary; and Ivan E. Allen, chairman of the Executive Board, met the previous evening and announced at 10:00 the next morning that they had ruled in favor of Joan, stating "that drivers, regardless of sex, who can qualify"[11] may enter in future race meets.

According to the press release, the track officials also added that "Disbrow can stay home if he is afraid to race against a woman."[12] They evidently had the opposite opinion of Joan's demeanor. LaCosta won the admiration of the board by refusing to make disparaging remarks about Louis Disbrow or any others who threatened protests. She would stand on her accomplishments, she told them, and hoped to set a new mile mark at the track. She was as good of an actor as Louis, and she played the valiant protagonist to perfection.

But there was one troubling sidebar. An accompanying article in the *Atlanta Constitution* that day mentioned that she was nursing a bum ankle. Apparently, while stepping off the pageant parade float the previous Thursday, she misstepped and twisted it. But, she said, "it won't keep me from racing at Lakewood track next Saturday."[13]

There was no mention from Joan about the upcoming small-market Birmingham race. As far as that Alabama event was concerned, the local papers were still heavily promoting her appearance there, and from all indications, Joan gave the impression that she was definitely going to be racing. The *Montgomery Advertiser* reported on her every move, even

INDICATIONS POINT TO MONSTER CROWD FOR AUTO RACES HERE THIS WEDNESDAY

JOAN LA COSTA

JOAN LA COSTA, feminine speed ace at the wheel of the racer with which she recently set up the fastest mark ever made by woman. She is entered in the May 12 Montgomery Playgrounds Motor Classic.

Some of World's Premier Speed Demons To Appear at State Fair Grounds in Speed Events Staged For Montgomery Playgrounds Benefit

Figure 5.2. Race promotion featuring Joan LaCosta in the *Montgomery Advertiser* of Montgomery, Alabama, on May 9, 1926.

MONTGOMERY ADVERTISER.

noting the ovation she received while she was cheering the home team at the Montgomery-versus-Savannah baseball game on Monday evening, two days before the races. The public schools were to be let out early the day of the big show as a sign of thanks and support.

Disbrow was doing his best to sell tickets. In an out-of-the-blue screed in the papers, he proclaimed that racing was a "man's game,"[14] and concerning the possibility of competing against Lacoste, he said he would be in "abject fear of an accident."[15] He also gave her several back-handed compliments, saying she was more fitted for the movies than behind the wheel of a race car because she was slight of build and not muscular or strong. He mentions that after seeing her on the beach of Daytona, he is convinced that she "drives on her nerves"[16] and hopefully can avoid injury so that she can "take up work which is offered her in the movies next fall."[17]

In the space of a few paragraphs, Disbrow had painted Joan as a feminine yet nervy and fearless driver with movie-star looks. Not a bad job of selling an exhibition race.

Louis feigned concern for the safety of LaCosta, but he never said she was a bad driver. And in the end, no matter what he proclaimed publicly, he always showed up to race against her (and lose if necessary) as long as it made headlines and filled the stands. His actions spoke louder than his pre-race promotional broadsides. He had also been part of the Alex Sloan stable for nearly 15 years, which meant that he'd participated in many races with female drivers before Joan, and he'd never been anything but game.

Joan played right along. On May 9, she told the *Atlanta Journal* that

> I know that Mr. Disbrow has many friends and followers in Atlanta and Georgia, probably more than any other section, and I believe he just thought he could scare me away. I would have given a lot not to have this argument come up, but since Mr. Disbrow started it he'll have to finish it and you just bet that he'll finish—second.[18]

Chapter Six

The Grudge Match

May 12, 1926 was the day of the big Birmingham benefit race. Schools and many businesses closed, and huge crowds were headed to the racetrack. The entire city showed up, except for Joan LaCosta.

She had come down with the "flu."[1] The quotation marks were courtesy of the angry publishers of the *Montgomery Advertiser*, who buried the LaCosta mention two-thirds of the way through their report on the race results and highlighted it with the snide editorial punctuation. Instead of looking at the faces of the hundreds of customers who ditched either work or school to see her try to break another record, Joan was looking out the window of the train headed back to Atlanta.

According to the *Atlanta Constitution*, LaCosta was overruled by her physicians, who begged her to stay in bed, which she acceded to in order "to be in condition for her match race against Louis Disbrow"[2] at the Lakewood Track on May 15. The illness also caused cancellations of public appearances in Atlanta, including a speaking engagement for the Junior Chamber of Commerce, though the M. Rich & Brothers department store still held out hope for an appearance from her for their reception on Friday afternoon, May 14.

Louis Disbrow reacted to the reports of Joan LaCosta's illness by offering to cancel their match race on Saturday, and he might have gotten a more positive reaction from LaCosta if he hadn't added that "this is Mlle. LaCosta's chance to get out of the race if she thinks she has more than she can handle."[3] Joan was indignant, saying that "it would take more than a bad cold to keep me from running against Disbrow now."[4]

"I'd stand on my head in the corner for two days to be sure of a chance to beat Louis Disbrow on the track at Atlanta."[5]

She was determined to keep all of her focus on the grudge match. Although she eventually canceled the M. Rich & Brothers appearance, she set about letting everyone know that she was in top shape for the race on Saturday and felt confident enough in her spirits to accept the honor of judging a Charleston dance contest for Georgia Tech at the Lakewood Casino on Saturday night after the match. She would not allow for any excuses that she wasn't at her best, even if she lost.

The honorary judge of local events was a consistent angle of Alex Sloan's promotional pushes. He had a habit of booking LaCosta in anything that might get a few free publicity inches of ink, including being an honorary judge at the Atlanta Marble Shooting Championships, an event noted by the Moline, Illinois, paper the *Dispatch*:

> Miss Joan LaCosta. Premier woman automobile racing driver, acted as one of the judges in a sectional tournament in the city-wide marbles championship contest being conducted by the Atlanta, Ga., Journal. In accepting the invitation to act she said: "All branches of sport are equally interesting to me and I know that it will take the same well developed control of the nerves and muscles and the same kind of coolness under great strain, to win the marbles championship as it takes to drive a fast car around a track at one hundred miles an hour."[6]

There would be no excuses allowed this time, and the papers trumpeted that fact.

Disbrow arrived in Atlanta early on Friday, May 13, ahead of LaCosta, but he promised that he wouldn't do any test runs on the oval until later in the day so as not to give himself an advantage in the race. He offered to cancel the match, but LaCosta declined by telephone before arriving in town that evening.

The buildup continued to the start of the race. Joan said she would be at the starting tape ready to leave Disbrow in the dust. Disbrow claims the track was in the fastest condition he'd ever seen and promised to take an early lead and keep stretching it. It was going to be a three-mile duel,

Figure 6.1. Headline in the *Atlanta Constitution* of Atlanta, Georgia, on May 14, 1926.
ATLANTA CONSTITUTION.

and the winner would get a silver championship belt and, more important, bragging rights.

The course that afternoon was damp, hard, and fast. It was good driving weather, with a crisp, brisk wind, and overcast with no blinding sun in the driver's eyes to worry about. There was just enough humidity in the air to keep the dust manageable. LaCosta and Disbrow were scheduled as the third event of the day, and the 5,000 shivering fans in the crowd were expecting a great event, and they got it.

Joan LaCosta's father, William, was in attendance at her race for the first time. The man whom Joan so wanted to impress all of her life watched as his daughter was presented with a bouquet of carnations by Mildred Malcolm, manager of the floral department at M. Rich & Brothers. Mr. Carver was gifted a flower corsage as well. The trio of the men who approved Joan's application to race at Lakewood were also the race judges, and they and thousands more cheered enthusiastically for Mr. William Carver's daughter.

LaCosta entered the track in a Miller 8, and she was garbed in her usual white, with white knickers, stockings, and sweater. When she pulled up to the starting line, she signaled to the official that she was ready to go, no warm-up necessary.

Joan immediately jumped out in front and led the bulk of the race. Louis turned on the afterburners at the last to make it exciting down the homestretch, but Joan won by a good 50 feet, putting Disbrow in his place in front of thousands of cheering fans. However choreographed the match might have been, those two pulled it off with aplomb.

Her final time was listed as less than a fifth of a second slower than Ray Lampkin's winning time over the same distance in the all-male event later that day. The large crowd roared; they'd gotten what they paid for. LaCosta had crawled out of her sickbed and struck a blow for women's rights, and she'd proved to the doubters that racing wasn't just for men. She was so exhausted by the event that she bowed out of the solo mile run that had been planned for her later in the day.

Louis Disbrow was a gracious loser. He congratulated LaCosta after the race, giving her a handshake and a big smile.

And Joan's father witnessed the entire spectacle as the track announcer proclaimed Joan LaCosta the greatest female driver alive. The stonecutter from Tennessee sat quietly, almost nonchalantly in the stands, as if he expected nothing less from his strong daughter. When the race ended, Joan invited her gray-haired father down to the track to pose with her and some of the other drivers. He stood there, in his matching light-colored suit, gazing down at his daughter, the most famous woman driver in the country.

Oscar Anderson did his part to make the show a sensation, setting a new Southern dirt track record with an official time of five miles at 4:10, beating Walter Cutcliffe by a full 10 seconds in their head-to-head matchup. In his mind, part of his victory was due to his lucky number, 44, posted to the side of his Mercedes.

But there were some dark clouds brewing to go along with the silver linings in Disbrow's life; a federal warrant was issued for his arrest in Florida, the same day as his race with LaCosta. In what he tried to label "a misunderstanding,"[7] the authorities were called in when Disbrow had verbally expressed plans to import alcohol into the state.

Disbrow's issue with spirits was well known. His ex-wife, Harriet Henry, had divorced him four years prior, telling the court that she had to leave the racer months before the proceedings because "he raced J. Barleycorn instead"[8] and had a violent temper when drinking.

Disbrow could not afford to miss the upcoming races that he was headlining (and probably getting a top salary for), so on May 17 in an arraignment in front of U.S. Commissioner Joe Abbott, he paid a $1,000 bond, with a hearing set for December 6 in the Jacksonville court.

Figure 6.2. Three photos of Joan LaCosta appearing in the *Atlanta Journal* of Atlanta, Georgia, on May 16, 1926. The bearded man in the bottom left photo is her father, William Carver, and the man in the bottom right photo is Louis Disbrow.
ATLANTA JOURNAL. IMAGE ENHANCED FOR CLARITY BY ADELIS SEGUNDO BRICEÑO.

One of those important races was the match in Jackson, Mississippi, which would be a rematch with LaCosta. Disbrow told the *Clarion-Ledger* of Jackson, Mississippi, on May 21 that he was willing to bet that the first race loss to LaCosta was a fluke, and he'd put up "money, marbles or chalk, or even his automobile against hers"[9]:

"But this isn't any alibi," he said, "and I know there's only one way to square myself with the fans and prove to Mlle. LaCosta that I can beat her—and that way is to beat her. With my own machine I'd run against her anywhere and anytime, but I want to make sure my car will be in shape before I tackle another match with her

RACERS BELIEVE NUMBER FOUR IS LUCKY

Speaking mathematically, four is to auto racing what seven is to dice tossing.

The numeral four is a signal of luck, started by Fred Horey when he was dirt track champion. Horey had cars numbered 4, 14, 24, 34 and 40, and, in spite of several bad spills, never has been seriously injured.

Oscar ("Swede") Anderson, long-distance champion and one of the entrants in the auto races at Lakewood Saturday, figures that if four is lucky, two of them ought to be better, and has numbered his big Mercedes "44."

Figure 6.3. Article appearing in the *Atlanta Constitution* on May 12, 1926.
ATLANTA CONSTITUTION.

"While I don't think there is any woman and probably not any men, who can beat me on a dirt track with even machines, I am not belittling Mlle. LaCosta. I have seen her drive on several dirt tracks, and mighty few men can handle a car like she does. I saw her when she crashed through a fence at Detroit, and kept the machine right side up after tearing down a couple of lengths of fence. I was in Florida too when she was running on the beach, although I didn't see her during her record trials, and I know that few persons of either sex can handle a car like she did there.

"I still don't think she can beat me on a dirt track, though, especially on a half-miler like Jackson has and if the track officials want a return match I'm willing."[10]

Once again, Disbrow did a masterful job of painting LaCosta as a fearless, possibly dangerous driver, possessing superb racing skills equal to any man. He sold the match while simultaneously declaring that the match was a bad idea. It was superb public relations and also a great distraction from his legal troubles.

It didn't mean that Alex Sloan was coasting in his duties. He was constantly releasing promo pieces to the local papers, always making sure that the lovely Joan LaCosta was prominently pictured. She was often photographed wearing spotless white racing gear, the better to be seen as she roared past the grandstand crowd.

By now, the papers touted that Joan was "born in France, but reared in Memphis,"[11] perhaps laying the groundwork for a future explanation as to why the "French" mademoiselle spoke with a Tennessee drawl. She was, in fact, at heart, still a small-town Southern gal. When she was traveling from Jackson to Birmingham during the Confederate Soldiers Reunion and Parade, she was obliged to take an upper berth and just climbed on up without a word of complaint. "Why shouldn't I take an upper or even sit up if it helped one of those dear old men in gray?"[12] she explained. "To me, the great parade I saw here will go down as one of the most beautiful sights I ever beheld and it brought the tears, too, when I thought how many of them might not be on hand for the next reunion."[13]

She felt at home in the South and had no problem taking on a full-race schedule, with her focus on her appearance at Jackson, Mississippi, on May 26. The usual suspects were also booked to appear, including Louis Disbrow and Ray Lampkin. Disbrow was a local favorite, having first raced there 12 years before in 1914.

Girl Champion to Try For Records In Jackson

Mlle. Joan LaCosta

Mlle. Joan LaCosta, "Queen of Speed" and who smashed all feminine speed marks by a 145.14 miles per hour clip, will go after southern and world half mile track records during the auto races to be run at the State Fair track next Wednesday, May 26.

The dainty little Miss, born in France but reared in Memphis, wants to hold all women's speed records, and with the straightaway time securely marked up, she expects to smash a record or two here next Wednesday.

Figure 6.4. Joan LaCosta pictured in the *Clarion-Ledger* on May 21, 1926.
CLARION-LEDGER. IMAGE ENHANCED FOR CLARITY BY ADELIS SEGUNDO BRICEÑO.

Disbrow wouldn't publicly admit that Joan was the faster driver on May 15 in Atlanta; instead, he blamed his defeat on having a slower car. As the race grew closer, the tenor of the promotion got more heated. "I still don't think she can beat me on a dirt track,"[14] said Disbrow.

The verbal kindling caught fire. The Disbrow–LaCosta grudge match was officially announced the next day by the race officials, who did yeoman's duty in pretending this wasn't a preplanned scenario. Joan was due to arrive on Monday from Birmingham just before the Wednesday race, but it still gave her enough time to "inspect and try out the track before she shoots for records."[15] Because of the buzz the match was generating, she showed up early, on Saturday May 22, just in case there were any skeptical observers who thought she might be "running out"[16] of the match because she feared the veteran racing king.

The papers were all aflutter regarding the appearance of the fastest woman in the world. The stories came with pictures and headlines referencing the world champion crown that Joan wore so comfortably.

The nightlife in Jackson was constrained by Prohibition liquor laws, so "private venues" cropped up to provide celebrations with spirits and music. On that Monday night, the Jackson Exchange Club held its annual soiree, with singers, dancers, and a cabaret at the Edwards House. The festivities ran well into the night, and one of the special guests of honor was "racing car driver, Joan LaCosta."[17]

In the last few hours before the race, the track team was busy with the water truck hoses, trying to get the dust down, give the dirt some traction, and hopefully keep the speeds as high as possible. The importance of the track condition was reported in the *Clarion-Ledger* of May 26:

> Mlle. Joan LaCosta, "Queen of Speed" who will match speed with Louis Disbrow in a special duel, rode over the track late yesterday and pronounced it in great shape for today's events.
>
> "If the track stays as fast, I'll beat Disbrow in the match race," she assured her friends, while Disbrow, after overhauling and repainting his powerful machine, declared that the finish this time will be different than at the Atlanta race, when Mlle. LaCosta beat him.[18]

The Alex Sloan "A" team was booked there, and some of the other big names on the bill were Ray Lampkin, Oscar Anderson, Arch Powell, and Al Cotey. But there was no doubt who the promoters thought was the big draw.

There could be only one headlining event, and it was going to be the sophomore match race between Joan LaCosta and Louis Disbrow. Everybody else was mentioned in small print. And LaCosta was billed first, of course, because she was the draw. The event was even gathering attention from outside the sporting world, enticing local government officials to share in the celebrity cachet of the event.

The political royalty of Mississippi showed up in force. Governor Henry L. Whitfield was the official referee of the match, and the mayor of Jackson, Walter A. Scott, was judge. Two women were also tapped to participate: Mrs. Julius Crisler as a judge and Miss Mabel Stire, the representative of the IMCA, who was in attendance to record the results. It was proof that auto racing was developing a sheen as the sport for the masses, and the electeds knew that the masses voted.

Race day broke sunny and hot. There was an enormous crowd, 5,000 at least, who came out on the warmest day of the year to see the highlight of the summer. The water trucks didn't make a dent in the dry track surface, so times weren't exceptionally fast, and the heat and the dust hid much of the spectacle contained on the half-mile oval. The reporter from the *Clarion-Ledger* provided the following account:

> Jackson's first annual spring automobile parade and show and speed car trials were staged at the Fair Grounds yesterday with a crowd of 5,000 to 6,000 in attendance.
>
> It was the hottest day so far this year, the track was dry and dusty, the drivers were uncomfortably warm while the crowded spectators sweltered—but take it by and large, it was the most successful affair of its kind ever staged in Jackson, from every point of view.
>
> No records were broken but the speed contests brought thrills. There were no spills or other accidents but the motors of the racing cars made plenty of noise, the cars generally took the turns half-skidding, and the spectators enjoyed every minute of it.
>
> Of outstanding interest was the speed trial of Mlle. Joan LaCosta and that of Ray Lampkin. Neither shattered any standing marks, the trials being made on single laps half mile only. The charming little lady driver was given uproarious greeting at her every appearance, and

especially was she given an ovation following her snappy defeat of the veteran Louis Disbrow in their match trials.[19]

Oscar Anderson and Ray Lampkin traded off wins in the other events, with Oscar winning the most entertaining match, the No Distance race, where the drivers weren't told how long the race was until the final lap (which turned out to be two miles over four laps).

Birmingham, Alabama, was next on the docket the following Saturday. Since it was a five-hour trip from Jackson to Birmingham and the race was in three days, it allowed little time for Joan to soak up the adulation. But the momentum was following her, and the ads in the Alabama papers were listing her—and her alone—above everyone else.

Once again, Joan *was* the event. That week Disbrow had slipped below the fold, tumbling down the bill to rank along the rest of the driver roster. Fortunately, this was a team that ran like clockwork. They were so comfortable with each other and with their machines and had such total trust in their fellow drivers that the audience was guaranteed a spectacular show for their admission tickets no matter who held the top spot on the fliers.

There seemed to be no begrudging Joan LaCosta's star billing from any of her teammates. The drivers were keenly aware that they had some of the best jobs in the world: tearing around a dirt track in souped-up tractors. Jimmy Malone was a former press agent for J. Alex Sloan in the early dirt track days, and he talked about the team aspect of the drivers back in the 1920s in an interview with the *Reading Times* on August 30, 1935:

> "Yes," Jimmy recalled, "they were teams in those days. Usually, we had 10 cars and eight drivers, two of the boys doubling on two different cars. Thus, Joe Doaks could also be Jim Smith for the racing score cards. It sounded like a bigger field."
>
> Sloan's team traveled from fair to fair in their own special railroad car, the racing machines following in a special baggage car. Their diet was prepared by a chef who traveled with the team.
>
> "Frequently we stored all our machines in one garage while waiting for race day," Jimmy recounted "In such cases the drivers would

always warn the garage attendants to watch over their cars and caution them to make sure that no other pilot tinkered with the motors. As if it mattered."

Figure 6.5. Advertisement for Auto Races appearing in the *Birmingham News* on May 28, 1926.
BIRMINGHAM NEWS.

Jimmy told of an incident that happened at Bethany, Missouri. "Our train was an hour late and the grandstand was packed and jammed with customers waiting for us to come in. At Bethany the railroad tracks are directly across from the grandstand, so that when we finally arrived and began unloading, we did it in full view of the crowd. It must have been apparent that we were just a bunch of barnstormers, all working together, but no-one ever said a word about it." . . .

In a few towns where they played, there would crop up local boys who had constructed their own weird speed creations and become infested with the speed bug. "We usually had to let them have their fling, but they never got anywhere," said Jimmy. "If they got through the first turn without giving up under the showers of dirt thrown at them by artfully skidded tires, good 'teamwork' always finished the job." . . .

Sloan was in a habit of sending his pilots in to win the prize money away from the other contestants, an easily accomplished performance. On one occasion in question, however, with the Iowa State Fair dangling exceptionally rich purses for the drivers, Ralph A. Hankinson, a rival promoter, decided to send his rival team in to battle it out with the Sloan contingent.

"That," declared Jimmy, "would have been a clash of the titans." But it never happened. "The night before the race Sloan got together with Ray Lampkin, Bill Claypool and several others of the featured Hankinson stars and hired them away for the remainder of the season. It was a crushing blow for Hankinson."

In time the amateurs who demanded a chance to compete when the troupers came to town increased in number. As they grew more numerous, their cars became faster, and the barnstormers soon learned to expect tough opposition at certain points along the circuit. At Topeka, Kansas, for instance, Johnny Bagley, an Omaha, Nebraska policeman showed up regularly. Des Moines became known as Gus Schrader's stamping ground. And in Edmonton, Alberta, Canada one year, a youngster named Emory Collins took on the whole team. Sloan promptly hired him.

"Of course," explained Jimmy, "when every town began to have its Emory Collins, Sloan could no longer employ them all. Too many. So, he did the logical thing, hung up good purses, and made them all run for the money."[20]

As long as folks showed up to watch, they got to keep that job, and if the crowds were bigger, they would get a little more in their pockets. If the grandstands were full, the sun shined on everybody's face.

Joan LaCosta had a big fan on the staff of the *Birmingham News*, and his byline name was Speedo. As befits a moniker like Speedo, his articles about the race fixated on the beauty of LaCosta, referring to her as "the feminine fairy of gasoline,"[21] and her match with Bobby Green was billed as a battle of looks, writing that "Green, due to his dapper appearance, is known as the 'Sheik of dirt track drivers,'" while "LaCosta's beauty is proving a magnet, which will likely get her a prominent place in the movies next Fall, following the close of the 1926 dirt track season."[22]

Dolly Darymple, the nom de plume of another *Birmingham News* staff writer, reportedly gasped at the slender, petite "feminineness"[23] of the driver in the May 28 edition. The interview was astounding in its patronizing of Joan's perceived girlish traits versus her driving ability: "Meet the 'Speed Queen,' Mlle. Joan LaCosta, and then hold your breath as you exclaim upon seeing this dainty bit of femininity 'like a doll in a tea cup,' all pink and white and lovely, as completely unlike a 'racer' as anything you ever beheld, although 'bubbling over' and 'Zev' could give her a handicap and then she'd beat 'em!"[24] (Zev was the Kentucky Derby winner of 1923; Bubbling Over won in 1926.)

The astonished Dolly Darymple then pulls out the thesaurus and continues to spackle on even more adjectives of the fairer sex by describing Joan as "a wisp of a girl," "petite as a ballet dancer," and "pretty enough to grace the heroine role of any movie,"[25] all before finally inveigling Joan to sit down at the piano to trill sweet tunes. After all, she was trained "at a renowned conservatory."[26]

It was a tack that publicist Alex Sloan could never have used with Elfrieda Mais or almost any other woman driver. But Joan had the raw charisma of a femme fatale and enough showbiz background to play the part of a siren to a tee.

Women in countries around the world were also hitting the racetracks, with the first official race for women in Poland taking place on June 27, 1926. The race, dubbed I Jazda Konkursowa Pan, was won by

Mlle. Joan La Costa, 'Meteor Maid,'
Disappointingly Unlike Auto Racer

MLLE. JOAN LA COSTA

Figure 6.6. Joan LaCosta pictured in the *Birmingham News* on May 28, 1926.
BIRMINGHAM NEWS. IMAGE ENHANCED FOR CLARITY BY ADELIS SEGUNDO BRICEÑO.

Lumila Boguslawski in a Lancia Lambda, while the acknowledged Polish pioneer of women's racing, Halina Toepfer, finished third.

There were also more movies being made with the now-familiar theme of a secret woman race driver who surprises all the men with her unknown talent. A perfect example of that genre, *The Checkered Flag*, starring Elaine Hammerstein, opened that season with Elaine playing a young woman who has to take the place of her absent lover at the race-track at the last minute and wins the race. The racing scenes were filmed at the Fresno, California, track, and reportedly many of the top West Coast drivers were in the movie.

Joan, not yet being a movie star, still had to race and win; no amount of puff pieces churned out by the Sloan machine would keep the mystique of a losing race driver alive. On May 29, 1926, at Birmingham, that formula was put to the test.

Birmingham was the "home court" for Joan LaCosta. She had set records there, her father had showed up to watch the crowds cheer her on, and it was only four hours away from Memphis, where she had spent most of her life.

On that Friday afternoon in May, the day before the races, Joan was a guest at a meeting of the Civilian Club, a local version of the Chamber of Commerce, where they celebrated local athletes by handing out gold watches to them.

The clouds blew in heavy rain later that day, and a downpour all night and the next morning turned the track into a muddy brown river for the matches Saturday afternoon. The deep, sloppy ruts kept both the speeds and the danger down and turned the highlight match between LaCosta, the "Meteor Maid," and "The Sheik" Bobby Greene into a slow slog through axle-deep clay. Joan won, of course, and all of the other racers did their duty and put on a show, but this was one of those days when that "fun versus work" ratio skewed less toward joy and more toward earning a paycheck. Being the troupers they were, the team battled the elements and the track and hurriedly changed out of their wet racing togs before jumping onto the train to Memphis.

Although the small market did not supply much press for the Tennessee event, the city proved to be the perfect canvas for LaCosta. She

Figure 6.7. Advertisement for the film *The Checkered Flag* in the *Messenger-Inquirer* of Owensboro, Kentucky, on May 28, 1926.

had roared out of the Southern circuit, leaving new world records behind in her wake, and walloped the competition up north. The Memphis event was planned as a celebration of the local gal made good.

Alongside Joan was master promoter Alex Sloan, busy prepping the local papers for her appearance there. According to the June 7 edition of the *Greenwood Commonwealth* of Greenwood, Mississippi,

> Memphis will pay tribute to Mlle. Joan LaCosta of this city at the Memphis Motor Classic Auto races here Saturday, June 12, when homecoming exercises will be held in conjunction with the speed events to crown the local girl, world's woman auto race champion, "Queen of Speed."
>
> City and state officials, augmented by representatives from adjoining states, will be on hand for the ceremonies which will be a part of the afternoon auto racing program. The affair will be in the nature of a tribute to Miss LaCosta's acquisition of the title.[27]

The "Queen of Speed"[28] had conquered Georgia and now Tennessee. She didn't break the mile record on the track, but she did capture the hearts of the city of Memphis with the effort, and they touted hometown girl Marion Carver in every story about LaCosta.

Chapter Seven

The Rise

The 1926 Wisconsin State Fair race was on Sunday, June 13. The Milwaukee dirt track was a fast one, and the conditions were perfect for a record attempt. The unofficial time for the women's world record for the mile on a dirt track was 56 seconds, just over 64 miles per hour, held by the great Elfrieda Mais. It is unclear if this was from a standing start or what they call a "rolling start," where the car is in motion as it approaches the starting line. A rolling start would result in faster times, but either way, to be tearing around a dirt oval at over a mile per minute in a shaky tin can had to be at once terrifying and exhilarating.

Joan LaCosta was timed at 49 seconds on this track, shattering the world record, cruising at an average speed of 73.5 miles per hour in a car that was likely a Harry Miller–built roadster. The papers had disclosed the week before that Joan drove a Miller on the ovals but had chosen an Auburn as her personal vehicle and that Harry Miller also drove an Auburn.

It was a good indicator of the sponsorship money that was accumulating. The car company wanted their brand attached to Joan LaCosta, and the perk of an Auburn luxury car to use for free seemed like a small example of what was possible for Joan.

The following week, on June 19, she was scheduled for a racing exhibition at the Minnesota fairgrounds. Through some fortuitous timing, it coincided with the appearance of the New York Yankees appearing in St. Paul on their own barnstorming tour. Joan loved baseball and had been

---◆---

Champion Woman Driver
Chooses an Auburn Car

Mlle. Joan LaCosta, world's champion woman race driver of motor cars, who recently set a mark of 145.14 miles an hour for a one-half and a one-mile race against time on the Jacksonville Beach, Florida, selected an Auburn Eight Eighty-eight sedan as her personal car while on her Florida racing campaign.

In her racing Mlle. LaCosta drives a Miller Special, made by Harry Miller of Los Angeles, who also drives an Auburn as his own personal car for general use.

Figure 7.1. Excerpt from an article appearing in the *Brooklyn Daily Eagle* of Brooklyn, New York, on June 6, 1926.
BROOKLYN DAILY EAGLE.

seen at local games throughout her racing career, but this was much more than a local game.

Babe Ruth was the biggest sports star in the country and a year away from setting one of the most revered baseball records of all time: slugging the most home runs in a season. Fans swarmed him wherever he went, and this game with the minor league St. Paul Saints promised to be a once-in-a-lifetime spectacle. Rarely would a major league team play a minor league team (the Saints were in the American Association league) in mid-season, but the Yanks had a day off and scheduled an exhibition match for some good local public relations and a little cash.

Unfortunately for the crowds packed into the stadium, the rain ruined the fun, and the game was called off. Always the showman, Ruth entertained the disappointed fans by launching baseball moon shots over the fences.

Besides the Bambino and his teammates, another guest made an on-field appearance: Joan LaCosta. The papers lined up to get a shot of the pair together. The most famous male athlete alive posed with the newest rising star in the celebrity galaxy. Joan appeared awestruck in the photo, decked out in a fashionable hat and a fox fur stole. Although some accounts had them meeting previously in Florida just before Joan set the world land speed record, it's highly doubtful they had ever crossed paths. There's no doubt that some enterprising beat reporter would have mentioned the Sultan of Swat and the Speed Queen keeping company, considering there were thousands of nickel newspaper copies just waiting to be sold on that sort of gossip.

Later in the summer, that photo of Ruth and LaCosta together was trotted out by the papers to drum up interest in her local race appearances, like the clipping shown here from the *Des Moines Register* on August 16, promoting Joan for the Iowa State Fair race.

Being so close to such athletic greatness must have inspired LaCosta because she went into the Minnesota State Fair on June 19 with a full head of steam. Six thousand people packed the grandstands that Saturday. As the boys ran their longer events, the familiar names came out on top as usual. Ray Shaw emerged the winner at 100 miles, while Ray Lampkin, driving the same Miller Special that Joan was using for her event, nearly set a 30-mile speed record before the race car overheated and he had to let it cool down, but he still managed to finish the race as the runner-up.

LaCosta took a warm-up lap after the Hundred Mile race concluded. Her blue Miller whipped around the track with a powerful smoothness that impressed the crowd and even the other drivers. There was a tense moment before the practice time was announced: 48 seconds flat! It was another record, beating her last one at Wisconsin.

But this was just her stalking horse run. Joan used that first lap as a measuring stick, figuring out where the dirt was softest on the track

Figure 7.2. Broadside advertisement for the New York Yankees–St. Paul baseball game on June 16, 1926.

HERITAGE AUCTIONS.

Two Stars in Their Line

"Babe" Ruth, who does things with the business end of a bat and who yesterday hit his thirty-eighth home run of the season, and Joan LaCosta, world's champion girl auto racer, expressed admiration for each other's prowess at a recent meeting. Each is after more records. Mlle. LaCosta will try to smash some of her own marks at the Iowa state fair races, Aug. 27.

Figure 7.3. Joan LaCosta pictured with Babe Ruth in the *Des Moines Register* of Des Moines, Iowa, on August 15, 1926.

for the tire tread to grab as she skidded through the corners. She took a break, cooled the engine down, and then got back into the cockpit. She took a gallop toward the start while revving through the gears and again smashed her own week-old record in the unofficial dirt track mile, tearing around the oval in 45⅘ seconds, or nearly 80 miles per hour. This was a full three seconds faster than her Milwaukee time.

The headline of the Minneapolis *Star Tribune* said it all: "Joan LaCosta Shatters World's Auto Mark at Hamline."[1] She was regularly smashing the track records now, and it was almost a letdown when she fell short.

Her old beau, Walter Martins, was also having success on the track, setting dirt records in the longer distances and covering 10 miles in 8:00 and 20 miles in 15:53.40. He competed against the best of the best, including Indianapolis 500 legend Wilbur Shaw, with whom he would trade wins on the Crown Point AAA track in northwestern Indiana a few days after Joan's Minnesota runs.

Walter mostly avoided the Alex Sloan circuit. Except for the occasional visit as spectators in the stands watching each other race, Joan and Walter rarely crossed paths in the dirt track universe. Walter kept busy in the Chicago area that summer, racing at the Thornton track at 175th and Halstead in two events around the Fourth of July week while Joan was appearing at other shows in the region. It would be easy to imagine a quick get-together in between their respective scheduled events, but there's no record of a joint race appearance.

The Montana State Fair in Minot was opening on June 28, and what better way to kick off the festivities than to hold an auto race? The usual pre-event buildup featured Joan and Louis Disbrow as the main attractions. But in a rare instance of being pushed out of the spotlight, LaCosta's appearance was overshadowed in the big papers by the mysterious saga of Aimee McPherson.

McPherson, a well-known "tent evangelist," made her reputation by traveling the country on the revival circuit. She was a charismatic, riveting preacher whose personal life was as enthralling as her public persona. A divorcée who traveled from city to city, without a man as an escort, she was viewed as both a hosanna-spouting voice of God and a witch. She

Miss Joan LaCoster, girl auto racer, at the wheel of her car with which she smashed the mile dirt track record for women at St. Paul recently.

Figure 7.4. Joan LaCosta pictured in the *Pittsburgh Press* of Pittsburgh, Pennsylvania, on July 11, 1926.
PITTSBURGH PRESS.

began preaching from an Oldsmobile in 1918 and then rented bigger and bigger spaces. Eventually, she built her own 4,000-seat auditorium in Los Angeles. She was easily one of the biggest celebrities in the United States, eclipsing even the famous white-suited evangelist Billy Sunday in popularity. She had an enormous influence on religious services, creating services that were full-blown theatrical productions with costumes, dozens of extras, and an orchestra.

She also mentored other women in the field, including a young girl by the name of Uldine Utley. Utley was born in 1912, and by the time the pale, flaxen-haired girl was in her late teens, she had sold out large venues

Dirt Record

Walter Martins, Chicago race driver, established new western dirt track records for 10 and 20 miles. Martins piloted his car over the 10-mile route in 8 minutes, bettering the old mark by 25 1-5 seconds. In the 20-mile event Martins' time was 15:53 2-5. The old record for the distance was 17:13 1-5.

Figure 7.5. Walter Martins pictured in the *Daily Times* of Davenport, Iowa, on June 21, 1926.

DAILY TIMES.

for her sermons across the country, including Madison Square Garden and Carnegie Hall in New York and the LaSalle Baptist Church in Chicago, where she was booked for two months in the fall of 1929. McPherson and her acolytes, like Utley, blazed a trail for many other younger female evangelists in the years that followed.

On May 18, 1928, McPherson went for a swim at Venice Beach, California, and disappeared. There was wild speculation on what had happened, and no body was found in the surf or otherwise. There was a nationwide search.

Then, on June 23, a bedraggled woman staggered out of the Mexican desert in Agua Prieta, Sonora, in front of two shocked residents. It was Aimee McPherson, spilling forth a mysterious story about being kidnapped, tortured, drugged, and held for ransom. The details of her travails were never independently verified.

* * *

In late June in Montana, after the whirlwind news of the kidnapped preacher had died down, Joan LaCosta was again the newspaper headliner, and though reports on the race results are incomplete, she did well enough there to get the royal treatment from the *Sioux City Journal* for her next appearance scheduled for the July 5 weekend. But before that Iowa State Fair appearance, the 1926 Fourth of July racing event in Illinois was squeezed into Joan's already tight schedule.

The Fourth of July in Chicago was special to Joan. It was where, racing as Marion Martins in 1924, she had made her breakthrough, winning her first two professional races over the course of the weekend. Since then, she always had a race on or near Independence Day, preferably near her former home in the Windy City.

One of the closest big tracks to Chicago in 1926 was about an hour west of the city in Aurora. Joan would celebrate her annual homecoming racing there on Independence Day. The ads in the *Chicago Tribune* highlighted LaCosta's presence at the Aurora track, placing her there on July 4 but not July 5, as she had a quick turnaround to her next race in Iowa.

The 1926 Iowa State Fair scheduled her for a race against the clock, running her car solo on the track. LaCosta hoped to beat her own

What to do with your 3-Day Holiday July 3-4-5

Auto Races Aurora July 4 and 5

The 2nd Annual 100-Mile Motor Classic

at Aurora July 5th, with qualifying runs July 4th. The famous woman driver, Mlle. La-Costa will be there.

Figure 7.6. Excerpts from an advertisement for the Chicago Aurora and Elgin Railroad in the *Chicago Tribune* on July 2, 1926.
CHICAGO TRIBUNE.

world record, which she had set in Minneapolis three weeks prior. There was a big slate of other drivers penciled in for the weekend, including Fred Horey and Al Cotey. The fearless aerial stuntwoman Lillian Boyer planned to perform her hair-raising stunt of climbing a rope ladder from a speeding automobile up into a waiting airplane, followed by a wing-walking demonstration.

Had circumstances been just a little different, perhaps if she'd been born just a few years later, Joan might have been one of those daredevils in the air. In an illuminating glimpse into LaCosta's fantasy life written up in the *Birmingham News* on May 28, 1926, she proclaims that she might have been an aviatrix if not for that first Chicago race:

> Speed driving was no kid-day ambition with me. In fact I favored the airplane until two years ago while visiting in Chicago at North Shore when I saw auto races and when they announced a girl's event the next week, I caught a fancy for the game and went out to enter and copped all the prizes on the first try.[2]

Chapter Eight

A Charmed Life

Alex Sloan had put together an all-star team for the 1926 Independence Day weekend event in Aurora, Illinois. Fred Horey, Al Cotey, Ray Lavigne, and, of course, Joan LaCosta were all on the docket for the Sunday show. Monday would be minus LaCosta, as she had to make an appearance at the Iowa State Fair races.

Joan ran against the clock, as she often did. It was a unique experience, just her and the machine, tearing around the dirt track at 60 miles per hour, kicking up a rooster tail of dust in the air without having to worry about the dirt from other cars in her face. She drove after the Red Grange Sweepstakes event, which starred the top male drivers and during which Les Allen tried to pass Fred Horey and Al Cotey at "death curve"[1] and crashed through the rail into a wire fence. He was unhurt, and Cotey ended up nipping Horey at the race finish by a couple of feet.

LaCosta ripped around the oval in 51 seconds in her Fourth of July event in front of 10,000 spectators, a "splendid time for the Aurora track,"[2] according to the *Chicago Tribune*, and then she practically flew out of the stadium to get to Des Moines for the state fair.

It wasn't a coincidence that the front-page editorial cartoon in the *Tribune* the next day was a paean to the liberated woman, replete with examples, like the woman with short hair, cigarette, and riding crop. In her boots, helmet, and goggles, Joan could have stepped out of this drawing and onto the racetrack, where she sought to be judged on her merits, not her gender, at a time when women were still fighting to attain equal legal and financial standing. While women had won the right to vote

Figure 8.1. Political cartoon by John T. McCutcheon appearing in the *Chicago Tribune* on July 5, 1926.
CHICAGO TRIBUNE.

just a few years before, and in 1926, women still weren't allowed to sit on juries. Women were barred from participating in many parts of civic life, and female workers were making, on average, 58 percent as much as male workers.

Joan's fight was for opportunity. Be it driving, riding horseback, or hunting, she didn't want her gender to determine what pursuits were available to her. Joan would take trips with friends to hunt and shoot in the Dakotas, where she was usually the only woman. According to one of the hunters, Joan could outshoot the whole party. "I've ridden horseback all my life, and I'm crazy about hunting," Joan later said. "I went on a hunting party on Lookout Mountain when I was home for a vacation. I have a precious bird dog named 'Jim.' You see I used to go hunting with Dad when I was little—he didn't have any boys, and I liked it."[3]

* * *

Next on her hectic schedule was Iowa, an auto racing epicenter in those days. Locals loved the summer events, and the papers played up the spectacle. The *Sioux City Journal* printed this breathless write-up of the "Queen of Speed"[4]:

> Mlle. LaCosta, "Queen of Speed," Turned from an Opera Career to the Thrills of Piloting Racing Autos. . . .
> Born in France, but residing in America since less than a year old, Mlle. LaCosta's life story is much the same as any American girl's up to the point where she began racing. She was raised in Memphis, Tenn., where she finished public schools and attended St. Mary's school for girls. Possessing a pleasing voice and an undeniable talent for music, she was sent to Chicago to study at one of that city's great conservatories. While there she became interested in flying machines, and, with the temperament typical of her, she decided to become a great flier.
> Until May in 1923 she had never seen an automobile race. She drove her own car, but never felt the urge to attend races, she says. But on her birthday a friend took her to a meet at the Robey speedway and then and there she decided that her career should be on the speedways. Two months later she started in the women's races which featured a three-day meet at North Shore speedway, and startled her own friends by taking first in two of the three meets.[5]

Promoter Alex Sloan's fiction-writing fingerprints were all over that one. Joan LaCosta was possibly going to be interviewed on radio or maybe make movies, so they needed to explain the French mademoiselle's soft Southern drawl.

Joan was remade as having been born in France, then raised in Memphis. In her bio, the paper stated that after she finished public school, she studied music at a noted Chicago conservatory. In reality, she dropped out of school at 15 years old and followed her teenage husband north for work and left her child behind in Memphis. But an "opera career"[6] made a much better headline and a more intriguing storyline of Joan's transformation from genteel artist to tough-nosed competitor. It worked.

The wild publicity drew an immense crowd of 5,000 spectators. Alex Sloan was there as the official starter, a responsibility he relished. The Thearle-Duffield Company supplied the usual evening fireworks display and also introduced a novel "daylights"[7] show to thrill the spectators. Instead of rockets and bursting shells, these projectiles released streamers and colored cloth as well as paper caricatures of celebrities and funny animals. Figures of giraffes and elephants, weighted at the bottom, floated down over the delighted crowd, who'd never seen such a thing. Red, white, and blue strips of material danced in the wind, zoo animals drifted down into the hands of children, and the race car engines in the infield below them revved a symphony of excitement.

LaCosta was scheduled for later in the show, the sixth event, mainly to keep the audience's fannies in the seats to sell more concessions. When she finally made her entrance onto the infield, the honor guard from the Monahan Post Drum Corps accompanied her.

Figure 8.2. Joan LaCosta pictured in the *Sioux City Journal* of Sioux City, Iowa, on July 7, 1926.
SIOUX CITY JOURNAL. IMAGE ENHANCED FOR CLARITY BY ADELIS SEGUNDO BRICEÑO.

Her appearance so late in the bill created technical problems. The slew of cars racing on the track before had made it a mess, so when LaCosta took her turn in the half-mile run, it was a slow trudge through the old tire ruts. No records were broken, and her time was an unimpressive 34.8 seconds, or about 52 miles per hour. There weren't any reports of unhappy crowd reactions, though. The *Sioux City Journal* even noted that "LaCosta's time, while not a record-breaking mark, was remarkable [*sic*]"[8] for the conditions. Teammate Ray Lampkin turned in his usual stellar effort, winning multiple races. Overall, it was an outstanding event; the fans were happy, and the box office tills were full.

Over the course of that July and August 1926, the team traveled the state fair circuit, but LaCosta wasn't always with them. She had been racing nonstop since her Daytona Beach adventures, and she needed breaks to recuperate. After the Independence Day celebration, she finally took a breather before her next big event.

She was penciled in for the Hawthorne oval in Indiana on August 15, which would have been a big career boost for her. This track was graced by the likes of all-time greats Wilbur Shaw and Ralph DePalma, and it would have supplied a much bigger platform for her talents on a big, fast circuit.

The Sloan publicity machine ramped up another "drivers protest"[9] angle aimed at Joan in the local papers to push ticket sales, but, as often happened in her life, storm clouds appeared at an inopportune time, causing the event to be postponed due to heavy rains. LaCosta's debut at Hawthorne would have to wait.

It wasn't just the disappointing cancellation of the high-profile racing opportunity that put LaCosta on the sidelines for almost two weeks. On August 13 in Chicago, Joan's former husband, Walter Martins, married her sister Helen. It didn't seem to strain the two sister's lifelong relationship, but Walter was putting a stamp on his past. The marriage date was significant. Like every driver, Walter had a lucky car number, and his was 13. Walter and his former wife Joan's marriage vows were recorded on February 14. This time, Walter chose his car number over St. Valentine's.

The next big event on LaCosta's calendar would be her Friday, August 27, return to Des Moines for the state fair races. She felt like she owed a better performance to the fans than her previous match there, and Alex Sloan was keen to make it possible. Beyond the relatively low likelihood of rain in late August, Joan had reason to be optimistic. The overseer of the event, A. R. Corey, secretary of the Fair Board, was the "official" timer of LaCosta's record-breaking runs in Florida. Having him holding the watch benefited Joan because he was part of Sloan's team as well. And the track length presented an opportunity for Joan to break a new record: the fastest mile on a half-mile dirt track. With nine races, the lineup that Friday offered spectators an exciting night ahead. They intentionally saved LaCosta for the second-to-last event, an exhibition attempt to break the dirt track speed record. A straw hat derby took place just before her run and did its usual popular pandering to the audience. Men raced around the track with a hat on, and the driver who crossed the finish line first without losing their hat was the winner.

This was clever planning on behalf of the show planners. With one hand securing their hats while the other was busily steering and shifting, drivers drove with more caution and at a measured rate around the oval. The casual, entertaining event slowed down the pace and dulled the audience's perception of the car speeds. When Joan followed by ripping around the course and sliding through corners, the audience leapt off their seats. The heightened danger caught the attention of every seat holder in the arena and those outside the track property without a paying ticket who watched from a distance. The dual crowds shouted and cheered, their combined voices echoing into the clouds.

That day, more than 40,000 folks came through the turnstiles, and the appearance of Joan LaCosta was a major reason. Early Saturday morning temperatures reached a scorching 96 degrees in Des Moines. During the heat wave, one local resident, Charles Belcher, a 42-year-old boilermaker, dropped dead from heatstroke while cleaning a furnace at the Des Moines Electric Company. Several women fairgoers fainted on the grounds, but it didn't stop the crowds from packing the Iowa State Fair.

Prominent on the bill was the heavily anticipated appearance of the aviatrix Lillian Boyer, the daring airplane stuntwoman still recovering from a nasty parachute accident the previous year that had put her in the hospital. Lillian reminded Joan of herself in many ways; she was fearless and just 25 years old (the same age as Joan), and they looked remarkably alike with the same dark hair, slight build, and thousand-watt smile.

And like Joan, Lillian had seen more than her share of death. As the most active of the post–World War I aviatrixes, Lillian Boyer was nearly the last survivor. Many of the others were killed in a variety of accidents. Pioneers like Myron "Fearless" Tinney, Laura Locklear, and Mildred Doran were dead, while others, like Ruth Law, retired as they saw the level of danger rise in the new stunts being rolled out.

On August 28, 1926, the amphitheater bleachers were packed shoulder to shoulder for the races that afternoon. Ray Lampkin carried the day, winning multiple events and setting a speed record over the five-mile distance. Oscar Anderson was an also-ran.

In the fifth event, Lampkin roared twice around the half-mile track in his Miller Special in a fierce attempt to break another speed record, but he came up short.

That left Joan to put the capper on the day, and she delivered in the very next event. Spurred on by the thousands of full-throated screams from the grandstands, her elapsed time was stunning, just a couple of seconds off Ray Lampkins's earlier mark. LaCosta's record came in the less-than-ideal dusty heat and in the face of the high-pressure expectations of the raucous crowd packed into the stadium. She tore around the dry dirt oval at top speed, lowering the mile standard for women racers on a half-mile track to 1:04.2, and the tens of thousands of people in the audience were witnesses to a very special memory that they could cherish the rest of their lives.

Published in the *Des Moines Register* was one of the best close-ups of Joan in action.

Basking in the moment's glory and the emanating adulation of her thousands of fans, Joan left the race drivers' area, slipped behind the wheel of her Auburn sedan, and pulled out of the stadium at a slow pace with a smile. But as she turned the steering wheel, she twisted her arm awkwardly and sprained her shoulder. The doctor told the papers that Joan needed a week to heal, but she was scheduled for Tuesday

Figure 8.3. Lillian Boyer as pictured in the *New York Times* on January 22, 1922.
NEW YORK TIMES.

Within the image:

BREAKING A RECORD. Ray Lampkin (on the left in this picture) broke the track record at the Iowa state fair grounds Aug. 27 by winning the five mile race in 5 minutes, 49 seconds. The car in the lead in this photo is driven by Johnny Watters and No. 9, close behind, is driven by "Putty" Hoffman. *Yates, Register, photo.*

ACE OF SPEED QUEENS! Joan La Costa, daring French woman, lowered the women's dirt track racing record two-fifths of a second in her exhibition at the Iowa state fair Aug. 27. This photo shows La Costa in action, driving directly into the camera's nose. *Yates, Register, photo.*

Figure 8.4. Joan LaCosta in action, pictured in the *Des Moines Register* on September 5, 1926.
DES MOINES REGISTER.

at the fair again. She had to skip the Tuesday races and perform that Friday instead.

"That's what I get for driving slow," Joan said. "If I'd been in a racing car I would have been all right."[10]

She was probably correct. Outside of a few fence scrapes and the Daytona Beach fire, she had led a very charmed life in a profession that killed many top drivers during the time she was competing. Joan LaCosta showed no fear of death when she was ripping around a rutted dirt track at 80 miles per hour in a motorized tin can, but speed didn't seem to scare her. She did remark one time that one of her biggest fears was mice. She was terrified of the little creatures.

Following her race was the big 30-lap Hawkeye Sweepstakes, starring the top drivers in the region. The action was terrific but anticlimactic. Make no mistake: it was the Joan LaCosta show.

Joan and Oscar were growing closer by the day. Being the only woman driver on the Sloan circuit, she was single and lonely for companionship. She had feelings for Oscar Anderson, but he was unavailable. She made some friends with a few aviatrixes, like Phoebe Fairgrave and Lillian Boyer, but they crossed paths only occasionally. Very few men outside of the auto racing world could understand the extraordinary but solitary life she led. And her ex-husband had just married her sister.

LaCosta returned for the September 3 event as advertised, but once again, the weather turned nasty. The raindrops poured down on Thursday night, and by Friday morning, with no letup in the deluge in sight, the fair officials called off the afternoon races. The few paying stragglers who braved the torrents were soggily serenaded by "Thaviu, his band, and his opera singers,"[11] who were backed by some wet and shivering Charleston dancers. After 30 minutes of playing in front of a deserted grandstand, the water started to come down in buckets, forcing the band to call it a day and retreat with the dancers to a covered shelter.

LaCosta benefited from the event cancellation, as it gave her an extra few days off on the schedule to heal the sore shoulder. She needed it if only to carve out a break from the pre- and post-race publicity chores. And her next engagements, the Nebraska State Fair the first week of September followed by a low-key week at the South Dakota State Fair in Huron, were going to be easy shifts, essentially by-the-numbers shows.

Oscar Anderson was also racing on September 6 in Nebraska. Unlike Joan, Oscar was prone to crashes due to his aggressive style. On that day, Joan's heart had to have skipped a beat when, in the first heat, Anderson hit a muddy patch of dirt at top speed and ended up taking out 20 yards of wood planks on the inside rail. But as usual, his hard head saved him, and he shook it off, grabbed another car, and finished the seven-lap event. He won in thrilling style, coming from four places back heading into the last lap. Joan LaCosta ran a two-lap exhibition, turning in a lackluster 1:09.75 mile time after her initial warm-up lap.

Friday, September 10, in Lincoln was a barn burner of an afternoon. After Ray Lampkin tied the track record for a mile in 60 seconds flat, Johnny Waters and Morris Tavlinsky went head-to-head in a scheduled three-mile grudge match. They didn't get it settled.

On the first go-round, Tavlinsky threw a wheel, causing a restart. In the second start, it was a dogfight through the first couple of laps, with Tavlinsky having the edge in raw speed but hindered by a lack of control in the corners. Finally, in lap 3, Tavlinsky lost his traction, sending his Ford Frontenac careening into the west fence. Waters, who was following close on his tail, tried desperately to avoid the carnage, lost control, and crashed into his rival. Tavlinsky suffered a broken arm, a leg gash, and torn tendons; Johnny Waters had a few scrapes and bruises.

The match race between Joan LaCosta and Oscar Anderson seemed anticlimactic in comparison. Oscar was not the type to play along, usually driving fiercely to win, and he topped Joan in the mile and a half in 1:46. Joan had to have been shadowing Oscar closely in this duel. The image of his slicing through the fence a few days before was still fresh in her memory, and the spectacular crash with Waters and Tavlinsky that had just occurred earlier that afternoon made her more cautious. She was less willing to push the speeds on her laps. She rarely lost in these exhibitions, but this was Oscar, the man she loved, and she was a step slower in pace than normal, likely out of caution. This was one of the moments where the thought of death might have colored her performance.

On September 13, Joan LaCosta was billed as appearing in a match race against "The Masked Marvel."[12] With the memory of Anderson's spectacular accident still fresh in her mind, Sloan set up a handful of races for any team member who felt like getting out on the track with Joan for a routine "make it close but lose" run. This allowed the racers to give the audience a good show but not risk their lives with any attempts at breaking records, and it also took away any stigma an individual driver might have felt about losing to a woman. Whoever took that defeat from Joan that day probably paid for the drinks on the train ride to the next venue.

The papers from Deadwood and Sioux City were filled with the standard pre-event hype advertisements for the fair races and even mentioned LaCosta arriving in Huron late at night before the show, but once the event was over, the state fair stories returned to cattle and hogs. Not a peep was mentioned about the auto race, a sure sign that it was perfunctory and uneventful. There were no write-ups of crashes or controversy at the event, which was a welcome break from the drama of the Nebraska shows.

It was the same postshow blackout with her midweek scheduled appearances at the Kansas Free Fair as well on September 15 and 18. Promoter Alex Sloan learned that if there are no crashes, controversy, or records broken, there was no write-up after the event. Yes, everyone on the team still got their paycheck, but the publicity momentum going into the next meet was a little softer.

It was the calm before the storm.

CHAPTER NINE

Luck Is a Leaf in the Wind

NEXT ON THE DOCKET WAS AN EXTRAORDINARY EVENT ON SEPTEMBER 18, 1926, in Miami, Florida. The city was in the nascent throes of an economic slump and about to be hit by one of the most powerful hurricanes to reach Florida's shores in recorded history.

The *Miami Daily News* heralded the danger in a rare alarmist headline, warning of a tropical storm headed toward the city, with the fear that it may pack hurricane-velocity winds by the time it hit the coast.

But the warnings were shrugged off. Most of the Miami populace were transplants from the North who had experienced nothing more than a weak tropical storm before, but this hurricane was an entirely different animal. As the front passed over the city, many clueless residents came out from their places of shelter and wandered the streets, oblivious to the fact that they were in the eye of the storm. In half an hour, the backside winds picked up, carrying with them a storm surge of water levels that flooded most of Miami, ripped the tops off more than 10,000 homes, and sent blades of corrugated tin metal roofs flying through the exposed crowds.

The barometric pressure, a key indicator of deadly power, was recorded at the peak of the cyclone at a stunning 27.75, which was lower than any cyclone or hurricane reading measured up to that time. Hundreds of people were killed. In today's dollars, the multibillion-dollar property damage, has never been equaled. The resulting economic damage sent Miami into a deep recession just ahead of the onset of the Great Depression. The civic leaders did their best to keep public spirits up, providing free concerts, parades, and dances, but putting on a brave face for residents was not enough. The *Miami Herald* posted an editorial cartoon on its front page the week after the storm, proclaiming that disasters often led to rejuvenation in stricken cities. It took a generation for Miami to fully recover.

Joan LaCosta had many memories of Florida, and she had many friends there. There had to be multiple phone calls and many sleepless nights as Joan reached out to those she knew were in the stricken areas. The state had been the setting for one of her most triumphant moments. There was an understandable break in the action for LaCosta for a good part of September as well as for much of the Southeast racing circuit.

But the racing world forged ahead in the North. The New Jersey show on October 2 was a rare appearance in the far Northeast for Joan and also partly explains the calendar gap on LaCosta's schedule. The route from the deep Midwest to the Eastern Seaboard was a long excursion by railroad and a logistical nightmare. Moving trainloads of cars and drivers and the ancillary squadron of pre- and postshow entertainers like dancers and musicians took a lot of patience and, most of all, time.

Featured at the Trenton Interstate Fair were a top contingent of racers, including Joan, the aviatrix Lillian Boyer doing her famous aerial stunts, and the fan-favorite auto polo team.

Joan LaCosta lived up to her notices and set a new Trenton track record for women, lowering the standard set years before by Elfrieda Mais. The dependable Fred Horey won the big event, and Lillian Boyer thrilled the packed grandstand with her climb from the back of a speeding automobile up into a low-flying airplane. It was another day at the office for everyone in some of the most exciting and deadly jobs in the world.

The appearance of Lillian Boyer was a highlight for Joan. Boyer was one of the most skilled daredevils of the air, and she wasn't competing against anyone but herself. LaCosta saw how the crowd held their breath when Boyer was climbing the rope ladder out of the car, the whirring blades of the biplane just feet away. It was a stunning routine, and that same month, the *Philadelphia Inquirer* was inspired to write about the performance in images that were rarely used to describe Joan's races:

Figure 9.1. Political cartoon by John T. McCutcheon appearing in the *Miami Herald* of Miami, Florida, on September 24, 1926, and originally published by the *Chicago Tribune*.

CHICAGO TRIBUNE.

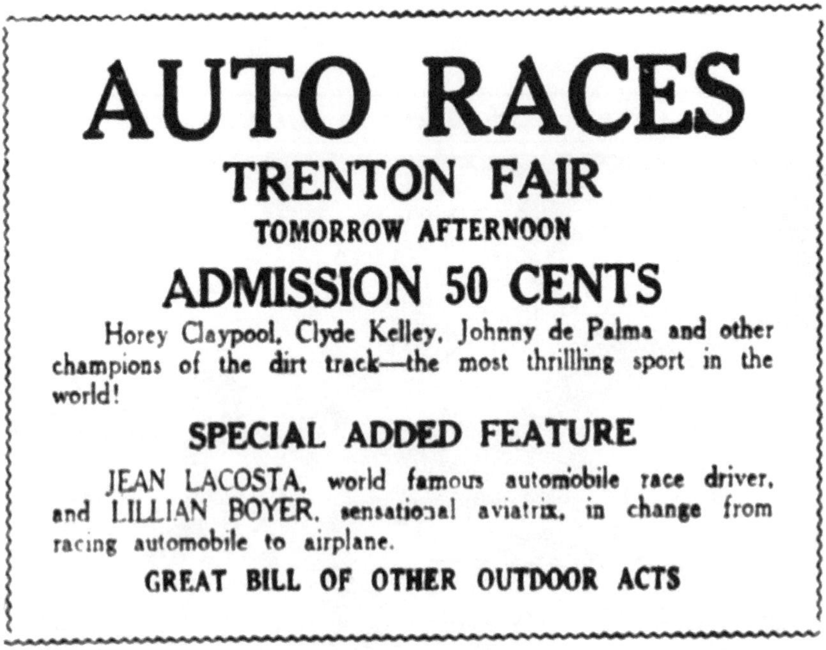

AUTO RACES
TRENTON FAIR
TOMORROW AFTERNOON
ADMISSION 50 CENTS

Horey Claypool, Clyde Kelley, Johnny de Palma and other champions of the dirt track—the most thrillling sport in the world!

SPECIAL ADDED FEATURE

JEAN LACOSTA, world famous automobile race driver, and LILLIAN BOYER, sensational aviatrix, in change from racing automobile to airplane.

GREAT BILL OF OTHER OUTDOOR ACTS

Figure 9.2. Advertisement for the Trenton Fair in the *Central New Jersey Home News* of New Brunswick, New Jersey, on October 1, 1926, promoting the dual appearance of Joan LaCosta and Lillian Boyer.
CENTRAL NEW JERSEY HOME NEWS.

> Lillian Boyer, acrobatic aviatrix extraordinary, swung from the end of a rope ladder fastened to the binding gear of her plane, as it sped over the bowl, and the crowd gasped, glad of a momentary diversion. The dusk was falling rapidly. The shades of night were settling slowly upon the land, darkening the eastern horizon, bringing into beautiful relief the tints and rich colors of the sunset. The chill of autumn was creeping into the air.[1]

On the other hand, the sentence in the Paterson, New Jersey, the*Morning Call* that headed the LaCosta Trenton race results was standard fare minus the poetry: "Girl Auto Racer Smashes Record."[2]

In these mixed shows, the Joan LaCosta name was now sharing the promo advertisements with other female pioneers with increasing regularity. Joan loved to fly, and she felt that being a pilot was actually less dangerous than what she was doing. She watched these performances in the sky and pondered.

After the long detour to the Northeast, it was a relief to get back to her home turf in Atlanta. It was here that she had first unveiled her Joan LaCosta persona and had her biggest on-track triumph there the prior May, the pasting of the legend Louis Disbrow before a huge crowd on the Lakewood oval. She was now a big enough star to draw crowds on just her reputation alone; there was no more need for a phony grudge match here. This time, Joan was gunning for a new speed record. As she told *The Atlanta Constitution*, "Southeastern sports fans have seen me drive in competition, now I want to show them what speed I can make with the track to myself."[3]

But it was also in Atlanta that the edges began to fray even more. On Thursday, October 7, two days before the show, the normally sure-footed LaCosta found herself on the wrong side of a wooden track rail. Her light dirt car spun into the whitewashed fence, which could have been deadly. Fortunately, it was at the beginning of the practice lap before she had built up to top speed. Physically, she was uninjured, but it had to have shaken her mentally.

She borrowed a Duesenberg, probably DePalma's, for the exhibition run for Saturday. She then turned the accident around into an ad for the Duesy, proclaiming it was "one of the finest looking cars I have ever seen"[4] and a potential record breaker for her upcoming run. It's remarkable that she had no reservations about jumping into a powerful Duesenberg on just 48 hours' notice. She had learned to race and made her living behind the wheel of the lightweight Miller and Frontenac Fords, and this was a king-size version of those cars.

The heavily modified DePalma Duesenberg was not the most stable auto to drive. A year later, DePalma himself, with many races piloting the big car under his belt, lost control of it in a Tampa, Florida, race, leaving him battered though alive but destroying the car. But Joan handled the dangerous machine beautifully.

On Saturday, October 9, 1926, Ray Claypool was scheduled to race with his big Peugeot, and Ralph DePalma's cousin Johnny wheeled out his favored Duesenberg. From her time on the circuit, Joan was familiar

MLLE. LA COSTA HAS ACCIDENT

Figure 9.3. Joan LaCosta after crashing during a pre-race practice lap in Atlanta pictured in the *Atlanta Constitution* on October 8, 1926.
ATLANTA CONSTITUTION.

with Team Sloan members such as Al Cotey. There was also an aerial show scheduled, which featured "Aerial McKay," a man attempting the same car-to-airplane climb that Lillian Boyer made famous and following that into a wing-walking, parachute jump maneuver. That stunt went awry and nearly ended in tragedy, but luckily, Aerial McKay ended up dangling in his parachute from a giant pine tree behind the grandstand.

Eight thousand people packed into the race stands, and twice that many watched from the low hills circling the track. The show was worth it. In the first 10-lap event, Johnny DePalma let the other racers jostle for the lead while he loped along at the back of the pack, and on the last lap, his powerful Duesenberg kicked down in gear and flew past the other competitors like they were standing still. The six-lap grudge match between Ray Claypool and Irvin Hoffman was a thriller that came down to the last 50 feet of track, where Hoffman pulled away and nipped Claypool by a nose.

The sweepstakes finale was anticipated as a repeat of the feared DePalma Duesey victory, but choking dust held back the airflow for the

DePalma car, and it couldn't repeat its majestic run from earlier. Instead, it was Hoffman and Claypool dueling once again, and once again, Hoffman edged out Claypool. Then came the interlude with the tumbling parachutist and a couple more races, and then it was Joan LaCosta's turn on the oval.

The dust was thick and noxious, and Joan's car spun up a dirt plume tail feather behind her as she flew around the track. The audience was on its feet. The cheers never stopped even though Joan crossed the finish line just short of a record time. They loved the spectacle, they loved the bravery, and they loved the huge smile of the tiny driver in the big car as she roared past the stands.

There was some concern over whether Joan LaCosta would appear at the Mississippi State Fair the following week on October 18 and 21. According to the *Clarion-Ledger* of Jackson, Joan was also penciled in for a Chicago run. But this may have been another planted story to whet the appetite of the locals by convincing them that the fair promoters were angling for a top celebrity racer.

In the end, the news was good. LaCosta was finally confirmed for October 18, and a record crowd poured through the gates. The conditions were perfect with clear skies, warm air, and dry, hard dirt. A car parade started promptly at noon from town and was watched by thousands of the locals. The procession led hundreds of folks into the fairgrounds, where Mayor Walter A. Scott was waiting to cut the ribbon. The crowd then scattered to the various exhibits, some of which were still being put together due to a transport train derailment that delayed getting building materials to the site that day. Eventually, they made their way to the grandstands of the racetrack.

The rumble of dozens of high-powered engines and the smoke wafting through the stands intoxicated the viewers. The backfiring "gunshots" of the motors echoed off the buildings throughout the fairgrounds and attracted the attention of hundreds. It was a dusty, noisy symphony that had seldom been heard by most of the attendees, and the excitement level ratcheted up with every glimpse and wail of a driver roaring past.

There was an adrenaline-pumping moment right off the bat when Ray Lampkin and Oscar Anderson (who else?) rubbed paint in a warm-up lap that sent both of their cars careening out of control. But being the masters that they were, each quickly corrected their steering, and no harm was done. It certainly woke the crowd up and reminded them that this was real racing and that it was dangerous, and it was happening right in front of them.

Jamie Clark's Scotch Band took center stage and regaled the crowd with a pre-race selection of popular tunes (with bagpipes played in lieu of the regular instruments in the original arrangements), and the drivers jumped into the cockpits and headed to the starting line.

The racing times that day weren't record breakers; the dirt track was rutted and rough, but the matches were still thrilling. The first two were elimination heats in the Magnolia State Sweepstakes, with the top two finishers in each moving on to the finals on Thursday. Collins, Waters, Lampkin, and Anderson were the top four, and then it was Joan LaCosta's turn.

The crowd was on its feet, cheering, waving hats, and mentally willing LaCosta to go faster and faster. But try as she might, the gravelly course and lack of traction in the corners kept her time down. The onlookers didn't seem to care. They were there to share the communal experience of watching a visual maelstrom of spinning tires throwing dirt in the air and to watch a dainty woman hanging onto a huge steering wheel for dear life as her car tore around the brown circle at dangerous speeds.

The afternoon of races wrapped up, and it had gotten on to early evening. The raffle ticket winners were announced; $50 went to Mr. McCurly of Stevenson. The crowds dispersed, heading by the hundreds to the food booths, and then they strolled through the grounds as night began to fall. The fairy lights clicked on in the dark, and half a dozen small bands began to play, their music accompanied by the cries of the carnival barkers and the constant rhythmic peal of the carousel calliope.

At last, the crowds slowly drifted back to the racetrack stands, the laughter and cries of the children dying down as their energy and attention waned, and they reclined on the wooden slats, craning their faces upward to see the first exploding firework. And then another. And then came a volley of whirling, whistling rockets that pierced the darkness. The small-town folks cheered with their friends, family, and strangers, staring up at the sparkling flares in the clear blue-black of the Mississippi night.

The fair continued to have unparalleled attendance numbers. The beautiful weather held, and the final auto races were held on October 21. LaCosta was now in all of the race advertising; word had gotten out about her performance on Monday, and many wanted a repeat show. Panhandle Gasoline, a big fair sponsor, certainly did. They ran a huge advertisement the day before in the *Clarion-Ledger*, touting the fact that Joan and the other drivers used Panhandle gas and motor oil. And though they claimed it was used by all the drivers, they used the picture of only one.

To give this slate of races a special air, they scheduled a match race between Joan and Oscar (the secret Romeo and Juliet of the track world) in a head-to-head three-lap duel. Joan LaCosta was the "Queen of Speed,"[5] and she got to drive the very fast Miller Special (the Ray Lampkin record-breaking speedster), which was a car that Joan was very familiar with. It paid off, as Joan sped to victory in the "grudge match," and Oscar probably had to buy the drinks after the event as Joan basked in her victory.

Lampkin, behind the wheel of the Miller, swept the other races as expected, and the big finale was a claiming race between a Chevrolet and a Star Company vehicle driven by professionals that was won by the Chevy. Both the Chevrolet and the Star were sold to the highest bidders in the stands after the race.

The relationship between Joan and Oscar was heating up. They headed to Waco, Texas, under the usual promotional heading of fierce competitors, but they were also seeing more of each other than just on the red dirt of the Texas racetrack.

October 26, 1926 was the Texas event on the calendar. The pre-race publicity highlighted the triumvirate of Sloan's main attractions: Ray Lampkin, Joan LaCosta, and Oscar Anderson. Lampkin was to go for the track record LaCosta for the women's, and Oscar was a favorite to win the conventional races. Waco was the far edge of the Alex Sloan circuit, and October was the tail end of the season and a chance for the

AUTO RACES

AT THE
STATE FAIR
JACKSON, MISS.
THURSDAY
OCTOBER 21st
Mlle. JOAN LaCOSTA
"QUEEN OF SPEED"
AND
RAY LAMKIN and OTHERS
WILL ATTEMPT TO SET NEW SOUTHERN AND WORLD HALF MILE TRACK RECORDS ON THE JACKSON TRACK

PANHANDLE GASOLINE
—AND—
PANOLENE MOTOR OILS
Were Used Exclusively
by LaCosta, Lamkin and Others Participating in the Races Monday

THE FOLLOWING LETTER SPEAKS FOR ITSELF—

Jackson, Mississippi,
October 18, 1926.

Panhandle Oil Company,
Jackson, Mississippi.

Gentlemen:

After the automobile races of the Mississippi State Fair, Jackson, Mississippi, this date, we can sincerely recommend Panhandle Gasoline and Panolene Motor Oil, which products we used in the operation of our cars in the races of this date.

Our cars performed beautifully and without a single delay or mishap.

We heartily recommend to the motoring Public, Panhandle Petroleum Products in the operation of their cars.

Miss Joan LaCosta	"Swede" Anderson
Ray Lamkin	Swan Peterson
Emory Collins	John Waters

PANHANDLE
IS BETTER GASOLINE
AND COSTS NO MORE

Try PANHANDLE GAS and PANOLENE MOTOR OILS
One Month and Note The Difference In The Performance of Your Motor

PANHANDLE
Is Winning Thousands of Friends Through
QUALITY AND PERFORMANCE
TRY IT!

Panhandle Stations Conveniently Located—

AMITE AND FARISH	PEARL AND GALLATIN	2767 WEST CAPITOL Farmer Jones	D'LO AND BRANDON ROAD Brook's Place
PASCAGOULA AND FARISH	WEST CAPITOL AND DELAWARE	WINTERS-WOODS-TERRY ROAD	

PERFORMANCE
A PRODUCT which cannot resell itself its own performance is not worthy of being sold the first time at any price. "One-Time Salesmanship" in a product is just as bad as "one-time salesmanship" in a salesman who cannot go back over his first route and produce a paying volume of business. PANHANDLE GUARANTEED GASOLINE has proven its ability to sell again and again, and to build an ever widening reputation for quality and performance.

PANHANDLE OIL COMPANY
521–23 EDWARDS HOTEL BLDG.   OF MISSISSIPPI   JACKSON, MISS.

Figure 9.4. Full-page advertisement for Auto Races appearing in the *Clarion-Ledger* on October 20, 1926.

CLARION-LEDGER.

drivers to show off one last time. It was also Joan's first racing trip to the state.

There were two show days. On Tuesday, October 26, LaCosta would run against the clock, driving by herself on the track, and then Thursday was the match race against another driver. The preshow publicity for the first day was standard fare, with the print ads touting the stellar lineup of professionals. The races went off without a hitch, and Joan, in the third slot, ran the course well but again didn't break any records.

On Wednesday, October 27, there was a sidebar in the Sports section in the Waco paper, decrying the taunting that LaCosta had received the day before during her run. She was incensed and demanded to race against one of the men. Oscar Anderson and his baby Fiat were chosen to face off against the Queen of Speed. It didn't matter who won because Joan and Oscar relished the few public opportunities that they had to be seen as a couple.

After the Thursday show, the team had a few days off before the Louisiana State Fair event. Some went ahead to Shreveport to prepare, but Joan and Oscar stayed over in Waco. That weekend, the pair had dinner with Mrs. Ennis Lorette from Chicago, then visited several Waco attractions. One of them might have been the Orpheum Theatre, which was showing the best double feature that could have encapsulated the fictional life of Joan LaCosta: *The Showgirl* and *The Speeding Venus*.

The Speeding Venus was the type of movie role that Alex Sloan must have been imagining when he dropped hints to the papers about Joan's future. Quite often, the actors in these films did the actual stunts, and being a professional driving dynamo like Joan LaCosta would have been a big plus. Before computer-generated images, the danger was palpable in the action scenes (a stunt flier in *Wings*, the first Academy Award–winning picture in 1927, was killed during filming), and part of the publicity was the idea that the audience would be watching the stars risking their lives for the viewers' entertainment. Joan never made the leap to the big screen, possibly in part because she didn't enjoy speaking in front of groups. The only place where she showed no fear was flying along at a mile per minute in a thin metal cone.

Figure 9.5. Advertisement for *The Speeding Venus*, 1926.
IMDB.

The last event on the books for many of the drivers that season was the Louisiana State Fair in Shreveport on Sunday, October 31, 1926, and the following Sunday, November 6. It was a last hurrah, and Alex Sloan was there to start the races (and maybe hand out a few bonuses). The big draw besides Joan was the 20-mile event, to be contested by Oscar Anderson, Swan Peterson, and Ray Lampkin. All three men delivered and put on a thriller of a race, making the finish a nail-biter with Swan Peterson winning by inches.

Joan then took center stage and drove alone on the oval. She ran against the timer, and while she did not set a record, she burned through the mile in a very respectable 55.40 seconds. Ray Lampkin, driving the Wisconsin Special, one of the fastest machines in the world and the same car that Joan had established her record in Daytona in, bettered Joan's time that day by a mere four seconds.

The crowds were so large and enthusiastic that the fairgrounds crew added 5,000 more grandstand bleacher seats for the following week's event, and another slate of races was added for Saturday in addition to the Sunday matches. Usually, LaCosta reserved her second appearance at an event for a "grudge match" against another driver, but for the added Saturday show, she would make another solo run at the clock. For Sunday's show, she suggested either Swan Peterson or (fingers crossed) Oscar Anderson. Her wish was granted, and she squared off against Oscar on Sunday.

It was a fantastic way to wrap up the season. The top drivers were there (except Louis Disbrow, who seemed to be otherwise occupied during the latter half of the Sloan season), and the weather was fair and warm, perfect for driving. The races were nearly carbon copies of the previous Sunday. The main event was a nail-biter, with the top three finishers separated by less than a foot. Oscar Anderson won the men's race, and Joan LaCosta ran her timed lap at 55 seconds flat. The buzz for their head-to-head matchup the next day was building, and Sloan bumped it into the headlining slot for closing night. The race would be the next-to-last event (before for the consolation match, the last chance for all of the day's losers to get some prize money), as it was guaranteed to keep the audience in the seats until the end of the show.

The *Marshall News Messenger* newspaper of Marshall, Texas, ran an interview with Mlle. LaCosta a couple of days before her match race. After the usual hyperbole describing her feminine and delicate attributes, they asked if she was ever afraid:

> "Of snakes, yes!" she answers, "but they're about the only thing. Racing cars? No! Nothing to be afraid of. If I ever get afraid, I'll quit driving. You can't take chances like that when you're afraid. I'm not afraid of the men drivers, either. I've driven faster than most of them and I can drive that fast again. They've matched me against Oscar Anderson for Sunday. Well, he's a terribly good driver. You know in the last few weeks he's driven so well that he's second, I believe, in the points of races for the 1926 championship. But he's never driven 145 miles an hour—and I have. I can beat him Sunday if the track is good; if it's real good I can run away from him, I think. Anyway, I'll try to. See you Sunday!"[6]

Sunday, November 6, was a barn burner of a show. Swan Peterson, who had thrilled the crowd the week before with his photo-finish win in the main event, came around the corner into the homestretch and broke an axle under the car, sending a tire careening down the track and forcing his sliding vehicle into the outer fence. Johnny Waters also had mechanical troubles in the first race when his engine exploded into flames, but the inferno was contained quickly without injury.

The match race between Joan and Oscar was superb. The track dirt was thick and slow, so Oscar's heavier Fiat had the advantage digging and holding the line into the corners, while Joan's lighter Miller Special outran the Fiat on the straightaways. It came down to the final homestretch, as it always did with these professionals, and Anderson floored the gas pedal to nip LaCosta at the finish, but it nearly cost Oscar control of his ride. The short amount of runway left after the finish line wasn't nearly enough for the final burst of speed of the accelerating Fiat, and Oscar nearly skidded into the outer fence. But he was used to getting out of tight spots and close calls, and his calm nerves saved the car and his life.

In the December 1926 issue of *Popular Mechanics*, a publication with a print run of more than 1.2 million copies per month, a picture of Joan LaCosta was included in a two-page spread titled "Woman Champions."

Helen Filkey, Left, Set Three World's Records in One Day; Gertrude Ederle, Above, Made Another

Mlle. Jean LaCosta, Famous Auto Racer, Who Set New Speed Marks on the Sands of Daytona Beach, and, at Right, Miss Glenna Collett, Holder of Many Championships in the Golf World

Figure 9.6. Joan LaCosta featured in a photomontage of female athletes titled "Woman Champions" in the December 1926 issue of *Popular Mechanics*.
POPULAR MECHANICS.

It heralded "Mlle. Jean LaCosta, Famous Auto Racer, Who Set New Speed Marks on the Sands of Daytona."[7] Her inclusion in the magazine cemented her status as one of the most high-profile female athletes in the country.

LaCosta, smiling in her roadster, was now in a million homes.

Chapter Ten

The Call of the Air

The year 1926 had been the most remarkable one of LaCosta's life. She had become a bona fide sports celebrity and had attained a professional level of respect that would have seemed impossible just 12 months before. She had been proclaimed the fastest woman in the world, and her picture had been plastered on the front pages of numerous newspapers. She was congratulated by and posed with Babe Ruth, and her own tough father had proudly witnessed her success.

She had also fallen in love.

Joan still projected an astonishing level of confidence in herself and her own courage, and with that came the belief that she could consistently achieve whatever she wanted.

On May 23, 1927, Joan LaCosta was noted as a special attendee at the Roby Racetrack, where she watched her ex-husband, Walter Martins, win a pair of races. An article covering the race described her as "Joan Le Coste of France, premier girl auto driver of the world."[1] She and Walter had separated paths years before. And now watching him perform on the track and cheering him on from the bleachers as he won race after race was a reminder for Joan of what her other path could have been. Instead of being recognized as the premier woman auto driver in the country, she could have been a racing spectator or a supportive wife, perhaps never experiencing her own life behind the wheel. Alex Sloan had planned for Joan LaCosta to appear in at least 20 events in the upcoming season. The circuit had done so well for Sloan that at this point, it was an obvious case of "if it ain't broke, don't fix it." The LaCosta shows had all been sellouts, in some cases with overflowing crowds, and there wasn't any reason to believe that this wouldn't be the case again.

Joan was secure in her role as the steady star of the Sloan shows. She was comfortable enough to allow herself some time visiting in the Chicago area, venturing out in the spring to see old acquaintances on the track.

Then, in May 1927, the world changed forever.

Charles Lindbergh flew from Roosevelt Field in New York, and a day and a half later, he landed in Paris at Le Bourget Field at 10:22 p.m., becoming the first man to fly solo across the Atlantic. The reaction around the world was astonishing, as hundreds of thousands of citizens in America and Europe took to the streets in parades and spontaneous celebrations. Suddenly, a daredevil woman in a car, racing along the beach a mile at a time, no matter how fast she went, paled to the feat of a lanky Minnesota pilot handling the plane controls in a cramped cockpit for a 33½-hour flight, with only a few sandwiches to carry him through, while the deep blue death of the Atlantic beckoned below.

The international spectacle changed LaCosta's attitude toward her career trajectory. She began to publicly proclaim her flying plans, and she seemed to button up her racing past.

She had decided that 1927 was to be her last year on the racing circuit, and she would put together a flying lessons fund, money that was saved from her race purses and selling off her few unnecessary possessions.

The new race season for LaCosta kicked off with a big event at the Hamline Track in Minnesota, scheduled for June 18. There was also a 100-mile race booked with a full contingent of 20 drivers, at least 14 from the Minneapolis area. The overwhelming local driver response required pre-race qualification heats to winnow the field down to the best of the best.

LaCosta was featured as usual, but the pre-event publicity in the papers mentioned that there was a local woman driver who had issued a challenge to Joan. This was a new wrinkle for her in these events. During the previous season, she had raced men or by herself against the clock. Was Sloan hedging his bets early, looking for a replacement for LaCosta

"LUCKY SLIM" LINDBERGH, THE "FLYIN' FOOL," AND HIS RYAN MONOPLANE

Figure 10.1. Charles Lindberg appearing with his plane, the *Spirit of St. Louis*, in the *Times Union* of Brooklyn, New York, on May 20, 1927.
TIMES UNION.

in case she left the fold? Or was it a ploy to keep her in the bit, to remind her that she wasn't the only woman who could drive a fast car for prize money?

Considering Alex Sloan's fertile promotional mind, he was probably poking around for a new selling angle. Joan LaCosta had raced plenty of men in the past six months; maybe the audiences would be enticed by a woman-versus-woman match.

In either case, Joan continued to soak up the adulation. On June 14, she was advertised as the star attraction at the Marigold Ballroom. She waded into the Minneapolis nightlife, danced up a storm, and, best of all, got paid for it by the sponsors. But the papers barely covered it.

On June 14, there were breathless reports on the radio, and the newspapers were packed with pictures of the huge ticker-tape parade that New York City had thrown for Charles Lindbergh in an official hero's welcome.

Between 3 million and 4 million people lined the streets and cheered out of the windows along Broadway, and even in far-flung Minnesota, the effect was transformational.

It was here, in an interview published on June 16 in *The Minneapolis Star* newspaper, that Joan lifted away part of her public persona veneer. The story notes that Marion Martins was Joan LaCosta, a rare public admission that seemed to imply that Joan was thinking about the end of her racing career and her legacy. The biggest revelation of the article, though, came in its title. Joan's ambition was becoming a pilot:

Girl Auto Racer Willing to Attempt Paris Hop.
Marion Martins Here for Test of Skill on State Fair Track.

An American girl whose age is the same as Col. Charles A. Lindbergh's and who, like the daring young airman, tinkered with and rode motorcycles and "junk" automobiles in extreme youth, today offered to hop across the Atlantic, unaccompanied, in an airplane, provided someone will accord her the same privileges enjoyed by Colonel Lindbergh and Clarence Chamberlin and underwrite the flight.

The girl is Miss Marion Martins, 25 years old, of Memphis, Tenn., known to the American dirt track auto racing public as Joan LaCosta, "daring French woman auto racer."

Miss Martins, who is of English and French parentage, would have preferred to have kept her plans for the flight secret until just before the intended hop-off, but the fact that she is practically unknown as an aviator and is a member of the so-called "weaker" sex almost precludes the possibility of obtaining the necessary backer for the flight unless her intentions are made known in advance of the proposed hop from New York, via "The Great Circle," to Paris.

"If I should fail in the attempt, there is my girlfriend, Phoebe Fairgrave, of Memphis, who would be willing to try it," Miss Martins declared today after her arrival in Minneapolis to prepare for participation in an auto race at the Minnesota State Fairgrounds Saturday with another girl. Miss Blanche Voge, of Robbinsdale, Minn.

"Phoebe is a licensed aviatrix, and I wouldn't be surprised if she would start out for Paris in her plane one of these days without saying much about it. Phoebe is like that, you know."

Marion Martins better known to public as Joan LaCosta.

Figure 10.2 Joan LaCosta/Marion Martins pictured in the *Minneapolis Star* of Minneapolis, Minnesota, on June 16, 1927.

MINNEAPOLIS STAR. IMAGE ENHANCED FOR CLARITY BY ADELIS SEGUNDO BRICEÑO.

Her "girl friend," she added, once jumped out of an airplane when it was 15,500 feet up in the air and descended safely to earth with the aid of a parachute.[2]

It was a bold statement. The fictional gig was up for Joan, and she willingly peeled away the "European champion" mask she had worn so long. She continued to race under the nom de guerre of Joan LaCosta, but she publicly acknowledged that it was an identity she had concocted.

There was no fallout from this bombshell; she would continue to be booked and recognized as LaCosta, even after her racing days, including that race in Minneapolis just two days later. But it also signaled that Joan was caught up in "Lucky Lindy" fever like most Americans, and in her mind, true immortality was going to be achieved by flying an airplane with an ocean below. In another interview later, she mentioned that it was only a matter of time before she would be getting a financial backer that would sponsor her for a solo flight across the Atlantic, and then she would leave this auto racing business behind for good.

At the Minnesota State Fair, the Saturday 100-mile open race was the lead draw, with the match race between Joan LaCosta and Blanche Voge promoted as an extra feature.

Blanche Voge, of nearby Robbinsdale, wasn't a professional, at least not at the level of Joan. She was slated to drive a Ford Frontenac belonging to her brother Don, who was a local racer, for the LaCosta match.

A used stock car race was also on the show bill. These were usually souped-up street cars piloted by inexperienced drivers. It would be a mix of new, fast cars and jalopies. The most dangerous conditions in a race are when the levels of equipment or skill are scaled far apart from each other, and this was the case in Minneapolis on June 18, 1927.

The early pictures of the event included one of Joan LaCosta, sitting proud and relaxed behind the wheel of her Miller Special. It really seemed that it was going to be another fun, exciting day, with some familiar names like Oscar Anderson and Cliff Woodbury making appearances. The weather was cool, in the upper sixties, typical May temperatures in Minnesota. There were an estimated 8,000 fans in the stands.

The big race had finally been chopped down for the main event, but it was still a packed field of 50 entrants. The crowd was loud and boisterous for the races, and they were as excited as the drivers were for the races.

Glenn Hiett of Chicago took the flag in the premier 100-mile contest, out-legging Oscar Anderson, who fought doggedly for the top position early on in the race as usual, along with second-place finisher Don Voge, who was piloting his Ford Frontenac. "Swede" Anderson finally lost his engine 12 miles in, and Hiett eventually held off Voge for the victory.

Figure 10.3. Joan LaCosta pictured in the *Star Tribune* of Minneapolis, Minnesota, on June 19, 1927.
STAR TRIBUNE. IMAGE ENHANCED FOR CLARITY BY ADELIS SEGUNDO BRICEÑO.

LaCosta had a relatively easy time of it, running her two laps at a leisurely time of two minutes and change, and breezed to the win over the rookie Blanche Voge.

The stock car race looked like the amateur show it was. The rules were open, "run what ya brung," and there was a mixture of vehicles at the starting line.

What was supposed to be a regulated but less strict event turned into a disaster. The cars were supposed to start in small, manageable groups for safety, but the pictures show roadsters and convertibles, some with additional passengers, throwing up the dirt as they take off elbow to elbow toward the first curve.

The car on the far right of the track is being driven by 25-year-old Arthur Van Vleet, a movie projectionist at the Summit Theatre in St. Paul, who had recently taken up racing as a hobby. It was the last picture of the young man alive.

John Berkey and his passenger, a Mr. Larson, in the white car near the inner fence, were taking the first corner at speed. As they went into the bend, Berkey lost control and flipped the car onto its side (throwing both the driver and the passenger clear), and the empty auto ended up skidding sideways across the track directly into the path of Van Vleet, who desperately tried to brake.

The eyewitnesses watching from the bleachers that day stated that there was some debris from the wreckage that Van Vleet collided with,

Figure 10.4. Arthur Van Vleet (far right) pictured racing in the *Star Tribune* on June 19, 1927.

STAR TRIBUNE. IMAGE ENHANCED FOR CLARITY BY ADELIS SEGUNDO BRICEÑO.

Figure 10.5. The John Berkey race car that caused the death of Arthur Van Vleet, pictured in the *Star Tribune* on June 19, 1927.
STAR TRIBUNE. IMAGE ENHANCED FOR CLARITY BY ADELIS SEGUNDO BRICEÑO.

and he lost control, flipping his car end over end. Clara Houdek, Arthur's fiancée, whom he was to marry the following week, was there that afternoon. Clara joined the crowd around the bloodied young man, and a physician, H. E. Whitcomb, rushed out of the stands to help. He pronounced Arthur dead from a fractured skull. Clara Houdek collapsed in grief.

His body lay beside the track for an hour until an ambulance arrived. The drivers, standing beside their own high-powered vehicles in the pits, had plenty of time to contemplate their choice of profession. The scene haunted Joan LaCosta for the rest of her life.

The rest of the stock car races that day were canceled. The front page of the Minneapolis *Star Tribune* on June 19, 1927, headline was posted in bold type: "Racer Killed at Fair Track."[3]

It was a sobering start to the season.

Until then, LaCosta had been fairly insulated from the deadlier side of racing. She was aware of fatal accidents, as all the drivers were, but it was different seeing the light leave a young man's eyes, killed right in front of you while doing the exact same thing you had been doing for years.

One way to push the tragedy of the dead driver out of Joan's mind was to keep working. The July Fourth weekend loomed, and it had always been a high point in her previous race seasons. But in Decatur, over that same Fourth of July holiday, the Macon County Fairgrounds was the setting for several horrific accidents that resulted in the death of one driver and multiple injuries for another. Six crashes occurred on July 5 on the dirt track, with the most disastrous one involving Robert Tippey.

A 27-year-old from Peoria, Illinois, Tippey was driving a new car that was unfamiliar to him, but he had made it to the checkered flag of his race, finishing third. However, the ignition was acting finicky, so Tippey kept going on the track, hoping to clear up the problem. On his last lap, he swerved at the bend to avoid another car and crashed into the fence, colliding with Orville Zook (who survived with burns and bruises). The supporting fence post transformed into a deadly spear, piercing the radiator, the dashboard, and Robert Tippey's right lung. He passed away later that afternoon.

Oscar Anderson was busy that weekend, being booked back-to-back, first on July 3 at the Sterling, Illinois, Speedbowl Park, where he was debuting his $10,000 Miller Straight Eight car, and then the next day on July 4 at Fox Valley Exposition Park. LaCosta looked forward to appearing with Swede at the Exposition Park event in Aurora, Illinois, where Anderson was the billed headliner in the 100-mile race and LaCosta was advertised in a matchup against Lillian Boyer in a five-mile race. That event would have been an odd but interesting crossover of worlds. There's no record of that head-to-head race happening, and Joan would have been extremely distracted after what happened in Oscar's July 3 event.

In 1927, Oscar "Swede" Anderson was on the cusp of attaining legendary racing status. He was a fast and fearless pilot, consistently finishing in the money. But that fearlessness spawned recklessness. He was known to wreck spectacularly in a fair number of his races. Those crashes weren't always his fault, but the reputation dogged him, and he drew good-sized crowds who came to the events hoping to see that danger that he emanated on the track.

On July 3, in Sterling, the big draw was the new monster-sized, eight-cylinder machine owned by Oscar Anderson. It was a big financial investment, reputed to have cost $100,000, and it came with a steep learning curve for Anderson, who was used to the quick maneuverability of his smaller "Baby Fiat."[4] This behemoth was a different animal, trading the Fiat's easier handling for raw speed.

The powerful car ran as advertised in the first three-mile race. Oscar won going away in a blistering 2:43. In his next match, the six-mile qualifier, he was again leading the pack when something went horribly wrong. He lost control of the Miller Eight, which flew 75 feet through the air, flipping end over end twice. The new car was completely destroyed; Oscar, as usual, escaped far less wounded than he had any right to be. There were three other crashes that afternoon, and all of the drivers received serious injuries, but Oscar Anderson was the most fortunate. He was a tough man, but the violent spill shook him up.

In Brazil, Indiana, on Sunday, July 24, 25 cars lined up at the Sunflower Speedway starting line, a very crowded field from the get-go. Driver Benny Bennifield had elbowed his way in front when he lost control of his rig at 75 miles per hour and flew over the embankment and into the crowd, scattering the spectators and breaking the shoulder of Mr. Kingery of Terre Haute. A following driver, Dick Boles, blinded by the resultant cloud of dust, crashed into another competitor, R. A. Hall, which led to a chain of collisions involving the nine cars following behind them.

Besides the injuries to the initial victims, driver Paul Weis was critically wounded; drivers R. A. Hall, Walter Ax, Al Jones, Ralph Swigart, Bob Slater, and Mark Billman were all moderately hurt; and spectator Mary Taylor of Danville was severely injured by the race car of Charles Crawford.

Another crash involving Oscar in Aurora on August 14 traumatized Joan.

Oscar was burning up the track in his Fiat and had just finished the race when he lost control of the car and spun out into the fence. Unlike his July 3 accident, this time, he suffered compound fractures of two ribs, and the severity of the injury earned him an extended stay in the hospital. He was sidelined for the rest of the season.

Joan was in the arena watching, and her heart dropped as the disaster unfolded. When Anderson took a turn for the worse a month later, Joan drove up to see him. She had suffered similar injuries in a few of her own rare accidents, like when she went through the fence on the Detroit track the year before. She had taken out more than a few fence rails in her career, but the one in Detroit and then another later in Atlanta would give her chronic pain,issues for years.

Oscar would be on the shelf recuperating for months, but he recovered enough to compete again at the top dirt tracks, returning halfway through the 1928 season.

LaCosta had raced in scores of events on dirt tracks around the country, and, of course, she knew (or knew of) many of these dead and hurt drivers. But now she had been a witness to it in person, following on the heels of watching a young man die in front of his fiancée just days before. It was no wonder that Joan LaCosta was seriously contemplating the idea of leaving the auto racing world for that of the skies.

It was an intoxicating thought for Joan. The everlasting fame would come with just one bravura act: there would be no more climbing into a train car over and over and waking up the next day at a county fair in Iowa, Alberta, or Alabama. She would be touring the country in style in her own private Pullman. And, according to an interview with the *Rock Island Argus* on August 13, all she needed was the backing of a local businessman to the tune of $25,000.

It's an oddly specific amount. She mentioned her friend Phoebe Fairgrave Omlie when interviewed on the topic of switching careers. Phoebe had just been granted the first federal commercial flying license for a woman and was married to a respected pilot, Vernon Omlie. On August 2, the *Nashville Banner* newspaper had printed an article that mentioned that Phoebe Fairgrave had been offered a sponsorship by a New York news syndicate to fly across the Atlantic. That sponsorship was $20,000.

Joan was competitive, even with her friends.

LaCosta wasn't alone in her grand plans of aviation immortality. There were many other brave, ambitious women with nerves of steel and the necessary physical athleticism needed for such an endeavor.

The usual suspects were prominently featured in various publications. They were referred to as the "Bird Women."[5] Among the most often mentioned was the intrepid Ruth Elder Law, who had set several U.S.

air-flight records, establishing the archetype of the female aviatrix seen at fairgrounds across the country. But she was 40 years old and considered a dark horse in the transatlantic race. Also in consideration was Thea Rasche, a German flier who was known for her hops around Europe in her 100-horsepower Siemens plane. And then there was one of the most unique personalities to take to the air, Gladys Roy.

Roy, determined to leave her past behind, was born Gladys Smith but was inspired to change her name when she learned that Mary Pickford had ditched her original last name, which was also Smith. Gladys took her husband's surname of Roy as her professional moniker. She was a photogenic, daring stuntwoman who grew up in the city of Minneapolis, Minnesota, along with her four brothers and two sisters.

Gladys Roy was one of the women who inspired Joan to take another dangerous leap for her career. Joan LaCosta jumped feetfirst into the flying fray on August 14. The *Moline Daily Dispatch* printed an interview about her own possible plans about soaring across the Atlantic:

"If I should get the financial backing that is essential, I would give up auto racing for the time being and go right into training for the flight," Miss LaCosta declared recently when interviewed by a newspaper reporter. "For I don't want to start out after making only haphazard preparations. I want to go about this thing in a business-like way, and that means months of preparation and experience in the air with my time devoted solely to flying.

"The expenses may come to $25,000 or more, but if some kind-hearted man will come forward with the money, I am ready to begin preparations at any time. But then men probably think a woman couldn't make a flight like that, so you see, it is going to be difficult for me to realize my ambition. Even tho I'm not going to give up my plans to make the flight unless someone comes forward with assistance.

"I have already been in the air more than 200 hours and Lieutenant Vernon Omlie, stationed at Memphis Airport, has said that I am now ready and fitted for 'solo flying' following a series of flights at Memphis during the past several months."[6]

Figure 10.6. Montage of female pilots titled "Bird Women" in the *Cuba Review* of Cuba, Missouri, on September 8, 1927.

CUBA REVIEW.

The upcoming Iowa State Fair in Davenport was a big event for LaCosta. It covered the span of a full week, and she would be thrown into the show earlier than usual, racing on the second day of the fair, Monday, August 15.

Stuntwoman Lillian Boyer was also on the bill and was scheduled as the co-headliner for Monday. She was always a crowd favorite on the circuit and was now regularly performing with Alex Sloan's team. Her pilot was William "Billy" Brock, and this show was to be his swan song in the stunt business, but his appearance was canceled at the last minute. According to Sloan, Billy Brock was "scheduled to attempt to hop around the world in 15 days soon in a semi-official flight, and . . . Brock asked government permission to fly Miss Boyer's plane, but was refused."[7] Lillian was without her trusted partner, and there was no quick substitute in such a dangerous undertaking. Her appearances were scratched.

On Monday, Joan still thrilled the crowd by ripping around the track in a record time for a woman, at 2:18.80 over the two miles. The "frail, winsome lass"[8] won an enthusiastic ovation from the stadium crowd.

Although Joan didn't know it, that same day, Monday, August 15, 1927, Gladys Roy was appearing in Youngstown, Ohio, to promote a film she was making, titled *The Queen of Ohio Meets the Queen of the Air*.

Roy was in her aviation togs, sitting in the cockpit of Delmar Snyder's plane, and Evelyn Wilgus, the newly crowned Miss Ohio, was standing beside the plane in her pageant getup when the photographer asked for one last shot of the two of them together by the plane.

Gladys Roy climbed down and absentmindedly walked into the invisible spinning blades. She had conscientiously kept the propellers turning while pictures were being taken so as not to clutter the shots, and being more passenger than pilot, she had a lapse of awareness that cost Roy her life. Lieutenant Snyder was there at the photo session, and he rushed to her side. It was too late. Part of Roy's skull had been ripped away, and she passed away that afternoon at a local hospital.

An incident involving LaCosta's friend Phoebe Fairgrave Omlie added to Joan's rough summer. On August 28, Fairgrave was flying a passenger around Armstrong Field in Memphis when the passenger accidently braced his foot against the rudder, sending the plane into a spin.

The skilled Fairgrave managed to crash-land the out-of-control aircraft near the field, and somehow both survived with moderate injuries.

Another Midwest stunt flier, Otto Smith, wasn't as fortunate. On August 29, he had just finished racing a car in his plane at the fair in Indiana when, after finishing the scheduled stunt, he decided to thrill the crowd at Montpelier by doing some spins and dives. His engine conked out, and though he managed to get it restarted at the last second, he couldn't control it. He pulled up out of the final dive about 20 feet from the ground, then nosed down into a field. He was dead at 25.

Suddenly, Joan LaCosta's world had gone from close calls that she could laugh off with her friends later to actually seeing and hearing of serious mishaps and deaths among friends and acquaintances. It hit home how quickly a life could be snuffed out, and even the most highly skilled fliers and racers were always on the knife edge of life and death, one slip away from the void.

CHAPTER ELEVEN

Falling Back to Earth

AFTER LILLIAN BOYER'S PULLOUT AND THE SHOCKING NEWS THAT ONE of the most popular aviatrixes in the country was dead, Joan LaCosta put her head down and soldiered on. It felt like the winding down of a routine that Joan had once found thrilling but that now made her mull the end of her race career, event by event.

Joan's blazing two-mile run on Monday was the prologue for her head-to-head matchup against the winner of the Glen Hiett–Swan Peterson race to take place the following Saturday. It was the usual twist that she participated in many shows before. LaCosta would have her speed exhibition first, then take on the men's race winner after. She was again slotted in a prime spot, the seventh race, toward the close of the event.

But her thunder was stolen that week by the biggest star in the world, Charles Lindbergh.

He was in the midst of a countrywide barnstorming tour, touching down in several cities, and August 19 was the Tri-Cities' turn. He flew in over Davenport and landed at the Moline airport, and there were approximately 10,000 people surrounding the hangar as he emerged from the *Spirit of St. Louis*, Joan among them.

That night, at the Rock Island Arsenal, along with 800 other guests, Joan ate, drank, and listened as speech after speech, award after award, was draped on Lindbergh, who accepted it all with his humble grace and little-boy smile. At some point, LaCosta buttonholed him for a moment, and they commiserated over the private price both had paid in their very public pursuits.

Joan dreamed of getting away from the staring crowds but understood that it was part of her job description. She said that Charles Lindbergh was sympathetic.

"Oh, I wouldn't mind the eyes," she said the pilot told her. "If they just wouldn't push me and smother me to death!,"[1] adding,

> The only pilot that people will stare at is Lindbergh. I shall never forget how I felt when I stood up to receive the first real trophy I ever won. It was out in Indianapolis in 1925, and I had just defeated Elfrieda Mais, the Canadian, in five automobile races out of six for the International Women's Championship.
>
> It was wonderful to win, but I was on the point of taking my car and driving off when the crowd began milling about and calling my name. I never got such a case of stage fright in my life. And when they stood me up high to present the trophy I could feel every eye on the field, and I felt as though I had little prickles all over.
>
> You get accustomed to being stared at, though. But it is nice to be up in the air where you can't see anyone and they can't see you, at the same time knowing that there won't be anybody but a few bored loiterers about the field when you land.[2]

On Saturday, August 20, Glen Hiett beat Swan Peterson. In the follow-up showcase match in the afternoon, Joan LaCosta took on Hiett in a two-driver duel. After she took a three-lap warm-up to adjust to her borrowed car, the Rube Reynolds "Balding Special," she sped through the course, giving Hiett a good run for the money before he slipped past her for the win.

Six days later, in her last appearance at the Mississippi Valley Fair, Joan again turned in a great time, running the half-mile oval in 33.20 seconds, almost two seconds faster than her previous record. She followed that up a solid three-lap time of 1:57.80 on Sunday.

The 1927 Iowa State Fair races were wrapping up on September 2. It was a stacked card, with 10 events and some of the big dirt track names competing, like Sig Haugdahl, the streaking Glen Hiett, Fred Horey,

Swan Peterson, and Joan LaCosta. Joan was scheduled on the card in an earlier slot than usual, the fourth race, and it was to be another matchup with her new nemesis, Glen Hiett, in a three-lap free-for-all.

There were also 15 circus acts performing at the fair, along with Sousa and his band and whippet dog races. The crowds were normally huge for the Iowa events, and on this Friday, the Labor Day weekend extravaganza was sure to pack them in.

The show didn't disappoint. Local teen Jimmy Nichols won the longest race, hanging with the prohibitive favorite, Glen Hiett, each swapping the lead in the blowing dust until Hiett had to make a pit stop and lost three laps. Nichols had to actually get special permission to even be in the race, as he was considered a young novice and was a last-minute addition.

The murky brown clouds on the track choked and blinded the drivers who weren't in front, making a speedy start and fighting your way to the front of the pack essential for victory. Dry, rutted ovals in the summer and early fall were brutal to run in, but they were typical scenarios on the dirt track circuit.

Sig Haugdahl was without his famous Wisconsin Special and instead drove Fred Horey's race car. It was more than enough in the hands of the great Sig, who piloted number 10 to the checkered flag in the dusty conditions.

Joan LaCosta was once again defeated by Glen Hiett, who seemed to have Joan's number. Neither one gave an inch in their three-lap, one-on-one match.

It's no surprise that LaCosta opted to have her next match against a different driver, and Arch Miller drew the straw. On Monday, the first day, September 5, she would have her usual run against the clock, then she would face off with Arch on the second day of racing at the Nebraska State Fair in Lincoln on Friday, September 9.

Because it was the Labor Day weekend, it was also the busiest time of the year on the tour. Monday, September 5, 1927, was the opening day of races at the Nebraska State Fair. Aviatrix Lillian Boyer was in all of the pre-event press releases, but there was no mention of Joan LaCosta's scheduled appearances.

Figure 11.1. The Iowa State Fair race pictured in the *Des Moines Register* on September 3, 1927.
DES MOINES REGISTER. IMAGE ENHANCED FOR CLARITY BY ADELIS SEGUNDO BRICEÑO.

Joan's standard weekly routine was now established. She would run her exhibition lap the first day, and later in the week, Friday, she would match up against Arch Miller head-to-head. It was the formula she had grown accustomed to in her state fair history, but now, toward the end of that career, it was bittersweet. The September 5 exhibition run was her typical one-mile time test. LaCosta ran it in a relatively slow 1:09.50, or about 52 miles per hour. That was not a normal speed for Joan, and in a very rare complaint, Joan said that "the track was too soft."[3]

Her Friday, September 9, return race against Arch Miller in Nebraska put her back in the win column. She redeemed her disappointing Monday performance earlier that week, coming back to beat Arch in a three-lap race in front of 15,000 fans. She drove efficiently, with her winning time just a hair over 1:48. The write-ups on her two races were tepid, and there was no post-match commentary in the media.

It could have simply been just a bad case of fatigue. Between her appearances in Lincoln, Nebraska, on September 5 and the 9, she ran an exhibition in Atlantic, Iowa, for the Cass County Fair on Wednesday, September 7, loping through a mile in 1:05.50.

The crowds at these two events were massive. Attendance records were smashed regularly. The Atlantic stands held 20,000 spectators, and another 5,000 stood in front. The numbers were also impressive at Nebraska.

The crowds still adored her, and she was always in demand, but her wounds, both physical and emotional, were exacting a climbing toll. Her love, Oscar Anderson, was still recovering from his severe injuries in August. Her friend Phoebe Fairgrave had dropped out of the sky in a plane crash and had luckily escaped with nonlethal injuries. Gladys Roy, the famous wing walker, had died in a tragic freak accident.

On September 18, Roy's regular pilot, Delmar Snyder, landed in Sterling, Illinois (two hours outside Chicago). He was there to paint his airplane and fly off to Michigan. He announced that he was going to be the new pilot for Lillian Boyer, the aviation stuntwoman who had done so many state fair shows with Joan. The daredevils of the air were getting more and more attention and attracting top talent to the profession.

Joan LaCosta was still on her own, with the race season wrapping up, and her carefully cultivated world champion persona was starting to peel apart amid her public complaints and excuses.

The Spencer Fair Races in Iowa were on the docket for Saturday, October 1, to be headlined by Joan LaCosta and Sig Haugdahl. A torrential downpour canceled the racing, and Joan was off to Atlanta earlier than expected.

* * *

Atlanta was the center of national attention in early October. Charles Lindbergh, fresh off his solo Atlantic crossing a few months before, was arriving on October 11, flying into Candler Field. LaCosta made sure she was part of the spectacle by getting herself booked as a headliner at the local Lakewood Race Track event on October 8.

The weather always played a big part in LaCosta's career. She bragged early on in her track appearances that rain always gave her an edge, that she drove faster and better in the mud. She was usually right. It was in a downpour a year ago up north in New York when she first crossed race paths with Louis Disbrow. She impressed him by choosing to go out racing on the drenched Rochester course, with the storm soaking her to the bone, and that had cemented their friendship and respect for each other, professionally and personally.

Her last professional driving appearance in the city that loved her the most, Atlanta, was set for Saturday, October 8. It was where she had been honored again and again and where the biggest paper in Georgia fawned over her and promoted her incessantly. The Atlanta Lakewood racetrack during the Southeastern Fair was where she would make her last run in Georgia.

In 1926, Alex Sloan had used the *Atlanta Constitution* to publicize the battle that LaCosta was waging against the inherent prejudice of the male racing circuit. He ghost-wrote race challenges, throwing down the gauntlet of head-to-head matches with other top drivers and published them under Joan's name in the paper.

A year ago, fresh off her well-publicized world-record run in Daytona, it had worked. She whipped Louis Disbrow on the field and then bathed in the adulation of the fans.

This time, in 1927, Joan sent an invitation through the paper to Curly Young for a one-on-one race. He was the hot driver out of Chicago, so it seemed like a natural matchup: two Chicago favorites dueling for the crown of the fastest driver in the Midwest. Young had been loudly campaigning for a highlight race at the event, so Joan offered him one.

"If Curly Young wants a race so badly, why not match him with me?"[4] she wired race officials.

She got no response.

It seems Curly was busy angling for matchups against stellar *male* drivers, like "Wild Bill" Purvis, so Joan had to race alone. She gave it her all as she always did, posting the fastest lap time of anyone on the track that day. And, of course, it was raining again, as if the sky was upset that it wouldn't have another sight of this dark-haired woman with gray eyes who floated round and round the red dirt circles of the South.

Her other competition for attention that day was the crowd favorite Lady Irene, a speedy greyhound that slid over the course earlier in the dog races:

Greyhounds Give Fans Big Thrill
Mlle. LaCosta Makes Fastest Time of Day in Special Race.

No speed records were broken during the automobile races at Lakewood oval Saturday, nor were any necks, which after all is the important feature when the soggy condition of the track is taken into consideration. The nearest approach to tragedy came in the dog races when Lady Irene, finding the rabbit too fast and the course too slippery, skidded and spilled her patrician hide over various points of interest along the home stretch.

There wasn't any speed stuff to write home about. We'd much prefer to talk about the courage of the boys and that one lone little lady who dared even venture on a track which was several degrees slicker than a lightning rod salesman. It would hardly have been safe for a centipede equipped with chains to appear on the red clay that was Lakewood Saturday, yet the racers succeeded in making creditable time.

Take Mlle. Joan LaCosta for example. They bill her as the "world's champion girl race driver," which, of course, doesn't mean anything in these days when every ward has its spinach-eating champ, or some other outstanding attraction, but this correspondent will recall for a long time Mlle. LaCosta's daring performance in the one-mile exhibition event.

In the first place her race against time was made in a driving rain. Slated to be the sixth race on the program, it was moved up to third position, because the race official believed a large portion of the crowd had come out especially to see this daring young lady handle her speed chariot. But wagering was about even that she would never succeed in finishing the mile, but she did and in doing so made the fastest time of the afternoon, circling the oval in 57 and one-fifth seconds. Her racer was wobbly throughout the mile, but expert manipulation on the treacherous curves carried her to success.

"I'm so ashamed," she declared upon being lifted from the machine. "I didn't make any time and I know those people up there wanted to see me burn up this track, but they simply do not understand how dangerous this business is today."

But the cash customers did understand and they gave the plucky girl a splendid ovation for the exhibition of courage she displayed. Atlanta likes Mlle. LaCosta and wants to see more of her.[5]

Joan finished her lap, climbed out of the mud-spattered car, and walked to the paddock. It was her last glimpse of the Lakewood Track as a driver.

* * *

The *Commercial Appeal* of Memphis trumpeted the appearance of their hometown hero. The Tri-State Fair in Tennessee was a huge event, filled with exhibits, new wares and tools for the house and farm, and spectacular entertainment, including a full day of auto races.

Joan prioritized the Memphis race on the calendar. After four years, dozens of races, several injuries and broken hearts, and an unofficial world speed record, she was ready to come home to where it all started. The 12-year-old who drove the family car was still inside her, still seeking the next adventure, craving the spotlight and the adrenaline. Memphis was going to be the culmination of a lifetime of pushing the boundaries. She did a quick exhibition run at the Arkansas State Fair on Tuesday, October 11, then on she went to Tennessee.

Saturday, October 15, 1927, was cool and clear in Memphis. The track was dry, with a light breeze, and the temperature was in the low sixties. It was the kind of day that reminded folks that both summer had ended and that fall was coming. Pumpkins were being trundled to the fair, and hummingbirds were on their way south. There were a handful of races left on the Alex Sloan circuit before the end of the season break, but this one was the most important to Joan.

Once again, Sloan pushed the narrative in the papers that no one wanted to race against a woman head-to-head. The difference now is that the underlying theme of the big, strong man humiliating the dainty female was missing. The other drivers accepted Joan as a fellow competitor, just not an appealing one.

It stung LaCosta. In 1926, when Louis Disbrow had publicly scoffed at the idea of racing against her, he took pains to not denigrate her actual talent. Before his first Atlanta match with Joan, he'd said, "I have seen her drive on several dirt tracks, and mighty few men can handle a car like she does . . . and I know that few persons of either sex can handle a car like she did."[6]

Some of the Stars In Auto Races At the Fair Today

FRED HOREY

JOAN LA COSTA

CURLEY YOUNG

CARL YOUNG

JOHN DE PALMA

Figure 11.2. Montage of racers at the Tri-State Fair in Memphis, Tennessee, pictured in the *Commercial Appeal* on October 15, 1927.
COMMERCIAL APPEAL.

But in the days before this event, LaCosta was still scrambling to find a foil for her appearance, as the *Commercial Appeal* reported on October 14:

After deliberating over the demand of Miss LaCosta that she be given a chance to drive in open competition instead of in merely an exhibition time trial, officials decided that a race be arranged for the Memphis girl in which she will have a chance to display her skill. She will not be permitted to compete in the Memphis Derby however, but is to be matched in competition with a star driver or two, the opponents to be determined by the judges on the track.[7]

There was fierce pushback from the other drivers. The biggest star attraction, John DePalma, flat out refused to entertain the idea, claiming that in case of an accident, he would certainly be blamed. If he won he would be called a poor sportsman, and if he lost, he'd have the stigma of having lost to a woman.

The judges publicly admitted that several drivers had this attitude, so a compromise was reached where Joan's opponent would be determined by a random drawing. There was no debate about her racing or not: she *had* to race. She was featured in much of the advertising, and just a solo trip around the track a couple of times wasn't what she wanted for her hometown crowd.

On the day of the race, LaCosta drew Swan Peterson as her opponent. Swan wasn't scheduled to race much during the event, so he probably appreciated the couple hundred dollars being thrown his way. He had a Peugeot, and Joan borrowed Fred Horey's Miller Special, a model she was familiar with. The three-lap match was slotted near the end of the event as the lead-in for the big Ajax Trophy race for the male drivers.

As Joan sat in the ribbed leather seat, staring up at the blue Memphis sky, she wondered what was next in her career. She had conquered the dirt, gliding on top of it faster than any woman alive, but up there in the sky, with the crows, there was no limit. Planes were chasing the 300-mile-per-hour barrier in the air, twice the speed record that had almost killed her on land, but flying seemed so much more ethereal, closer to heaven, like the birds.

Joan pulled her goggles down, waiting for the start of the race, and put the Miller into gear.

Next to her, Swan gave a wave and a smile. The starter, Jimmy Malone, dropped the flag, and both cars sent up a quick plume of dust. Joan, in her light and nimble Miller, quickly shot to the inside and swept around the bends, leading the first lap. Peterson, in the powerful Peugeot, put his foot into it and pulled into the lead on lap 2.

On the last lap, it was LaCosta cutting the corners and Swan powering through the straightaway until they crossed the finish line neck and neck. The judges huddled.

Finally, in a controversial finish, Swan Peterson was declared the winner by inches. Joan climbed out of her car, congratulated her foe, and took off her racing gloves for the last time. She glanced up at the sky. Off in the distance, there were clouds on the horizon.

Joan arrived back in Atlanta that weekend. She attended a concert and dance at the Biltmore Hotel with Sig Haugdahl (it was his "Wisconsin Special" race car that had nearly roasted LaCosta alive on Daytona Beach) and prepared for her next career move.

On October 30, 1927, the *Atlanta Constitution* printed a one-paragraph notice on page 10. It was the retirement notice of Joan LaCosta, reporting her transition to the world of aviation. She was signing up under the tutelage of noted air racer Doug Davis, and she would be taking lessons locally at Candler Field straight away.

She had raced for four years, and four was a lucky number for many racers, including her favorite, Oscar Anderson, who even had 44 painted on the side of his race car for double the magical power. Perhaps LaCosta had a nagging feeling that her luck was on the wane, and five years would be pushing it.

The announcement of Joan LaCosta leaving the race car world to become an aviatrix could have originated only from the *Atlanta Constitution*, her stalwart ally. It was a parting gift from Alex Sloan. He knew that Joan was gone from his stable for good, and he wanted her to succeed in her new challenge. He always spoke warmly of her years later in interviews about his promoting career, and he would remark wistfully about how well she could have done as a professional driver at the top levels.

CHAPTER TWELVE

Love in the Clouds

ON HALLOWEEN WEEKEND OF 1927, A NEW FEMALE FLIER WAS IN Atlanta. Beth Beri, the famous Ziegfeld Girl with the Million-Dollar Legs, had been soaring in and out of the Candler airport in a Doug Davis plane. She was on one of her many "whistle-stop" tours where she would fly in, do her show, and jump in a plane to her next gig. She was dubbed "The Flying Venus."[1]

Beth Beri was one of the most famous of the Ziegfeld Follies girls. Born Elizabeth Kislingbury, she was raised in Hollywood, California, and as far back as her high school days, she was singled out for her expressive and evocative dancing. She was beautiful, ambitious, and adventurous, and, besides her Follies career, she was famous for her live movie theater preshows, where she and her two dozen handpicked dancers would perform choreographed routines before the main attraction movie showed on the screen that night. It was at the end of one of those bookings in Atlanta on October 30, 1927, that she and Joan LaCosta crossed paths.

They had much in common. In later years, Joan would talk of her stint in the "Artists and Models"[2] show in Chicago, which was a risqué production consisting of live classic works of art presented as tableaux before an appreciative audience of mostly male aficionados. If the characters were nude in the inspirational painting, well, accuracy was paramount, and the performers onstage tried to live up to the original works in every way.

BETH BERI' FLYER

Figure 12.1. Beth Beri pictured in the *Evening Journal* of Wilmington, Delaware, on October 30, 1927.

EVENING JOURNAL. IMAGE ENHANCED FOR CLARITY BY ADELIS SEGUNDO BRICEÑO.

And both were attracted to flamboyant, driven men. Joan had married a race car driver, fallen in love with yet another driver, and was now attracted to the dashing Doug Davis.

Beth Beri was a free spirit who was supported in her plane hopping, both financially and creatively, by her paramour Con Conrad, a Tin Pan Alley composer who penned memorable ditties like "The Continental" and "Margie." She was also unabashedly using Doug Davis's expertise to promote her "dangerous chanteuse" image.

The meeting at the Atlanta airport that afternoon before Halloween was fortuitous for Joan. She was beginning her training at the Doug Davis school, and Beth was being ferried to Atlanta by Davis to her next gig, where she was booked to play the Loews Theatre from October 26 through October 29. Davis had flown Beth Beri into town in his own plane on October 25 after he heard that her flight was grounded due to mechanical issues in Spartanburg, South Carolina. They were joined in the flight by her ever-present mascot terrier, Kelley.

After arriving in Atlanta, Beri was booked into the luxurious Biltmore Hotel for the week. She was accompanied by 25 performers for her song and dance revue, including Milton Berle. Beri was a former chorus girl living the kind of life Joan could only imagine. Instead of ending each public appearance covered in red dirt and then climbing into a tiny train berth week after week to head off to another water stop on the railroad schedule, Beri was enjoying the financial security of a sponsorship by the Blue Jay bunion foot treatment company.

Beri had revues lined up in Norfolk, Virginia, and Kansas in the following weeks, but her constant travel was well worth it, as she was earning the current equivalent of more than $60,000 per week for these shows.

Joan had tuned her tabletop wireless set to the big-city evening radio programs and listened to Beri's breathless accounts of her solo plane trips. Beth Beri was accompanied on the airwaves by her famous composer boyfriend Con, who played jazzy background music during the show, adding an evocative atmosphere to her stories. And at the same time that Beri was soaring through the blue skies on her way from one dazzling nightspot to another, Joan LaCosta was eating the mud thrown up from

Beth Beri, Aviatrix, Vaudeville Dancer Arrives by Plane for Engagement Here

Prominent Atlanta officials interested in commercial aviation greeted Miss Beth Beri, famous Ziegfeld beauty, who arrived by airplane at 10:50 o'clock at Candler field from Wilmington, Del., to fill a vaudeville engagement at Loew's Grand theater. In the picture Miss Beri is seen just after arriving in a plane piloted from Spartanburg, S. C., by Doug Davis, Atlanta flier, who had gone to meet Miss Beri and offered her his own plane to finish the trip to Atlanta after Miss Beri's ship developed a broken oil line. In the picture are Dr. H. B. Kennedy, president of Junior Chamber of Commerce; Henderson Hallman and G. C. Bowden, of the chamber of commerce aviation committee; Miss Beri with her dog "Kelley;" Manager Thomas H. James, of Loew's Grandtheater; Pilot Doug Davis and C. B. Yancey, of the Junior Chamber of Commerce.

Figure 12.2. Beth Beri (back) and pilot Doug Davis (second from right) pictured in the *Atlanta Constitution* on October 25, 1927.
ATLANTA CONSTITUTION.

the car ahead of her on the wet and dangerous racetracks in small Midwest towns on gray afternoons. Beth Beri was being escorted off into the evening like royalty on the day before All Hallows' Eve, while LaCosta was counting her pennies, hoping she could continue to pay for flying lessons with Doug Davis.

As Davis trundled Beri off into the air that Sunday afternoon, Joan watched, and it dawned on her that she was an afterthought to the gathered press, experiencing something foreign to her in her life as a celebrity. She was yesterday's news.

In the same article printed in the *Atlanta Constitution* that mentions that Joan was taking flying lessons, the story closed with aviatrix and vaudeville dancer Beth Beri having "appeared at the Grand theater during the past week."[3] Joan was mentioned as the "noted feminine dare-devil auto racer."[4]

Speeding over the red clay was thrilling to Joan in 1924 but had become repetitive to her in 1927. The constant pressure, heightened by the terrifying deaths she had witnessed in person, had intensified her stress in her last few months of racing. She yearned to be far from the bloody earth and into the air again.

She ached to fly.

Joan attended flight school at Candler Field in 1927 and 1928, but by the time she started, there were already other, younger versions of herself in the cockpits, women who hadn't tasted the blood from their wounds or had felt the sensation of hard metal crashing into earthbound obstacles. They were who Joan once was, five years before.

Doug Davis seemed to attract remarkably similar women to his aerial school, or perhaps a certain type of woman was drawn to him and his tutelage. They were generally young, dark-haired, and a little dangerous. Doug Davis was a real-life Jack Armstrong. Earlier in his career, he flew over 35 states advertising a candy company before becoming a repre-sentative for the Curtiss-Wright Airplane and Engine Company. As a candy rep, he flew low through cities and dropped candy bars attached to little parachutes, causing near riots in places like Pittsburgh, which then passed laws banning such inciting advertising stunts. In one run through Miami, a distributor talked Davis into taking his son along with him on the flight. That boy, 12-year-old Paul Tibbets, was so swept up in the experience that he later said, "From that day on, I knew I had to fly."[5] In World War II, Tibbets was the pilot of the B-29 Flying Fortress that dropped the atomic bomb on Hiroshima.

Davis accumulated more than 12,000 hours in the air and was con-sidered a conservative pilot, not prone to taking unmeasured chances. He was often in the papers, featured in stories about "flying in Santa Claus"[6] for local promotional appearances or taking a grieving young man to his dying father to beat the lengthy train ride time. "No pilot in the country was better liked"[7] was the consensus among other flyers. He was also getting involved in air racing, a newer sport that involved racing around designated pylons visible from the air. And he was quite good at it, a natural flier who took both his career and his competition seriously, and he was just as skilled at passing that knowledge on to his pupils.

In late April 1928, the national newspapers ran an interesting syndicated article from the *Atlanta Constitution*. It was the "official" retirement notice of Joan LaCosta. She was posed in front of a plane, evoking *The Birth of Venus*, with her arms draped around a propeller that covered her modesty. It was an appropriate juxtaposition; she was comforted by machinery, almost as if the metal protected her from the world at large. It was also the first update about the former star in months.

A few days later, the papers ran another, related story, but this one was on the front pages. On April 26, 1928, Frank Lockhart was attempting his second mission to break the land speed record on Daytona Beach. Lockhart was quickly becoming a legend in speed sports, having won the Indianapolis 500 race in his rookie attempt in 1926, and was leading most of the 1927 race before mechanical failure ended his sophomore effort. He also held several speed records over varying distances. The one goal that eluded him was the title of the Fastest Man on Earth. His previous record attempt a couple of months earlier had ended with a crash into the surf. According to the February 23 edition of the *Evening Journal* of Wilmington, Delaware, Lockhart vividly recalled the entire event: "Lockhart from his bed in the hospital last night told the story of his crash on the beach here yesterday to William F. Strum, his representative, in which he blamed poor visibility as the sole reason for the mishap that sent his special Stutz Blackhawk racer into the surf."

His story as related by Strum substantially was as follows:

"I was traveling down the beach at a terrific rate of speed when I glanced at my tachometer to learn how many revolutions the motor was making. It was turning over 6500 at the time (between 220 and 230 miles per hour) just a few seconds before the accident happened.

"I drove through a bright place in the atmosphere, where the sun was shining. Then all at once I ran into a rain and the visibility was completely gone. I could not see. The next thing I knew was when I was in the ocean."

Joan LaCosta, youthful women's champion of the automobile race track, is retiring—retiring to the air, according to Associated Press dispatches from Atlanta, Ga. She has left the racing oval forever and is completing the flying hours necessary for a commercial pilot's license at Candler Field. She looks upon aviation as a career and has no intention of attempting to be the first woman to cross the Atlantic by air.

Figure 12.3. Joan LaCosta pictured in the *Lima Morning Star and Republican-Gazette* of Lima, Ohio, on May 1, 1928.

LIMA MORNING STAR AND REPUBLICAN-GAZETTE. IMAGE ENHANCED FOR CLARITY BY ADELIS SEGUNDO BRICEÑO.

Strum, who examined the car after the accident, advanced the theory that Lockhart, blinded by the sudden poor visibility, had jammed his brakes on too quickly, causing the car to swerve.[8]

According to some of those close to Lockhart, he wanted to get back on the sand as soon as possible, as another competitor had just upped the record to 207 miles per hour. The Stutz repairs were quickly finished, and at the end of that April, Lockhart was racing the clock along the waterline once more when, on his return, he again lost control at more than 200 miles per hour. This time, instead of being thrown into the water, Frank Lockhart was catapulted from his Stutz Black Hawk Special headfirst into the hard-packed sand and died instantly.

Not since Jimmy Murphy had such a young, prodigious talent been cut down in their prime. It was also another stark reminder to Joan LaCosta that she had been balancing on a knife blade for several years, driving at ferocious speeds in rickety metal buckets on spindly wheels.

Her ambitions were still bold. She intended to be the first female pilot to fly across the Atlantic, and it didn't seem unrealistic. Most of the early fliers, like Gladys Roy, Beth Beri, and Gladys Poole, had fallen away from contention. There was still time for LaCosta to be a star again.

In mid-1928, everything still seemed possible for Joan LaCosta. She had been a tremendous success as a racer, and with a few more lessons from Doug Davis and Vernon Omlie, the next phase in her life looked to be more and more exciting. She knew that she had the one thing on her side that the other candidates did not always possess: an abundance of sheer luck.

But over time, the memories of death and mayhem seemed to weigh on Joan's mind. By April, the month that had always signaled the beginning of her race season, she was hedging her bets and not so sure of her ultimate goals. She seemed burned out and wanted to settle into a more sedate, lower-profile lifestyle. She was now telling the press that she looked on aviation as a career and had no intention of attempting to be the first woman to cross the Atlantic by air.

"I am pretty tired of taking risks, and I don't want the sort of glory the female Lindbergh is going to get. I want a job, and I think there is a future in aviation,"[9] she told the wire services.

Joan LaCosta took flying lessons for six months from Doug Davis and from Vernon Omlie, husband of her friend Phoebe Fairgrave. Phoebe, who was always a role model for Joan whenever she thought about being a pilot, suffered a major accident on October 15, 1928. Fairgrave was piloting a small plane in the company of a passenger named E. Z. Newsome when her monocoupe lost altitude, and she crash-landed from a height of 250 feet. She was seriously hurt, breaking both of her legs, while Mr. Newsome suffered internal injuries. It had to have shaken Joan since Phoebe was a much more experienced pilot than LaCosta and yet had nearly lost her life in the cockpit that day.

In the racing world, Alex Sloan wasted no time in getting his barnstorming show back together in Chicago without Joan. He brought back Elfrieda Mais to replace her, and soon the papers were peppered with stories of Mais beating LaCosta on the track to capture all of the Fastest Woman on the Continent titles. Joan even suffered the ignominy of one paper using her picture mistakenly labeled as Elfrieda Mais to tout an upcoming race.

There are no clues on how Joan was earning a living all of this time. She'd been involved with race cars since she was a teen, and now, deep into her twenties, she didn't have any other real skills for making money to pay for her expensive flying lessons. The largesse of her friends could last only so long. She was unmarried, hundreds of miles away from her family (including her daughter Helen), and at age 26, she was quickly being supplanted by the younger generation. After a spate of announcements in the papers about her taking to the air, her high-profile celebrity cachet had quickly dried up. It seemed that here was always another young flier, another daredevil stunt, and another thrilling story of danger to fill the insatiable headline machine of the national papers.

An accident stalled her lessons with Doug Davis. Joan also claimed that seeing a friend in an airplane mishap caused her to have an emotional episode and that she was advised not to take her test by the accreditation authorities. She claimed that they asked her to take a six-month

Girl Champion Will Race Here

Elfrieda Mais of Indianapolis, billed as the world's champion woman auto racer on dirt tracks, who has entered her name in the automobile racing events at the Rutland fair on Saturday.

Figure 12.4. Joan LaCosta misidentified as Elfrieda Mais in the *Rutland Daily Herald* of Rutland, Vermont, on September 6, 1928.
RUTLAND DAILY HERALD. IMAGE ENHANCED FOR CLARITY BY ADELIS SEGUNDO BRICEÑO.

break until early 1929 instead and to try again later. Shaken, she left the program and headed back to Chicago.

In 1929, the daily circulation of the *Chicago Tribune* was huge, with approximately 850,00 copies sold every day. In order to stave off the upstart dailies nipping at its heels, every news cycle became a race to find the most salacious stories printable. Splashy write-ups on murder, gang crime, and tragedy always sold, but the heat quickly dissipated from each previous hot story of the day. Children would disappear from their family-home stoops, and within 48 hours, it was as if that mystery never existed. The next front-page headlines would be splashing the particulars of gangster bodies found executed in speakeasy cellars, leaving no column space for follow-ups on the missing-child tragedies.

And aircraft stories, whether they involved crashes or heroic exploits, were a sexy new subject that fascinated and terrified the average reader. The *Chicago Tribune* printed a front-page editorial cartoon spotlighting the saturation of airplane reports, signifying the topic's ongoing battle with crime as the subject most likely to be splayed across the mast of the

Figure 12.5. Political cartoon by John T. McCutcheon appearing in the *Chicago Tribune* on September 9, 1929.
CHICAGO TRIBUNE.

big-city chronicle. A typical example was the headline accompanying the cartoon in the *Tribune* on September 9, 1929: "Find All Dead in Air Liner,"[10] screamed the huge banner, "Charred Bodies Carried Down Mountainside—Explosion Followed Crash in Storm."[11]

The story relayed the gory details of the bodies, grotesquely burned to a crisp, identified only by dental charts. This was the public atmosphere that circulated around LaCosta's life. She had made many bold claims about how her expertise in racing would translate to her new career in flying the big commercial planes, and now her psyche was being bombarded with the latest reports on fiery crashes and horrible deaths from planes plummeting from the clouds.

Figure 12.6. Advertisement for *The Man and the Moment* appearing in the *News & Observer* of Raleigh, North Carolina, on December 15, 1929. *NEWS & OBSERVER.*

Original

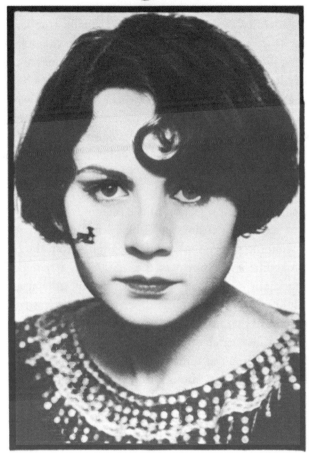

Gladys Roy, aviatrix, not only
adopted a crest but had it made
up into a beauty spot. What's
more, she wears said spot, as
shown.

Figure 12.7. Gladys Roy pictured in the *Burlington Free Press* of Burlington, Vermont, on October 30, 1924.

BURLINGTON FREE PRESS. IMAGE ENHANCED FOR CLARITY BY ADELIS SEGUNDO BRICEÑO.

The film industry was quick to pounce on the public's new obsession. A new movie making the rounds in Chicago in 1929 was *The Man and the Moment*, the Billie Dove vehicle that involved an aviatrix in a plane crash, a false identity, society's high life, and, finally, true love. It was in this film that Dove had patently based her on-screen character on Gladys Roy, the tragic flier. The press illustrations made no bones about the dangerous, sultry looks of Roy that they were exploiting.

Movies about heroines behind the wheel of hot rods were old news; now the most thrilling stories on the screen featured planes and aerial stunt work. The winner of the very first Academy Award for Best Picture was *Wings*, a film based on the romantic and deadly World War I aviator battles, directed by William Wellman, himself a veteran World War I pilot. Audiences were mesmerized by the use of Magnascope technology, which enlarged the projection of the picture from the typical movie house theater screen dimension of 12 by 18 feet to 30 by 40 feet, thus providing a stunning panorama of aerial dogfights from the cockpit view. It was the first film ever shown at the 1,500-seat Erlanger Theater in Chicago, and it ran for almost two consecutive months at a time when more than 2,000 movies were released per year, and it wasn't uncommon for theaters to have two new films showing on their screens every week.

Joan sat in the theater on the weekends, staring up at the endless celluloid heroines while the audience around her cheered and applauded. Daring pilots flew biplanes through tunnels and under bridges, rescuing helpless children and old matrons and snatching victory from the clutches of the evil land barons. LaCosta knew she was as brave and physically talented as the women she saw on the screen, and all she needed was to get her pilot license, and she could be working in Hollywood herself. But she was getting older, 28, and she was flat broke.

CHAPTER THIRTEEN

The Crash

JOAN LACOSTA WAS FIGHTING TO SURVIVE IN A CITY THAT WAS CHANG-
ing at a breakneck pace. In 1929, Chicago welcomed more than
60,000 new residents, and it was a magnet for artists, musicians, gang-
sters, the wealthy, the poor, and immigrants from around the world. It
was a rough-and-tumble town in many ways, one where the weak and
unlucky were quickly culled. They either were left behind or left the city.

Oscar Anderson was working on his comeback. His 1927 season
had ended with a horrific crash in the last lap of a 100-mile race in
Aurora that had nearly killed him. After several months in the hospital,
he emerged halfway into the next auto season, determined to retake his
place in the racing spotlight. With both Oscar and close friend Phoebe
Fairgrave having now been seriously injured in a space of a few months,
LaCosta was mentally and emotionally staggered. She was also struggling to find steady employment, hampered by her nagging injuries and
double pneumonia, and winter was coming on hard.

Every big city in the country had a high-crime district, populated
with formerly grand hotels that had become stooped and cracked, but
occasionally there were some properties that attempted to put an illu-
sionary cheery face on their withered façades with new paint and a good
scrubbing. But, much like Dickens's Miss Havisham, it was an even more
sad reminder of their glorious heyday. These areas were a magnet for the
folks on the edge who were trying to straddle that life that exists between
sleeping on the streets and having a home. They were addresses for the

Figure 13.1. Joan LaCosta shortly after her arrest on October 3, 1929.

hobos, alcoholics, jailbirds, con men, drug addicts, and those who were just temporarily down on their luck.

The Hotel Lorraine was well known in Chicago and not because it was a tourist attraction or landmark of the city. The run-down, threadbare building on 411 South Wabash Avenue was where the have-nots lived and where they drank and fought. The hotel had the reputation of being the residence of the artists, actors, and performers of the city.

"If you were never in the Lorraine you have never met the other side of theatrical life. In its dingy precincts live the obscure thespians who work when they can and eat likewise,"[1] wrote the *Chicago Tribune* in 1920.

There was a speakeasy in the basement, and the upper floors were filled with pretty young actresses, clothing models, traveling salesmen, and part-time Ziegfield girls. The local newspapers printed stories of suicides by pistol, near deaths from sleeping pills, overdose fatalities from rat poison in the "dingy"[2] rooms, and narratives about innocent young women coerced from distant small towns into joining the dangerous community of the Lorraine, with voyeuristic pictures included.

At one point while Joan LaCosta was renting a room in the hotel, a squad of agents called "the Drys"[3] (which was the nickname that the local Prohibition officers were known by) tore through a narrow passage underneath the hotel and arrested two men who were tending bar in an underground nightclub that was overflowing with whiskey and beer. It wasn't a rare occurrence.

Joan had returned to Chicago in November 1928, with $1,400, about half a year's worth of an average worker's income, hoping to gather enough scratch and build enough courage to resume her flying lessons.

She was most likely taking those lessons at the Edgewater Flying Club at 357 North La Salle Avenue. Established in 1928 as a lower-cost alternative to private lessons, the school was a nonprofit cooperative that pooled resources and kept costs and tuition as low as possible. The club had an array of practical classes, including Introductory Aviation, Private Pilot License, Limited Commercial License, Transport Pilot License, Mechanics (Airframe and Engine) License, Aerial Photography, Celestial Navigation, and Stress Analysis. The enrollment fee was $150, and the club's ads estimated that license costs were $300 for the private pilot, $550 for the limited commercial, and $1,500 for the transport pilot. They offered both day and night classes, and they were located just a 25-minute walk from where Joan was living.

As she hiked up Van Buren, then turned right on La Salle toward the school, she glanced up at some of the most impressive addresses in Chicago. They were tall buildings—steel and almost entirely built for business. The massive Chicago Board of Trade stood like a sentinel at 141 South LaSalle along her walk, silhouetted against the sky-blue background above her and reminding Joan of the vast gulf between her financial plight and those who were much more successful.

Even with the school's reasonably priced approach, the $1,400 that Joan had come to Chicago with wouldn't have lasted long paying for flying lessons on top of her living expenses. There was a recession this summer and fall, and people were being cautious about their money, so work and money-earning opportunities weren't easy to come by. Joan was out of work. After eight hard months of expensive flying lessons and scraping by without her former profession to count on, she went betting at the horse tracks, possibly the new one at Washington Park. It was a desperate gamble, and she lost her remaining funds.

The country was rumbling in 1929. In Chicago, bombs were being used to settle personal scores, close down competitors' businesses, and assassinate rival gang members. Burlesque houses like the archly named Academy (which was located just a mile from Joan's residence) were being attacked in an escalation of price wars and customer poaching. Explosions occurred almost every other day. The Windy City was in constant upheaval.

The fickle stock market was adding more and more financial uncertainty to the national economy, even as the wealth in America was being quickly consolidated by business behemoths like John D. Rockefeller Jr.

The mass introduction of automobiles into crowded urban life led to the unnecessary deaths of hundreds of pedestrians and drivers in Cook County. There was also a rise of gang-based violence and a growing economic gulf between the upper class and blue-collar workers. The city's chaos was becoming a bellwether for the impending disaster that was looming over the country as a whole.

A desperate Joan turned to old acquaintances in Chicago, like Hyman Bobbe, whom she remembered from her racing days. She was willing to trade her pride for any help she could get.

Bobbe was a furniture salesman on University Avenue. He shared one vice with Joan: he had been arrested years before on illegal gambling charges. LaCosta and Bobbe first met in 1923, just as her driving career took off, and both were racing fans. She trusted him enough to make a personal plea for cash. They scheduled a lunch in early September where they caught up on Chicago gossip and enjoyed one of the last warm days of the season, and then Joan made her pitch.

Hyman was flattered by the attention from Joan, but he couldn't help his young friend. If only he had as much money as his brother Joseph, he said, he would gladly help her out.

LaCosta questioned Hyman about his rich sibling Joseph and his finances and also about the jewels that Joseph gifted to his wife. Joan was living just blocks away from the J. Bobbe Painting and Decorating business on Wabash Avenue and had walked by it often, peering into the shop's beautiful interior. The opulence of his shop magnified the personal riches she imagined he must have, so a plan percolated in Joan's mind. She concocted a scheme to go to his home residence and, in her words, "ask for a loan."[4] Hyman was completely unaware of Joan's desperation, and he admitted later that he was as shocked as anyone by her actions.

October 2, 1929, was a cool, cloudy fall day. It was in the low fifties when LaCosta first went to the Chicago Beach Hotel, where Mr. and Mrs. Bobbe resided in an upper-floor suite.

It was a tour into a different world.

The Chicago Beach Hotel was the extreme opposite of the run-down Lorraine. The building was still as opulent as it was when it was first built in 1892 in the Hyde Park area to capitalize on the upcoming Chicago Exposition. It had private access to the lake and boasted a selection of "six hundred light, airy, elegantly furnished rooms."[5]

It was a luxurious, on-the-beach tourist magnet favored by the rich and the superrich, drawing in well-off families, couples, and high-society singles. There was also a year-round upper-class stratum of women who socialized together on the lakeshore, ran their households, and held dinner parties with their friends, all while their chief executive officer husbands traveled for business, met in offices downtown, and pulled the economic levers of the great city.

Most of the hotel's original construction from the 1890s had recently been demolished, and in its place were high-end apartments designed for Chicago's elite social circle and moneyed vacationers from around

CHICAGO BEACH HOTEL, Chicago

Where Your Delights

Are Studied in a Hundred Ways

ONE of the most inviting hotels in America is the Chicago Beach Hotel, with its 16 acres on Lake Michigan, almost in the heart of Chicago. It has a quarter-mile of bathing beach in summer, with vast sandy playgrounds for the children. Three tennis courts, which are made skating rinks in winter. Sun parlors, putting grounds etc.—all that can add to anybody's joy. Living rooms which are luxurious and comfortable. A cuisine which is nowhere excelled.

There is no hotel which studies more the likes of people, their joys and recreations, than the Chicago Beach Hotel.

One of their features is La Touraine Coffee. It greets you there at every breakfast, every dinner. And the manager states that he has never known a person whom that coffee did not delight.

You cannot bring to your home all the delights of the Chicago Beach Hotel. But you can serve the coffee which they serve. Your grocer supplies it. And you owe it to the people at your table.

Figure 13.2. Advertisement for the Chicago Beach Hotel appearing in the *Barre Daily Times* of Barre, Vermont, on April 14, 1927.
BARRE DAILY TIMES.

the world. The 12 floors that overlooked Lake Michigan featured beautiful imported mahogany wood, illuminated with the latest in art deco lighting fixtures and filled with artisan furniture. There was an acclaimed restaurant, a ballroom, and a recreation area for both children and adults. The Grand Lobby was spacious enough to host a car show, as it did on occasion. Whether patrons were full-time residents or tourists soaking up Chicago's beaches and architecture, the Chicago Beach Hotel had every amenity one could desire.

For entertainment, it had three tennis courts (converted into ice rinks in the winter), a golf putting green, world-class restaurants, and even a house band, Al Katz and the Kittens, who broadcast live over radio station WQJ. It was the primary home of many Chicago luminaries, like Judge Kenesaw Mountain Landis, the first Commissioner of Baseball and the man who oversaw the resolution of the Chicago "Black Sox" World Series scandal.

Part of the hotel was devoted to these private residences, with prime monthly rents topping $700 per month (more than $10,000 in 2024 dollars). It was consistently rated by the printed traveling guides as one of the top half dozen hotels in the city.

Joan's apartment at the Hotel Lorraine was $90 per month.

When Joan walked into the lobby of the Chicago Beach Hotel, she was overwhelmed. This was where *she* should be living, hobnobbing with the rich and famous, playing tennis, and soaking up the sun on a private beach.

She girded herself, headed up to the eighth floor, went to room 802, and knocked. There was no answer. She waited a moment or two and then took the lack of response as a sign that perhaps she really shouldn't be there, and she left.

If she had listened to her conscience then, trusted the instincts that had guided her throughout her racing career, perhaps she would have returned home to Memphis or tried her hand at showbiz. She could have crawled back into the cockpit of a Frontenac Ford and maybe sparked up some of that old magic again. Instead, she came back the next day with a fake gun and a chloroform rag.

It wasn't easy to get a real pistol in the 1920s, but toy guns were popular and cheap. They were a tempting choice for young criminals because the penalties were less severe for those caught with a fake pistol than a real one. It got so out of hand that Chicago instituted a ban on the sale of toy guns for underage buyers in the Hyde Park area. The availability of the chintzy replicas was leading to an increase in strong-arm robberies by the youthful crime element, and police were afraid that the thrill of exhibiting a fake firearm would inexorably lead to the desire to pack real heat.

In Joan's case, she bought a novelty cigarette holder that dispensed cigs at the pull of a trigger. It might have fooled a victim in a dark street alley, but it wasn't quite as convincing in the hallway light of a fancy hotel. Some of these novelties were good "10-footers," and at a reasonable distance, they might pass as a deadly weapon. The "weapon" Joan packed was a cheap toy, but the blatant fakery of the contraption did give her the cover of plausible deniability if her plan did go south.

The next day, October 3, broke cool and clear, about 60 degrees. The ride from downtown to Hyde Park on the swaying Elevated Line was about half an hour, and Joan arrived at the Chicago Beach Hotel address in the afternoon.

She once again rode up in the elevator to the same room and knocked. Mrs. Bobbe opened the door. She was dressed up for the day, draped in $20,000 worth of jewels.

A trembling Joan stood before her, clutching what looked like to be a silver automatic in her hand.

"Don't scream or make a noise, and you will be safe,"[6] Joan said and reached forward to grab her necklace.

Mrs. Bobbe, an older but still healthy woman, took in the sight of the shivering, 100-pound young lady in front of her and took her chances. She fought back.

They wrestled to the ground. Mrs. Bobbe felt tremendous blows striking her face, a shock considering how slight the woman on top of her seemed. Bobbe's eye was blackened, and twin bloody gouges appeared beneath it. Joan tore at Rebecca's neck while her free hand pushed the chloroform-soaked cotton wad toward her victim's mouth, and both of Bobbe's hands were violently cut and bloodied in her desperate self-defense. The pistol fell to the floor.

A maid heard Bobbe's screams from the other room, and she rushed to help her employer. Elevator operators and bellhops nearby, along with those passing by in the hallway, also responded to the commotion, and hotel security was quickly alerted. It took a swarm of men, alongside the exertions of Rebecca Bobbe, to gain control of the flailing young woman. Arriving Chicago police officers took her into custody, and her wildcat demeanor quickly dissipated. Instead, she trotted out her easy Southern charm, and, as happened often in her life, the men around her fell under her sway.

Joan was brought into the booking building and held at the same time as an 18-year-old flapper by the name of Josephine Dobscher.

Dobscher, who had earned the sobriquet of the "Red Slicker Bandit,"[7] was one of the roughest characters booked into the women's jail, having just been arrested for a strong-arm robbery that occurred while she was out on bail for a previous felony. But she proclaimed to anyone who would listen that the string of stickups weren't really her fault, that she had been forced to commit the robberies by her newly minted husband, William Levinson, who had threatened to kill her if she didn't follow his commands:

"I was forced into it,'" the girl cried while on the witness stand. "William Levinson forced me into it. Later he forced me to marry him so that I could not testify against him in the event he was captured."

After the robbery, for which she was convicted, the girl said Levinson drove toward Crown Point, Ind, and on a lonely road stopped his machine, saying:

"This is a good place to bump you off, women have too much tongue."

"No, no, no!" I shouted. "I'll do anything you want if you won't kill me." Then he said I would have to marry him or die, so I married him and have never seen him since."[8]

The Red Slicker Bandit

Josephine Dobscher, eighteen and pretty, of Chicago, known as the "Red Slicker Bandit," as she appeared in court on a charge of first degree robbery.

Figure 13.3. Josephine Dobscher, the "Red Slicker Bandit," pictured in the *Belvidere Daily Republican* of Belvidere, Illinois, on November 5, 1929.

BELVIDERE DAILY REPUBLICAN. IMAGE ENHANCED FOR CLARITY BY ADELIS SEGUNDO BRICEÑO.

Joan LaCosta, who tried on and discarded personas like seasonal outfits all of her life, was a quick learner. She immediately co-opted Josephine's spiel.

In the Saturday, October 5, edition of the *Chicago Tribune*, the mysterious and beautiful criminal was already drawing ink from the reporters. A story on page 3 exclaimed that "she's the coolest redhead the Hyde Park police ever clapped into a cell. Hardly a hundred pounds of her, but she has the entire district stumped. . . . Half the Hyde Park police say she is 'taking the rap' for a man. The other half says there isn't any man."[9]

She proclaimed to the detectives that her name was Josephine Rust and that she was the wife of a handsome bootlegger fresh out of Canada by the name of Thomas Rust. Thomas (in Joan's imaginary world) was tall, blond, blue-eyed, and obviously a cad who had coerced her into the strong-arm robbery and then fled the scene when the police arrived. He was a garage mechanic by trade but a bootlegger when times were slow. He was a student at the University of Alabama for two years, and the couple were married nine years. The pair had only recently arrived in the city, she said, and they had been staying at a West Side hotel; the name of the establishment escaped her. On Wednesday night, she had slept in someone's private garage. When they had money, they lived well; when they didn't, they didn't. Where was her husband now, she was asked? Probably hightailed it out of the city, she replied, leaving her holding the bag and taking the fall. Her husband had planned the robbery but lacked the courage to carry it out, so she tried her hand at it.

She spun a fictional turn of events that read like the inner monologue of a pulp fiction gangster's moll. Only once or twice, however, was there anything resembling a Southern accent in her voice:

"Desperate for money, of course, or I'd never have tried it. . . .

"It was my first attempt—he said it would be easy. . . .

"I'm twenty-four I was raised in the south—Birmingham. Was a day pupil at a convent there. My husband is thirty-six. We've been on the move almost constantly, in practically every large city. No, I don't know where to find him. I only know he won't be back after me. It's my guess he's out of the state by this time. . . .

"Hope it won't be too ho'hid. They say I can get life for it—but there's nothing to do but take the medicine. At least I'll know what the next day's going to be." . . .

Sergt. Egan holds that here is a sweet girl graduate of "the rackets." She purchased chloroform, she looked over the hotel the previous day, he says. She probably hasn't any husband. And he admits: "She's one of the nicest girls I've ever saw—and a slick one."[10]

The character she fashioned in interviews was at stark odds with her demeanor. The reports that came out at the time described her as soft-spoken, undeniably intelligent, and unusually well educated; she was tastefully dressed and her manner was as gentle as that of a nun. She was convent bred but not a Catholic, she said. To police observers, she was "the direct antithesis of the hardboiled gun girl in whose shoes she has been stepping."[11]

In 1920s-era Chicago, the processing of robbery suspects included one very populist wrinkle. Joan and other arrestees were paraded in front of hundreds of crime victims, all of whom were called in to identify possible suspects in their own cases. On this Sunday night, Joan was shouldered in between a hardened 60-year-old grandmother who boasted a 20-year rap sheet and cast contemptuous looks at the crowds and the slouching, fierce 19-year-old strong-arm robber Josephine Dobscher.

LaCosta stood out among them; she was a thin, nervous dark-eyed waif surrounded by tough parolees and hardscrabble criminals. She wept uncontrollably as the attending sergeant barked out directions to the spotlighted prisoners.

"Face the front . . . turn to the left."[12] This public humiliation left Joan shaken and probably hastened her capitulation to the authorities. The persistence of disbelieving detectives and her own frayed physical condition finally took a toll. Her eyes were sunken and dark from the stress and lack of sleep, and her battle with pneumonia weakened her resolve. She was never a quitter, but this time, Joan gave up the charade. Late Saturday night, on October 5, after 36 hours of intense nonstop grilling by Chicago's lawmen, the facade finally crumbled in the interrogation room. Joan broke down in sobs and confessed that her real name was

Joan LaCosta of Memphis, Tennessee. "Josephine Rust" was a fictional character invented by LaCosta to hide her real identity and to save her family from disgrace. She wore a dark green dress and was curled up in the big leather chair in Captain Thomas's office, her dark red hair buried into her arm. She sobbed out her story to the captain and Sergeant Egan.

"You'll get it all anyway," she told them. "I might as well 'spill.'"[13]

She told the officers of her meeting with Hymann Robbe and how she had teased out specific information about his wealthy brother Joseph:

> I told him of my racing interests, and found he had similar ones. I have met him off and on for lunches and dinners since then. A few weeks ago, I told him I was completely broke, and discouraged. He said that if he was as rich as his brother, Joseph Bobbe, President of J. Bobbe & Company, he would be able to help me out. He said that his brother lived at the Chicago Beach Hotel, and told me something about his habits and those of his wife. What he didn't tell me, I asked. He did not know it, but right there I decided to attempt that robbery. I needed money desperately.[14]

LaCosta broke down in tears more than once while detailing her confession to the detectives that night. She pleaded with them for a new start with a clean slate, and she stated that the hotel incident was the first time that she had ever strayed from the straight and narrow. She mentioned that she had been spending the last of her funds on flying lessons at local airfields and trying unsuccessfully to enhance her bank account by betting on the horse races.

"'I have no idea what caused me to try such a thing as robbery,' she sobbed. 'I must have had a brain storm.'"[15]

The police were unmoved despite calling it "a remarkable exhibition of misdirected nerve."[16] She couldn't charm her way out of this. Her mentor Alex Sloan couldn't pull any strings for her, and she had no former partners or lovers for emotional support. She was broke and desperate and possessed nothing but bravery. And finally, it had failed her, too.

The police brought in Hyman Bobbe and his wife. He identified Joan and confirmed their dinner meeting, but he professed his ignorance of the robbery plot, and he was let go without charge. Joan was then arraigned on felony charges of assault and attempted burglary.

Word spread quickly in her hometown of Memphis. The *Kingsport Times* in Tennessee ran an article on October 6 about its local celebrity and mentioned how surprised her family was at this turn of events. LaCosta's father, Mr. Carver, was particularly shocked. He had seen Joan cheered by tens of thousands of fans just a couple years before in Alabama; now he was being interviewed by reporters asking about his criminal daughter:

> Relatives today rallied to the aid of Joan LaCosta, girl automobile racer, under arrest in Chicago on a charge of attempted robbery. A sister planned to leave today for the Illinois city to help the young woman in her plight.
>
> Miss LaCosta is the daughter of Mr. and Mrs. W. M. Carver of Memphis. Carver is employed as an engineer.
>
> "We can't believe it is true," the parents of the girl told newspaper men today.
>
> Mrs. Carver said she had not heard from her daughter since her arrest in Chicago Thursday.
>
> "The last letter we had from Joan was two weeks ago," Mrs. Carver said. "In a letter she told us she was coming home soon. All we know is what we have read in the paper."[17]

Joan's sister Helen traveled to Chicago and became a constant companion during the ordeal, appearing in news accounts and occasionally in trial photos. Throughout the trial, she went by her middle name, Jeanette, and used her former husband's last name, Johnson, but she was more commonly known as Helen Martins. This adapted moniker was a convenient way to avoid bringing any reminder of Helen's husband, and Joan's ex-husband, Walter Martins, into the courtroom.

The court system moved quickly at the time in Chicago, and the arraignment in the grand jury process took place on Monday, October 7. A visibly nervous LaCosta sat next to her attorney as Rebecca Bobbe took the stand and described how Joan, armed with the fake gun and chloroform, had pushed her way into the apartment. They grappled, Bobbe said, and her screams alerted others nearby.

LaCosta took the opportunity to lay out her own version of the events and, while agreeing that she was forceful, proclaimed that it grew out of sheer desperation.

She stood up at the table in front of the court and softly explained her situation:

"I came here last November with $1,400 I'd won in auto races," she said, "that was all gone. I couldn't find work, and I needed money. So I thought about this robbery. I started out one day to go through with it, but lost my nerve. The next day I went all the way and got caught."[18]

"I never did anything like this before," she told the judge. "I never did. All I want is another chance. I'll go straight, I'll never do it again!"[19]

Judge Joseph Borrelli recognized the unlawful actions taken by Joan, and he didn't hesitate to hold her over for trial. "Well, we'll have to try this case the same as any other."[20] "'You deserve no more consideration than a man,' said the court. 'Your assault on Mrs. Bobbe was cruel and unprovoked.'"[21] "So I will hold Miss LaCosta to the Grand Jury under bonds of $25,000."[22]

Joan LaCosta crumpled to the floor in a dead faint. She was out for so long that she was eventually carried to the anteroom, and from there, the court staff could hear her muffled wails of anguish. When she reemerged from the waiting room, the tears were gone, replaced with the cool demeanor that had kept the Hyde Park police at bay for three days. She was fingerprinted and photographed. The reporters in attendance immediately fed the story to the wires about this dramatic turn of events, and the arraignment was in papers around the country the next day from New York to Los Angeles. LaCosta was once again the headline-grabbing celebrity. But there weren't any action shots of her in racing togs; the accompanying picture of her in those articles was that of the dark Joan: unsmiling, perched in a chair, and wearing her plain outfit, emotionally alone, her gaze aimed off in the distance.

She was offered a plea deal: If she admitted her guilt, she would receive a one-year probation and no jail time. LaCosta, always supremely confident in her ability of persuasion, turned down the offer and chose to take her chances with a jury.

Chapter Fourteen

The Trial

Joan LaCosta's sister Helen was at her side for the entire legal journey. She was the support system that Joan had recently lacked in Chicago. When the trial began, Helen sat close by, next to her sister and Joan's attorney. She was also very involved in the rehabilitation of Joan's public image. Both she and LaCosta were dressed plainly in all court appearances, wearing clothing considered modest even by local standards. It was one of the conscious choices that was subtly aimed at influencing the trial proceedings. At the scheduling for the trial on October 17, Judge David, who had gotten word of the ragged, unkempt woman who'd been arrested, didn't even recognize Joan.

"Where is the defendant?"[1]

"Here."[2] LaCosta replied, standing calmly next to her newly appointed attorney.

Of all the interventions of fate in Joan's life, one of the luckiest was the assignment of Michael A. Romano as her public defender. Mr. Romano was a former assistant deputy prosecutor for the state of Illinois, and he had been instrumental in convicting a notorious killer by the name of Martin Durkin in the first-ever homicide of an FBI agent. After that high-profile case, he and another state assistant attorney, Louis Blumenthal, resigned from their government positions on November 29, 1926, and teamed up as partners in the lucrative private practice field. It didn't take much cajoling for Romano to take this "public service" case, as it was front-page news in the Chicago papers for days and also dovetailed in with Romano's natural flair for drama. Aiding Mr. Romano in the

Figure 14.1. Joan LaCosta (center) pictured with her sister Helen (Jeanette) Johnson née Martins (right) and her legal team, Michael Romano (left) and Robert Fischer (back), in October 1929.

CHICAGO SUN-TIMES/CHICAGO DAILY NEWS COLLECTION, CHICAGO HISTORY MUSEUM.

LaCosta trial was Robert Fischer, who, besides being an attorney, was a fellow part-time actor in local radio and stage performances.

Michael A. Romano was a part-time actor who used his sonorous voice and dramatic delivery to great effect in cross-examinations and always took great pains to be in sartorial splendor in the courtroom while addressing the jury. He was also a veteran of numerous amateur theater shows around town. Later in his career, Romano earned steady work as a second banana on local radio programs like *Bachelor Life* and *Today's Children*, and on more than one occasion, his dramatics frustrated the judges on the bench, who in return would make less-than-subtle cracks about his dual profession. One judge in particular, tired of his exaggerated hectoring of a witness in a trial, suggested that "the court direct this smart guy with the 'stach to keep his smart remarks to himself or go back to the movies.'"[3] Michael Romano took it as a compliment.

He was also a personal friend of the legendary film star Rudolph Valentino and was a pallbearer at the actor's funeral. He had known Valentino for several years, and in 1923, he was part of the wedding party when Valentino rewed Natacha Rambova in Indiana. He wrote the introduction to *My Private Diary*, the supposed personal notes of Valentino gathered in book form after the star's death, and even penned the memoriam for the public tribute to Valentino that was held September 1, 1926. He and legendary vamp actress Pola Negri accompanied Valentino's body on the funeral train as it was transported from New York through the Chicago area on its way to Hollywood.

The LaCosta trial began on October 21, 1929. A ferocious storm off the lake was about to slam into Chicago that evening. It was predicted to be one of the worst in years, but there was no delay for Joan. She appeared in the courtroom right on schedule, primly dressed in very sober attire.

She looked small and slim in a black chiffon velvet dress with a white collar. She sported a striking double string of pearls around her neck with a pearl pinned on her black felt hat. Her black cloth coat, with a high standing collar that partly shielded her face, was removed and checked when she entered the courtroom.

She sat down between her sister Helen and her counsel, Romano. She was noticeably ill at ease and shivered in her chair. When Judge

Figure 14.2. Michael Romano and Joan LaCosta on a break during her trial in
October 1929.
CHICAGO SUN-TIMES/CHICAGO DAILY NEWS COLLECTION, CHICAGO HISTORY MUSEUM.

David opened the court proceedings and mentioned her name, she dug her fingernails into her hands. LaCosta was nervous as she watched juror after juror leave the box, but she did have a brief smile for a female friend whom she saw in the well-filled courtroom. Shortly after the proceedings started, Joan began to shiver violently, and she asked a bailiff to bring back her coat. She wrapped it around her shoulders and pulled the black monkey fur collar around her neck.

Judge David was in a much better humor than the young woman. One of the 12 jurymen in the box declared at one point that he'd like to be excused, as he worked for the Commonwealth Edison Company, which he insisted needed him.

"Ah, Samuel Insull needs you," Judge David said sarcastically, "you'll serve."[4] Samuel Insull was the magnate who owned Edison Commonwealth, the largest electric company in the Midwest. Then the judge added, "We'd better call Samuel up and ask how important you are."[5]

Jury selection proved difficult in this case, as most of the available pool, all men, seemed to shy away from the thought of possibly sending the dark-eyed beauty in front of them to prison. According to the *Chicago Tribune*,

> Veniremen called into Judge Joseph David's court yesterday to be qual-ified as jurors in the trial of LaCosta did their best to be gallant toward the defendant by evading service on any and every pretext. They looked at the chic young woman, a former automobile racer, who is accused of an assault and attempted robbery of Mrs. Rebecca Bobbe of the Chicago Beach Hotel and decided they didn't care to sit in judgment against her.[6]

Judge David's impatient criticism of one after the other of the unwilling jurors finally achieved the desired results, and the jury was at last complete. The state would begin the presentation of its case the morning of October 22. Opposing Joan LaCosta's counsel were prosecutors Charles Bellows and Samuel Clawson. Both of the men had combative reputations, and they were not swayed by the magnetic persona of the lovely woman who sat across from them.

Mrs. Rebecca Bobbe was the main witness for the prosecution. She was still recovering from the physical wounds suffered in her fight with Joan, and she sported a plaster cast on her neck. She testified about how LaCosta came to her apartment the afternoon of the event and knocked on the door and, when Bobbe opened it, Joan pushed her way in and shoved the barrel of a pistol into the victim's ribs. Bobbe described the fierce struggle as LaCosta tried to force the chloroformed rag into Mrs. Bobbe's mouth. The gun that Joan produced was dropped to the floor in the fight, and eventually the screams from Bobbe and her maid brought reinforcements from down the hallway. Mrs. Bobbe, still sporting the vestiges of the cut under her eye, gave a compelling account. The judge paused the proceedings for the day, and the next morning, the defense would begin presenting its case.

Chicagoans woke that Wednesday morning, October 23, to a scene of unfathomable destruction. Gale-force winds of more than 50 miles per hour on Tuesday night, in tandem with the highest Lake Michigan water levels on record, combined to cause millions of dollars of damage to the city's frontage area. Lake Shore Drive was paralyzed by two feet of standing water on the roadway. The toll of the damage on the Lake Michigan shipping sector was high, including the sinking of a Milwaukee freighter, which was transporting goods with a crew of more than 50 men, all of whom were lost in the calamity. Wednesday also brought the coldest temperature for the date in 12 years, with a slushy snowstorm blanketing the morass of mud and rubble.

On October 23, 1929, the stock market closed in a frenzy of sell orders and plummeting share prices. The ticker tape ran an hour behind, causing traders to panic, as they had no reliable price information. Shares of big companies like Montgomery Ward and Bethlehem Steel tumbled in value. Traders on the pit floor were bewildered by the volume of trading and the losses that stacked up, but they were reassured by the fact that there had been big stock drops before.

Joan was called to the stand that day and quickly painted herself as a misunderstood charity seeker who had simply come to the Bobbe door for a handout.

She answered the questions posed to her in a clear voice, but she wore a worried expression. Joan recounted her career arc as an artist's model and then a race car driver and mentioned that she had switched to aviation. The jurors, all men, were rapt as she recounted her daredevil adventures.

Her attorney, Michael Romano, gently put LaCosta through her paces, unspooling the narrative of her hardscrabble life. He gently prodded her to describe her upbringing and how she arrived at this sad point in her life:

> She told of her marriage at the age of 15, of her subsequent divorce, and of a second marriage in Chicago several years ago. Then she related how she had taken up racing automobiles, her avocation leading to an estrangement between her husband and herself which resulted in a second marriage.
>
> After a racing career of the last few years she had taken up aviation, when she had a nervous breakdown.[7]

The jurymen were spellbound. This woman had been a successful driver on the tracks against an entirely male lineup, and she was now flying planes, another starkly masculine avocation. It was mind-bending to them, as they tried to reconcile the fact that this daring résumé was attached to the shivering, pale defendant in front of them.

Her money and health were gone, she explained to them, and with only $5 in her pocketbook, she turned in desperation to her last hope, Mrs. Bobbe, whom she knew through Hyman Bobbe as a wealthy philanthropist.

Joan explained that she had gone up to Bobbe's room to ask for a loan, but Mrs. Bobbe "apparently misunderstood my mission, and tried to resist."[8]

"There was a struggle, . . . and Mrs. Bobbe fell on the floor, hurting her nose. Then the house detectives came up and arrested me"[9]:

"Did you have this toy pistol and this bottle of chloroform with you when you called on Mrs. Bobbe?" Romano asked her.

"I did. The pistol I had had for some time. I used it as a cigarette case."

"What were you going to do with the chloroform?"

"I was going to take it," she replied in a low voice, hanging her head.

"Did you intend to rob Mr. Bobbe?"

"I did not. When I stepped inside. I said to her, 'Mrs. Bobbe, I want to appeal to you. I need money.' And I guess she thought I meant to rob her and screamed. Then we struggled, and I was arrested."[10]

A tough cross-examination by the prosecutor Charles Bellows followed, who worked mightily to shake out the image of a distraught and delicate flower from the jury's minds and to portray the accused as a common criminal. And LaCosta fought just as ardently to maintain her emotions under the relentless grilling, exhibiting the ice-cold composure she always showed on the racetrack, until she was finally excused from the witness box. She stood up unsteadily, took a few steps toward her table, and then collapsed in a heap directly in front of the stunned jury.

"Take her out! Take her out!" Judge David shouted. "What kind of a court am I running here?"[11]

Michael Romano and Helen rushed to her aid. With the help of the court bailiffs, she was carried into the anteroom and revived after nearly an hour. Her velvet dress and silk stockings carried long rents from her contact with the table as she fell.

"'This is awful!' she moaned again and again as she regained consciousness, 'this is awful!'"[12]

The jury was instructed by the judge to disregard the incident, and the trial was adjourned until the October 25.

By the next day, October 24, 1929, the collapse of America's economy was in full swing. It would forever be known as Black Thursday, the largest sell-off of stocks in the history of the United States. The market plummeted in a free fall, and the ticker ran three hours behind, only allowing the traders to see the wreckage that had already unfolded and that they were powerless to change. The 3,500 men on the floor of the New York Stock Exchange needed dozens of police to handle the surging crowds gathered outside the building who were trying to make their way into the exchange. Every trading record was smashed; General Motors and AT&T combined for more than half a billion dollars in value that was wiped off their respective ledgers.

There was no turning back; the country was careening toward the Great Depression.

On Friday, October 25, closing arguments were made in the court-room before the 12-man jury, and while the defense attorney Romano pleaded for sympathy, the state prosecutors urged the jury to treat her like "'any other prisoner,' and asked that the jury disregard her sex and beauty."[13] Joan sat watching, silent and nervous.

The jury convened for four hours. Joan passed the time talking to friends in the court and waiting in Chief Justice D. J. Normoyle's chambers (the same official who had reduced her bond from $25,000 to $2,500).

Uldine Maybelle Utley also made an appearance in the courtroom. The 17-year-old evangelist had arrived in the city on October 3 and was booked into the LaSalle Street Baptist Church for a multi-week preach-ing engagement. She was a national sensation, known for her dramatic sermons and her ghostly white attire. The teenage evangelist was always scheduled months ahead in the biggest venues and cities in the country.

It was a perfect publicity opportunity for both parties, as Utley was being associated with saving a high-profile "sinner," and Joan LaCosta (and her sister Helen) were snapped in a press photo supplicating for forgiveness with the "angel in white."

Uldine sat beside LaCosta at her table during the deliberations of the jury. They were all very well aware of the importance of cultivating their proper public personas but none more than the Queen of Reinvention, also known as Marion Carver, Marion Martins, Josephine Rust, and, ultimately, Joan LaCosta.

The night before, in front of packed pews at the LaSalle Street Bap-tist Church, Uldine had made Joan LaCosta the topic of her sermon, promising to help her at the trial and to help her "to find the strength that she needs now."[14]

"She is a victim of the age—speed. A racing driver, an aviator, she was courageous as long as she was speeding. But when she had to face a big moral issue, she broke down."[15]

Figure 14.3. Joan LaCosta, her sister Helen (Jeanette) Johnson née Martins, and Uldine Utley (left to right) on October 25, 1929.

The last view the jurors had before they filed into the jury room was that of Joan, shivering, her eyes wet with tears. Uldine Utley, clad in pure white, stood close, her arm around Joan; in Utley's other hand was a Bible, bound in white leather. She caressed the book as she spoke to Joan in soft, whispered tones, urging her to be brave.

In the afternoon, Judge David called the jury back into the court-room and asked if they had reached a verdict. The jurors said they stood 10 to 2 and thought a verdict could be reached in a few minutes. It was not announced whether the majority was for conviction or acquittal. Miss LaCosta apparently had gotten an inside tip because she laughed and talked gaily with her attorney Michael Romano and others while she waited for the jury to return with the expected verdict.

Shortly thereafter, the jury announced its decision: guilty of assault with intent to commit robbery.

Joan was stunned. Her trembling hands went up to her face. Her head slowly dropped, hiding her necklace of pearls. She wept.

She swooned and collapsed into her chair and was once again carried off to the antechamber, where her body-racking sobs could be heard throughout the court. After a delay until LaCosta could regain her composure, the sentencing phase was convened. The shock never left Joan's face, even as Judge David asked the jury if they felt this case was a candidate for leniency.

"Gentleman, in view of the circumstances, that this young lady has never been in trouble before and has no previous record, would you con-sider this a case for leniency?"[16]

The jury partially acceded, and the judge asked again. This time the vote was unanimously "yes."[17] The judge said he would consider proba-tion at the sentencing. LaCosta would otherwise face a stretch of one to 14 years in the Joliet State Prison.

The prosecutors were outraged and urged that Miss LaCosta be treated like "any other prisoner."[18] Assistant State Attorneys Charles A. Bellows and Samuel Clawson said they would oppose any move for probation. If the judge granted her liberty, it will be over their strenuous objection, they said.

Joan quickly recovered and spent the next hour laughing and chatting with the friends she had made in the criminal court since her trial began. She was then released on her original bond pending her sentencing on November 8.

It's a testament to LaCosta's charisma and Romano's emotion-based strategy that the defense swayed an entire courtroom's sympathy (aside from the disbelieving and angry prosecutors). The state's team actually ended up facing disciplinary action for their vociferous antipathy toward LaCosta, with both fines and possible suspensions on the table against them. It was maddening to the duo that they could have a prima facie case against Joan with several witnesses, physical evidence, and a confession from the defendant only to have her tears and "fainting habit"[19] derail their conviction. She was found guilty, but in the process, the prosecutors had created a sympathetic criminal.

The other *Chicago Tribune* front-page case that month was that of Josephine Dobscher, "The Red Slicker Bandit,"[20] who was facing similar charges and whose plaintive story Joan had "borrowed." She asked for and was denied the same deal that was initially offered to LaCosta, which was to plead guilty in exchange for probation. Instead, according to Prosecutor C. Wayland Brooks, the 19-year-old bandit would receive no special consideration despite her gender. "Too many girls are running around committing hold-ups," Brooks said when Miss Dobscher offered to plea bargain. "She will receive the same treatment as a man who commits a similar offence."[21]

On November 1, 1929, Josephine Dobscher was found guilty of robbery and faced a sentence of one year to life.

"It seems Juries are finally deciding to treat women criminals the same as men in this community,"[22] said Assistant State Attorney C. Wayland Brooks, who, with Prosecutor Nat Ruvell, opposed probation in return for a plea of guilty. Miss Dobscher, through her attorney, had offered to take a sentence in the Bridewell (which was a county workhouse as opposed to the state prison) rather than face a jury. The offer was rejected.

"This girl did not cry when she participated in the crime, and you men should not be swayed by her false tears of repentance at this

WOMAN AUTO RACER CONVICTED OF ROBBERY.
Joan La Coste, who was found guilty of entering room in
Chicago Beach hotel. She may be placed on probation.
[TRIBUNE Photo]   *(Story on page 2.)*

Figure 14.4. Joan LaCosta pictured in the *Chicago Tribune* on October 26, 1929.
CHICAGO TRIBUNE.

time,"[23] Brooks said in his closing plea to the jury, referencing when she
had wept on the witness stand.

The jury deliberated for two hours before returning the guilty verdict.
In this case, it was the jurors, not the judge, who had asked for instructions about leniency, but they were told that "this was none of their
concern."[24]

The very next day, despite the begging from Josephine and pleas of mercy from her mother, Judge Dennis Normoyle passed sentence: life imprisonment with the possibility of parole after 11 months. It was the harshest judgment ever meted out to any woman in Illinois for that crime, and Assistant State Attorneys C. Wayland Brooks and Nat Ruvell refused to listen to her pleas.

In a cruel twist, the imagined husband whom she had blamed for her criminal deeds turned out to be very real. He was taken into custody by the police the month after her trial. After a two-month search, William Levinson, 34 years old, the spouse and alleged robbery companion of Josephine, was captured in his room at 3001 Washington Boulevard by the police early in the morning of December 11.

Perhaps if he had been arrested earlier, his wife's plaintive but far-fetched story might have seemed more believable. Levinson refused to step forward for months while his teenage wife was in the process of being tried, convicted, and ultimately sentenced to life in prison.

It was just a few days after Doebscher's trial, on November 8, that Joan LaCosta faced the same dilemma as she returned to the courthouse for sentencing. Her fate hinged on the judge's opinion of what he felt would best serve the interest of the state in regard to the young woman in front of him. His decision shocked the press corps. The AP wire story was a dramatic finale to a theatrical trial:

> Today the motion of the girl's attorney, Michael Romano, for a new trial was overruled, but his motion for probation was granted despite the protests of the Assistant State's Attorney, Charles A. Bellows. . . . The State's Attorney was censured by the court for having pressed a felony charge against the girl, stating that the evidence merited only a misdemeanor.[25]

"'You have had a hard life and some hard luck,' said his honor, 'I believe you deserve probation. This is your one chance. Remember this court gives but one. Your tears will be of no avail a second time. There will be nothing but the penitentiary.'"[26]

Joan LaCosta, decked out in a new stylish brown ensemble (and not in her standard trial fare of a black frock with lace collar), took her probation and Judge David's lecture with a smile, signed her own $1,000 bond, and promised to continue her aviation studies.

"'I intend to take my examination for a commercial airplane pilot's license immediately,' she said after thanking the judge for his clemency. 'Friends have come to my aid financially and with what I am earning in the air, 1 hope never to be in want again.'"[27] She celebrated her release with her sister and friends with a party at an apartment at the Surfridge Hotel. The hotel had been the scene of a dynamite attack a few months before, adding to the atmosphere of excitement and danger that Joan had just escaped from:

> "Almost everyone has been so kind to me," she told reporters, "that I can't be anything but happy. Of course the verdict was a disappointment, because you know I didn't really do what they said I did.
>
> "Two big aviation companies have offered me contracts to fly for them. You know there are only seven women licensed to fly commercial planes in the country and I will be the only one in Chicago."[28]

CHAPTER FIFTEEN

Dust to Dust

LACOSTA'S TRIAL ENDED ALMOST SIMULTANEOUSLY WITH THE COL-
lapse of Wall Street. On October 29, 1929, the stock market crashed
on Black Tuesday, and though there were sputtering recovery rallies for
weeks, the damage was done. America's economy was gravely wounded,
and the Great Depression swept over the country. Joan's situation was
emblematic of the problems at large.

She was destitute. There were court fines to pay on top of her every-
day expenses, and she was still broke. She had family and friends supporting her financially to some degree, but she needed a steady job. And her
body hurt every day. After racing almost every week on the tour for four
years, her injuries never had a chance to heal. She was in nearly constant
pain from the damaged ribs from her fence crash in Detroit.

She eventually found work in the Loop in downtown Chicago, not
far from the Hotel Lorraine, where she was living. She sold stationery
and writing supplies at one of the nearby department stores (most likely
the Carson, Pirie, Scott & Company store, noted for its paper goods)
while she slowly recuperated physically and mentally. She enjoyed being
away from the public spotlight for a while, operating in and out of the
store's back rooms. Her face had been front-page news for years, and now,
as she sorted invoices and billings, she could hide away. It was a new start
for Joan at the Carson store, whose map location happened to be the
nexus for all the addresses in the city. Based on Chicago's grid system,
every destination in town was measured from that spot where she stood
every day.

In 1930, she met Joe.

Joseph Maurer was a former dental student at Loyola University who had just moved out of his Phi Mu Chi fraternity house and was living back home with his parents and three siblings. He was excited about his prospects in the train industry, and he worked during the day as a railroad clerk.

Joan and Joe met up and swapped office stories during their walks along the nearby beachfront. The Shedd Aquarium and Adler Planetarium were brand new, and the crowds on a Saturday afternoon made Joan feel both anonymous and lucky, fortunate in a more emotional way than during her racing adventures. They walked hand in hand, laughing at the excitement of the children running down the esplanade. On a summer day, the crowds passing around her were smiling back at an obviously smitten woman and her date, not at "Joan LaCosta." She scanned the faces of the young men and women walking by and realized that she and Joe were no different from them. They were just another couple in love. There were no loudspeakers announcing the arrival on a track of the European speed champion; instead, it was the cries of herring gulls begging for bread, the yelling of parents calling out to their children who wouldn't slow down, and the rhythmic putt-putt of car engines slowly passing them by.

On October 3, 1931, two years to the day from her Chicago arrest, Joan LaCosta married Joseph Maurer, the railroad worker six years her junior. Joan was proud enough to contact the *Chicago Tribune* with the big news, which the paper printed October 10, that Joe and Joan were moving into an apartment together on Diversey Parkway.

"I could have spent many more years in racing, but at the end I might have a lot of money, or only a little. I'd rather have this,"[1] she laughed and flashed her thin wedding ring.

Within two years, they moved to Indiana and bought a small home with a horse stable and a few horses, and they turned their focus to their family and their quiet small-town life out of the spotlight. Joseph became an engineer for the Pennsylvania Railroad, and Joan worked as a crew dispatcher. She took his last name, Maurer, but she kept the first name Joan the rest of her life. It was the last vestige of the exciting, fictional

Figure 15.1. 1930s postcard depicting the Shedd Aquarium in Chicago.
SHEDD AQUARIUM.

character that she had inhabited so perfectly for the past five years. Joan LaCosta was a record-breaking speed demon who was photographed leaning on Babe Ruth's arm for the front pages of the newspapers. Marion Carver, the little girl with the birdhouse in Memphis, was just a memory.

Alex Sloan continued to hunt for the right replacement for LaCosta's rare blend of beauty, talent, and ambition. He turned once again to Elfrieda Mais, the Racing Queen whom Joan had dethroned on her own road to stardom. Mais still exhibited the same sedate attitude that kept her from rising above the noise in the early 1920s. She was a skilled driver with courage, but she was quiet and wouldn't resort to the showy back-and-forth banter that stoked racing rivalries.

Mais had left dirt track racing, but she was eventually talked back into the daredevil show circuit by her husband, Ray La Plante, and Sloan. Instead of racing against men or other women, which had lost its novelty, she would perform a wild stunt to top off race events. She was asked by Sloan to do the routine, but given the social and legal status afforded women, Mais undoubtedly felt the pressure from her husband and also from the promoter who had made her a celebrity.

The act was immensely dangerous. Mais, wearing only a football helmet and safety goggles, would race her car at 70 miles per hour through a wall of wooden boards. The boards were soaked with oil and gasoline and were then set on fire.

In January 1934, the papers remarked that she was about to do her "unlucky"[2] thirteenth run through a wall at a local event. Elfrieda laughed it off. She even had "E1" painted on her speedster, which is the mirror image of "13." The event went off without a hitch. But there were more foreboding warning signs, one of the starkest being the Chippewa Falls Independence Day Fair that year, where Al Wright had been killed doing the same stunt.

At the Alabama State Fair on September 24, 1934, Elfrieda Mais strapped on her helmet and goggles and tore off at a mile a minute toward a wall of fire.

The automobile crashed through the fiery boards, and Mais lost control and caromed off a guardrail surrounding the track and went over an embankment, into a road grader, and finally through the fairgrounds wall. Mais was pronounced dead on arrival at a local hospital.

Three other people were hurt in the accident, which was witnessed by the crowd at the fair. Two boys, John Draper and Duncan Davenport, sitting on top of a parked car outside the fairground, were slightly injured when Miss Mais's car plunged through the fairgrounds fence and struck the car they were standing on to view the event. Jenks Hoagland, a fair performer, hurt his arm as the flaming auto careened through the wall.

Her husband saw the crash. He said he believed his wife was burned as the car went through the burning wall, which distracted her. She had been burned similarly by a flaming board the year before at a Tampa, Florida, show.

Alex Sloan didn't seem to comprehend the seriousness of the accident or Elfrieda's injuries. Harry Vance recalled Sloan coming into the fair office that afternoon with the next day's programs in hand. He'd seen the event in person that day, and even though he saw Mais being taken away to the hospital, he told Harry that Mais would be performing the same stunt the next day. When Harry told him that "she was a corpse," Sloan "slumped forward in his chair." "Sloan had seen a thousand wrecks. He'd guessed wrong on this one."[3]

Mais was paid $25 per day for two performances to drive through the fire and risk her life. She was 42.

At her memorial service in Alabama, Sloan, Sig Haugdahl, and 10 others posed for a picture behind a black and white checkered floral wreath in the shape of a flag, signifying the end of the last race. The service was held at midnight because, as the *Birmingham Post-Herald* reported, "It was only after their day's work ended that the group of friends gathered at Johns Funeral Parlors for the final rites. They knew she would have wanted it that way and so the funeral hour had been arranged shortly before midnight to allow them to go through with their acts."[4]

Her body was transported that night to her hometown, Indianapolis, to be buried.

Alex Sloan didn't miss a beat. After Elfrieda Mais was killed in the horrific accident on Monday, the following Thursday, the event was added back into the program. The *Birmingham News* on September 26 summed it up:

The show must go on.

That is a phrase emblematic of those who risk their lives and give of their talents daily to thrill and entertain.

Thursday afternoon in front of the grandstand at the Alabama State Fair Stephen "Skip" Fordyce, whose home is in Seattle, will crash the board walls in front of the grandstand at the Alabama State Fair on a motorcycle going at 70 miles an hour.

Steve "Skip" Fordyce, a trouper in the truest sense of the word, will be "subbing" for Elfrieda Mais, gathered unto her fathers in the tragedy of Monday night.

"The show must go on!" said "Skip" Fordyce, known as "the Human Bullet," to the show world Wednesday. "I'll go through that board wall Thursday afternoon at the Alabama State Fair Grounds, or know the reason why. Not only that, but I'll shoot the barricade of wood and nails on a motorcycle.

"The spirit of Elfrieda Mais must live!"

"Skip" Fordyce was speaking to Alex Sloan and Harold "Chick" Hagen, who have brought the auto races and this part of the State Fair thrills to Birmingham.

"If you'll do that," replied Mr. Sloan, "a phrase known to every trouper in the show world will spring into actual materialization." So, Messrs. Sloan and Hagen produced a contract, "Skip" Fordyce signed on the dotted line, and "the show goes on."

Fordyce will crash the walls on a motorcycle in front of the grandstand Thursday afternoon while hurling himself on a motorcycle at 70 miles an hour.[5]

The show went on.

The life raft for Joan in the aviation world was the flying ace Doug Davis. It was Davis who had taught Joan how to fly, and it was Davis whom she had fallen in love with after her race career. He was cut from the mold of all great pioneers. He was daring, fearless, and innovative.

Davis had carved out a strip for his planes at an Atlanta racetrack and called it Candler Field, where he taught Joan and other pilots starting in 1926, when it wasn't much more than a cow field. He was the first person in the state to give flying lessons, and it was hard not to be infected by his unabashed joy in the air.

Doug Davis was one of the premier air racers of the early 1930s. In late August 1934, he had just set a new transcontinental speed record and was the favorite coming into the Labor Day Weekend Nationals scheduled for Monday, September 3.

But he had misgivings, particularly over the short length of the course. Instead of the customary 10-mile circuit, it was shortened to 8⅓ miles for the viewing benefit of the grandstand audience. Davis had a premonition, telling others before the race, "The course is too short, I've half a notion not to enter at all. I think the course should be lengthened to at least ten miles. Someone's going to get killed."[6]

He was right. On September 3, 1934, Doug Davis was thrilling the enormous crowd of 125,000 spectators at the Thompson Trophy Race in Cleveland, increasing his lead on the 8⅓-mile course, cutting around the pylons closer and closer, until he just missed one; being a fierce competitor, he banked his plane upward sharply, attempting to swing his aircraft in an arc around the lap marker again. Witnesses saw the plane shoot up, then dive dramatically, and Davis, an ace to the end, almost managed to pull the nose up just before hitting the ground, but he ultimately failed, and the plane cartwheeled through the dirt. He was killed instantly. The first event crew members to respond to the scene found Davis in the cockpit, the parachute still strapped to his back and a satchel of letters in his hand: souvenirs for fans who wanted a postmark from the race day.

William Reeve was an eyewitness to the accident and marveled at how dangerously close Doug Davis was flying his race plane to the pylons:

> Doug Davis had plenty of nerve, believe me.
>
> I was right under the back-stretch pylon during the whole Thompson trophy race. I watched him shoot that red plane around the pylon time after time, so close that I thought sure he was going to hit it.
>
> No wonder he was out in front. He gained yards and yards on every turn.
>
> I could see him gain altitude after the pylon at the end of the straight away a mile away. Then he'd start to dive, and he would make the turn where I was located with his lower wing so close to the ground that 1 thought several times he was going to hit.
>
> I said to my wife: "That fellow sure has got what it takes." He was flying on pure nerve. But his luck couldn't last.
>
> The last time he came around he miscalculated a little and cut inside the pylon. Evidently, he realized his error, and decided to make a complete turn, round the pylon again, and continue.
>
> But he was going too fast. His plane shot upward, started to curve around, then plunged down as straight as a plumb line.
>
> It all happened so fast that I don't believe he ever knew what hit him.[7]

Doug Davis was 35.

Chapter Sixteen

Twilight

Joan Maurer stayed out of the papers until 1937, when the *Tal-lahassee Democrat* reported on August 4 that she was returning to her "home town" of Memphis for "treatment for a heart and nerve disorder"[1] at St. Joseph's Hospital. The years of stress and racing injuries had taken a toll on the 36-year-old.

"'It doesn't date back to any one thing,' she said of her physical condition, 'but comes of living under too great a strain and too much excitement over a period of years.'"[2]

The memories of her speed achievement at Daytona were still fresh in her mind as she spoke to the reporter: "'I'm sort of proud of the fact that record still stands and that I was the only woman ever to use the Daytona Beach track,' she said, admitting however, she is prouder of the way her husband has bragged for six years about her Italian spaghetti."[3]

She didn't retire completely from tackling physical challenges. There were numerous instances of her mettle and pain tolerance being tested while working in her barn doing chores and keeping up with her household duties. Joe was usually on a traveling train engineer assignment, so Joan often ran things at home by herself.

She had numerous incidents with intemperate horses on their modest property. She rode them whether they wanted her to or not. The ponies were another representation of speed and freedom for her, and it was one of her few local newsworthy events when she and her husband sued a pair of local horse trainers for breach of warranty and damages in the late 1950s.

There was also emotional pain.

On May 10, 1937, J. Alex Sloan, the master promoter, manager, and imagineer, died after a mysterious yearlong illness. The nagging symptoms had seemed minor at first, but in early May, he suffered a sudden medical relapse and a drastic turn for the worse. Despite immediate treatment and several transfusions, he passed away in the Evanston Hospital in Illinois, just as his beloved wife had 18 years before. He was 57. The man who had promoted the first state fair automobile race in Birmingham, Alabama, in 1907 left behind a staggering legacy. In his final year, he promoted 72 race events in 50 cities. He also conjured an imaginary French racing champion out of thin air, and Joan had stepped in and put on the fictional crown.

As for the "flaming machine"[4] that made her nationally famous, Sloan took possession of the Sig Haugdahl Wisconsin Special in 1930 and stored it at his Joliet, Illinois, garage until he died. Had Joan been sentenced to prison instead of probation, she would have served her sentence in the Joliet State Prison, which was within walking distance of her most infamous ride. Both the driver and the car would have been locked away in similar-sized boxes.

It was the end of the LaCosta racing era but not the end of the continued path for women in traditionally male-dominated sports and avocations. Amelia Earhart proved that it wasn't just men who had the stamina and mental fortitude to fly solo across the Atlantic. Babe Didrikson Zaharias was one of the greatest athletes ever, male or female, and after setting Olympic records, she took up golf at a late athletic stage in her life and was still so dominant that she actually took part in a PGA event against men, something that wouldn't be repeated for another six decades.

And in Joan's field, motor racing, women rose to the upper echelons in automotive sports, eventually competing in drag racing (Shirley Muldowney), land speed competitions in both cars and motorcycles (Paula Murphy and Joy Houston, among many others) and even the Indianapolis 500 (Danica Patrick). Joan LaCosta carved a path for hundreds of other women to follow.

Joan and Joe navigated one more surprise turn with the arrival of the couple's daughter, Toni Loretta, in June 1948, when Joan was 47 years old and her first daughter, June, was 31. With two daughters more than 30 years apart in age, Joan initially let the young Toni believe that her sister June was, in fact, her aunt. While her racing career kept her away for much of June's childhood, Joan kept her daring days on the track from her younger daughter. When Toni was in her teens, she thumbed through a book at home. She found a yellowed newspaper clipping used as a bookmark that was an account of one of her mother's racing exploits. Toni had been unaware of her mother's competitive career until that moment. She had been exposed to all of her mother's racing after-effects—the moods, the nerves, and the trembling at the sound of lightning storms—but she was unaware of the depth of the danger that Joan had been through. Her mother had hidden that past away, and the other old clippings and awards were lost or taken. Toni had to put together her mother's racing life piece by piece.

Her mother's nostalgia surfaced in other ways. Joan danced to popular music from years ago, inside her locked bedroom, as she swayed in time on the creaking floorboards, the tunes wafting out from under the door. The trophies and memorabilia were long gone, but Joan's youthful memories were still vivid. She always loved the jazzy songs of the 1920s and 1930s and listened to them when in the dark when the stars came out, and in her mind, she would drift back to that beach in Florida when Oscar, that handsome young man, pulled her out of the surf as the cameras rolled and the engine of the big race car conjured a genie of swirling black smoke.

Joan LaCosta saw the return of Halley's Comet in 1986, and the two astral events bookended her life. It was a neat little hello waving back at her from the nine-year-old Marion. When she was looking up at the dark sky as a child back then, did she imagine seeing that brilliant white flare again? And what memories would she have made in between?

Perhaps an even more fitting comparison to her life's journey was that other mysterious, once-every-9,200-year comet that she watched swing by in the chilly January air in 1910, a few months before Halley's appearance. It blazed through the southern sky of Kentucky, lit up a swath of the country, and awed the city of Chicago. That visitor was unexpected and spectacular, and no one here will ever see it again.

The January 27 edition of the *Paducah Sun* of Kentucky that year printed an editorial on the unique Great Daylight Comet:

> Whence come the comets, and where do they go? We know not, but we do know they have their habits and they appear periodically, much like some people. The irregular ones have their habits just as the normal commonplace people, who appear regularly, like the stars set in heaven, each in his appointed constellation. . . .
>
> But a comet swinging athwart our orbit, coming out of the unknown, illimitable space, manifesting phenomena unusual in the heavens of our vision, and passing with its train of attendant circumstances back into that space, piquing our curiosity, but throwing no light on the mystery whose existence its presence only emphasizes, attracts more attention than do the stars we know are always there. Yet that comet is composed of the same material that composes the other stars, obeys the same laws and eventually must pass through the same transformation. Some influence has exaggerated its eccentricity, that is all.[5]

* * *

After all of her dalliances with pilots and race car drivers, it was the solid and dependable railroad engineer, Joseph, who finally made her happy. On their gravestone, it's a train that is carved in a simple relief, not a hot rod. They were married 60 years, and Joan, as usual, finished first, passing away on December 29, 1993, with her husband following her two days later on New Year's Eve. They lay side by side in Brazil, Indiana.

NOTES

CHAPTER ONE

1. "Woman Champion Turns Robber," *Reidsville Review*, October 7, 1929, 1.
2. Kathleen McLaughlin, "Girl in Cell as Bandit Baffles Police Quizzers," *Chicago Tribune*, October 5, 1929, 3.
3. "Woman Auto Racer Caught in Attempted Jewel Robbery," *Commercial Appeal*, October 6, 1929, 16.
4. "New Marble Shop," *News Democrat*, December 27, 1901, 4.
5. John W. Bortle, "The Great Daylight Comet of 1910," *Sky & Telescope*, January 13, 2010.
6. "Artists and Models," *Chicago Tribune*, May 10, 1926, 29.
7. "Girl Driver Is Proud of Her Title," *Marshall News Messenger*, November 5, 1926, 5.
8. "Tommy Milton Tells of His Racing Experiences," *Fort Wayne Sentinel*, March 6, 1920, 4.
9. "Tommy Milton Tells of His Racing Experiences."

CHAPTER TWO

1. "Woman Daredevil Killed in Stunt," *Brooklyn Daily Eagle*, September 25, 1934, 13.
2. "Famous Woman Auto Racer to Drive in Wichita Races," *Wichita Beacon*, June 28, 1916, 14.
3. "Her Smile Robbers' Lure," *Chicago Tribune*, September 30, 1923, 2.
4. "Gas!" *Chicago Tribune*, May 18, 1924, 25.
5. "Pretty Jean on Trial," *Daily Independent*, October 21, 1929, 3.
6. "Sig Haughdahl and Mlle. Martens, French Pilot, to Head Program of Events," *Democrat and Chronicle*, August 29, 1925, 23.
7. "Marion Martin Challenges Lady Auto Racing Champion," *Calgary Herald*, July 8, 1925, 14.
8. Bob Lawrence, "James Jim 'Jimmie' Costa, Jr.," Bob Lawrence's Vintage Auto Racing Web Ring for Kansas Racing History, https://kansasracinghistory.com/tripod/Costa/Jimmie-Costa.htm, accessed February 25, 2024.
9. "Mrs. J. Alex Sloane Succumbs to Burns," *Jackson Daily News*, April 18, 1919, 8.

10. "Girl Auto Pilot Flirts with Death When Mount Flashes through Fence," *Star Tribune*, July 5, 1924, 13.

CHAPTER THREE

1. "Sports," *Forest Park Review*, July 12, 1924, 7.
2. "Joan Falls in Faint as She Leaves the Stand," *Chicago Tribune*, October 24, 1929, 5.
3. Elinor Hillyer, "Settling Down in the Air," *Atlanta Journal*, April 15, 1928, 87.
4. Hillyer, "Settling Down in the Air."
5. "Pilot Is Killed in Speed Trial at Roby Track," *Chicago Tribune*, June 8, 1925, 21.
6. "Cliff Woodbury Wins Auto Race at North Shore," *Chicago Tribune*, June 15, 1925, 25.
7. "Track Fit for 'Dust-Dogs' to Go Their Best," *Leader-Post*, July 2, 1925, 11.
8. "Famous Woman Auto Racer to Drive in Wichita Races," *Wichita Beacon*, June 28, 1916, 14.
9. "U.S. Lady Champ Loses to French Girl Race Driver," *Leader Post*, July 3, 1925, 8.
10. "U.S. Lady Champ Loses to French Girl Race Driver."
11. "Sweepstakes to Feature Jubilee Auto Race Meet," *Calgary Albertan*, July 10, 1925, 8.
12. "Marion Martin Challenges Lady Auto Racing Champion," *Calgary Herald*, July 8, 1925, 14.
13. "Marion Martin Challenges Lady Auto Racing Champion."
14. "Marion Martin Challenges Lady Auto Racing Champion."
15. "Speed Fans Howl Their Mightiest as Cars Roar around Exhibition Oval," *Edmonton Journal*, July 14, 1925, 15.
16. "Daredevil Drivers Here for Auto Meet," *Montreal Star*, August 21, 1925, 14.
17. "Auto Racing Tomorrow," *Gazette*, August 22, 1925, 15.
18. "Disbrow in Montreal," *Gazette*, August 20, 1925, 13.
19. "Sig Haughdahl and Mlle. Martens, French Pilot, to Head Program of Events," *Democrat and Chronicle*, August 29, 1925, 23.
20. "Famous Veteran of Dirt Track Drivers to March Skill against Lampkin," *Democrat and Chronicle*, August 30, 1925, 40.
21. "Watters Here for Fair," *Atlanta Constitution*, October 7, 1925, 19.
22. Toni Cooksey, interview, April 30, 2019.
23. "Horey, Watters, Disbrow and Girl Driver Entered in Fair's Closing Events," *Atlanta Constitution*, October 17, 1925, 8.
24. "Woman Driver Will Try to Break Dirt Track Records," *Clarion-Ledger*, October 22, 1925, 9.
25. "Mile a Minute Pace Made by Youthful Woman Pilot Great Crowd Cheers Racer," *Clarion-Ledger*, October 23, 1925, 11.

CHAPTER FOUR

1. "Wreck Reenacted as Cameras Click," unknown newspaper, April 15, 1926.
2. "Woman Driver of Racing Car Has Test of Nerve," *Bridgeport Telegram*, April 30, 1926, 17.

3. Sec Taylor, "Sittin' In with the Athletes," *Des Moines Register*, June 17, 1936, 9.

4. "Car Burns; 'Will Drive Wheels Off,' Says Woman Racer," *Journal Times*, April 16, 1926, 34.

5. "A Lesson in the Curriculum of World's Records," Skandinaviske Berliner Korrespondez, April 14, 1926.

6. M. L. Woodard, "On Automobile Row," *Lincoln Nebraska State Journal*, September 5, 1926, 35.

7. Elinor Hillyer, "Settling Down in the Air," *Atlanta Journal*, April 15, 1928, 87.

CHAPTER FIVE

1. "Veteran Auto Race Driver to Appear in Classic at Fair Grounds May 12," *Montgomery Advertiser*, May 4, 1926, 7.

2. "Two Foreign Stars to Appear in Auto Races Here May 12," *Montgomery Advertiser*, April 30, 1926, 7.

3. "Montgomery to Have Auto Races on May 12th," *Weekly Herald*, May 6, 1926, 1.

4. "Louis Disbrow Refuses to Race against LaCosta," *Atlanta Constitution*, May 4, 1926, 10.

5. "Louis Disbrow Refuses to Race against LaCosta," 10.

6. "Louis Disbrow Refuses to Race against LaCosta," 10.

7. "Another Star Enters Races at Lakewood," *Atlanta Constitution*, May 6, 1926, 14.

8. "Disbrow Jealous, Is Reply of Girl Racing Driver," *Atlanta Constitution*, May 6, 1926, 28.

9. "Speed Queen Will Arrive Here Today," *Atlanta Constitution*, May 7, 1926, 11.

10. "Race Board Declares LaCosta Is Eligible for Lakewood Events," *Atlanta Constitution*, May 8, 1926, 8.

11. "Race Board Declares LaCosta Is Eligible for Lakewood Events," 8.

12. "Race Board Declares LaCosta Is Eligible for Lakewood Events," 8.

13. "LaCosta Suffers Injured Ankle," *Atlanta Constitution*, May 8, 1926, 9.

14. "Disbrow Unwilling to Meet Woman Speed Champ in Local Racing Classic," *Montgomery Advertiser*, May 8, 1926, 6.

15. "Disbrow Unwilling to Meet Woman Speed Champ in Local Racing Classic," 6.

16. "Disbrow Unwilling to Meet Woman Speed Champ in Local Racing Classic," 6.

17. "Disbrow Unwilling to Meet Woman Speed Champ in Local Racing Classic," 6.

18. "Mlle. LaCosta, Speed Queen, Accepts Louis Disbrow's Challenge for Match Race," *Atlanta Journal*, May 9, 1926, 26.

CHAPTER SIX

1. "Lampkin Sets New Dirt Track Records in Auto Race Classic," *Montgomery Advertiser*, May 13, 1926, 7.

2. "Lampkin Sets New Record in Montgomery Race," *Atlanta Constitution*, May 13, 1926, 18.

3. "LaCosta to Race Disbrow Saturday despite Illness," *Atlanta Constitution*, May 14, 1926, 9.

4. "LaCosta to Race Disbrow Saturday despite Illness," 9.

5. "Lampkin Sets New Record in Montgomery Race," *Atlanta Constitution*, May 13, 1926, 18.

6. "What the Marble Shooters of Other Cities Are Doing," *Dispatch*, June 4, 1926, 14.

7. "Disbrow Arraigned in Federal Court on Liquor Charge," *Atlanta Constitution*, May 18, 1926, 6.

8. "Louis Disbrow 'Soak' Wife Says in Petition," *Tulsa World*, December 6, 1922, 10.

9. "Disbrow-LaCosta Match Is Likely," *Clarion-Ledger*, May 21, 1926, 9.

10. "Disbrow-LaCosta Match Is Likely," 9.

11. "Girl Champion to Try for Records in Jackson," *Clarion-Ledger*, May 21, 1926, 8.

12. Dolly Dalrymple, "Mlle. Joan LaCosta, 'Meteor Maid,' Disappointingly Unlike Auto Racer," *Birmingham News*, May 28, 1926, 37.

13. Dalrymple, "Mlle. Joan LaCosta, 'Meteor Maid,' Disappointingly Unlike Auto Racer," 37.

14. "Disbrow-LaCosta Match Is Likely," *Clarion-Ledger*, May 21, 1926, 9.

15. "LaCosta-Disbrow Will Match Speed on Local Track," *Clarion-Ledger*, May 22, 1926, 8.

16. "Speed Car Events Promise Exciting Races Wednesday," *Clarion-Ledger*, May 23, 1926, 9.

17. "Exchangeites Honor Ladies at Banquet," *Clarion-Ledger*, May 25, 1926, 2.

18. "Auto Speed Stars Ready for Trials at Fair Grounds," *Clarion-Ledger*, May 26, 1926, 3.

19. "Auto Speed Trials Draw Great Crowd, No Records Broken," *Clarion-Ledger*, May 27, 1926, 8.

20. Gordon Williams, "In the Realm of Sports," *Reading Times*, August 30, 1935, 22.

21. Speedo, "New Marks Promised for Half-Mile Oval," *Birmingham News*, May 28, 1926, 23.

22. "LaCosta Will Pit Her Skill against Green," *Birmingham News*, May 27, 1926, 20.

23. Dolly Dalrymple, "Mlle. Joan LaCosta, 'Meteor Maid,' Disappointingly Unlike Auto Racer," *Birmingham News*, May 28, 1926, 37.

24. Dalrymple, "Mlle. Joan LaCosta, 'Meteor Maid,' Disappointingly Unlike Auto Racer," 37.

25. Dalrymple, "Mlle. Joan LaCosta, 'Meteor Maid,' Disappointingly Unlike Auto Racer," 37.

26. Dalrymple, "Mlle. Joan LaCosta, 'Meteor Maid,' Disappointingly Unlike Auto Racer," 37.

27. "Memphis Will See Young Woman Racer," *Greenwood Commonwealth*, June 7, 1926, 1.

28. "Memphis Will See Young Woman Racer," 1.

CHAPTER SEVEN

1. Chandler Forman, "Joan LaCosta Shatters World's Auto Mark at Hamline: Woman Driver Sets World's Mile Record," *Star Tribune*, June 20, 1926, 25.

2. Dolly Dalrymple, "Mlle. Joan LaCosta, 'Meteor Maid,' Disappointingly Unlike Auto Racer," *Birmingham News*, May 28, 1926, 37.

Chapter Eight

1. "Les Allen Hits Fence in Auto Race at Aurora," *Chicago Tribune*, July 5, 1926, 20.

2. "Les Allen Hits Fence in Auto Race at Aurora," 20.

3. Elinor Hillyer, "Settling Down in the Air," *Atlanta Journal*, April 15, 1928, 87.

4. "Mlle. LaCosta, 'Queen of Speed,' Turned from an Opera Career to the Thrills of Piloting Racing Autos," *Sioux City Journal*, July 5, 1926, 10.

5. "Mlle. LaCosta, 'Queen of Speed,' Turned from an Opera Career to the Thrills of Piloting Racing Autos," 10.

6. "Mlle. LaCosta, 'Queen of Speed,' Turned from an Opera Career to the Thrills of Piloting Racing Autos," 10.

7. "Legion Adds Day Fireworks," *Sioux City Journal*, July 3, 1926, 16.

8. "5,000 Thrilled by Daring Pilots at Legion Races," *Sioux City Journal*, July 6, 1926, 8.

9. "Drivers Protest Woman in Race," *Odgen Standard-Examiner*, August 6, 1926, 9.

10. "Speed Much Safer Than Driving Slow, Says Champ Woman Auto Driver after Accident," *Des Moines Tribune*, August 28, 1926, 2.

11. "Fair's Crowds above Average despite Rains," *Des Moines Register*, September 4, 1926, 3.

12. South Dakota State Fair, advertisement, *Daily Deadwood Pioneer-Times*, September 12, 1926, 5.

Chapter Nine

1. "Survivors of Many Struggles Bring Back Grim Days of War," *Philadelphia Inquirer*, October 13, 1926, 6.

2. "Girl Auto Racer Smashes Record," *Morning Call*, October 4, 1926, 19.

3. "Joan LaCosta Arrives Today for Big Races," *Atlanta Constitution*, October 6, 1926, 11.

4. "Joan Lacoste to Use Duesenberg Racer," *Atlanta Constitution*, October 8, 1926, 9.

5. "Mlle. LaCosta, 'Queen of Speed,' Turned from an Opera Career to the Thrills of Piloting Racing Autos," *Sioux City Journal*, July 5, 1926, 10.

6. "Girl Driver Is Proud of Her Title," *Marshall News Messenger*, November 5, 1926, 5.

7. "Woman Champions," *Popular Mechanics*, December 1926, 182.

Chapter Ten

1. "Martins Wins Two Races at Roby Speedway," *Chicago Tribune*, May 23, 1927, 21.

2. "Girl Auto Racer Willing to Attempt Paris Hop," *Minneapolis Star*, June 16, 1927, 2.

3. "Racer Killed at Fair Track," *Star Tribune*, June 19, 1927, 1.

4. "Speed Kings Say Roby Track in Excellent Racing Conditions," *Photo News-Tribune*, October 25, 1926, 5.

5. Elmo Scott Watson, "Bird Women," *Cuba Review*, September 8, 1927, 7.

6. "Miss Joan LaCosta, World's Champion Racer, Makes Bid for Ocean Flight," *Rock Island Argus*, August 13, 1927, 15.

7. "Mlle. LaCosta Sets Two-Mile Auto Record of 2:18 4–5 on Fair Track," Boyer Air Act Off; Pilot Not Here," *Daily Times*, August 16, 1927, 20.

8. "Big Crowd Is Pleased with Fair," *Quad-City Times*, August 16, 1927, 1, 11.

CHAPTER ELEVEN

1. Elinor Hillyer, "Settling Down in the Air," *Atlanta Journal*, April 15, 1928, 87.

2. Hillyer, "Settling Down in the Air," 87.

3. "Auto Races Pull Overflow Crowd," *Lincoln Journal Star*, September 6, 1927, 10.

4. "Mlle. Lacoste Enters Races at Lakewood," *Atlanta Constitution*, October 6, 1927, 19.

5. Cliff Wheatley, "Greyhounds Give Fans Big Thrill," *Atlanta Constitution*, October 9, 1927, 22.

6. Disbrow-LaCosta Match Is Likely," *Clarion-Ledger*, May 21, 1926, 9.

7. Joan LaCosta Will Drive in Fair Races," *Commercial Appeal*, October 14, 1927, 24.

CHAPTER TWELVE

1. "Flyer and Dancer on Jaycee Program," *Atlanta Constitution*, October 27, 1927, 4.

2. "Artists and Models," *Chicago Tribune*, May 10, 1926, 29.

3. Ben Cooper, "Atlanta's Airport," *Atlanta Constitution*, October 30, 1927, 10.

4. Cooper, "Atlanta's Airport," 10.

5. Eric Malnic, "Pilot Launched Atomic Age over Hiroshima," *Los Angeles Times*, November 2, 2007.

6. "Plane Brings St. Nick Here," *Pensacola News Journal*, December 23, 1928, 24

7. "Tragic Death of Doug Davis Closes Colorful Air Career," *Atlanta Constitution*, September 4, 1934, 1, 10.

8. "Racer in Auto Dives in Sea at 225-Mile Pace," *Evening Journal*, February 23, 1928, 8.

9. "Auto Racer Quits Track for Clouds, Seeking a Career," *Clarion-Ledger*, April 22, 1928, 17.

10. "Find All Dead in Air Liner," *Chicago Tribune*, September 9, 1929, 1.

11. Robert Redwine, "Charred Bodies Carried Down Mountainside," *Chicago Tribune*, September 9, 1929, 1.

CHAPTER THIRTEEN

1. "A Mother's Love Never Dies; an Old, Old Story," *Chicago Tribune*, November 7, 1920, 5.

2. "A Mother's Love Never Dies," 5.

3. "Dry Raids in Loop Area Net Agents 2 Trucks of Liquor," *Chicago Tribune*, November 30, 1929, 5.

4. "Joan La Coste Goes on Stand before Court," *Daily Chronicle*, October 23, 1929, 10.

5. "The Chicago Beach," *National Hotel Reporter*, August 21, 1928, 1.

6. "The Pretty Girl Auto Racer Who Turned Burglar," *San Francisco Examiner*, December 8, 1929, 106.

7. "Girl Red Slicker Bandit Gets One Year to Life," *Austin American-Statesman*, November 1, 1929, 3.

8. "Bandit Tells of Forced Marriage," *El Paso Times*, November 1, 1929, 2.

9. Kathleen McLaughlin, "Girl in Cell as Bandit Baffles Police Quizzers," *Chicago Tribune*, October 5, 1929, 3.

10. McLaughlin, "Girl in Cell as Bandit Baffles Police Quizzers," 3.

11. McLaughlin, "Girl in Cell as Bandit Baffles Police Quizzers," 3.

12. "Joan La Coste, Famous Woman Auto Racer Who Appeared at Fair Here, Held in Chicago for Robbery," *Daily Times*, October 7, 1929, 4.

13. "Woman Auto Racer Caught in Attempted Jewel Robbery," *Commercial Appeal*, October 6, 1929, 14.

14. "Woman Auto Racer Caught in Attempted Jewel Robbery," 14.

15. "A 'Brain Storm,'" *Fort Worth Record-Telegram*, October 7, 1929, 1.

16. "Woman Champion Turns Robber," *Reidsville Review*, October 7, 1929, 1.

17. "Girl Racer under Arrest as Robber," *Kingsport Times*, October 6, 1929, 16.

18. "Joan La Coste, Champion Woman Auto Speed Driver, Is Detained after Hearing in Theft Case," *Times*, October 8, 1929, 1.

19. "Woman Daredevil Wilts in Court," *Joplin Globe*, October 8, 1929, 1.

20. "Woman 'Speed King' Is Held for Holdup," *Miami Herald*, October 8, 1929, 3.

21. "Girl Auto Race Driver Arrested for Robbery," *Morning Call*, October 8, 1929, 1.

22. "Woman 'Speed King' Is Held for Holdup," 3.

CHAPTER FOURTEEN

1. "Friends Go to Aid of Accused Race Driver," *Commercial Appeal*, October 18, 1929, 13.

2. "Friends Go to Aid of Accused Race Driver," 13.

3. Rita Fitzpatrick, "Court to Rule on Review of Borins' Battle," *Chicago Tribune*, November 22, 1946, 22.

4. "Judge in Good Humor as Joan's Trial Is Opened," *Messenger*, October 22, 1929, 5.

5. "Judge in Good Humor as Joan's Trial Is Opened," 5.

6. "Many Dodge Jury Duty in Trial of Girl, Ex-Auto Racer," *Chicago Tribune*, October 22, 1929, 19.

7. "Joan Falls in Faint as She Leaves Stand," *Chicago Tribune*, October 24, 1929, 5.

8. "Joan La Coste Goes on Stand before Court," *Daily Chronicle*, October 23, 1929, 10.

9. "Joan La Coste Goes on Stand before Court," 10.

10. "Joan Falls in Faint as She Leaves Stand," 5.

11. "Joan Falls in Faint as She Leaves Stand," 5.

12. "Joan Falls in Faint as She Leaves Stand," 5.

13. "Demand Prison Term for Woman," *Times*, October 25, 1929, 3.

14. "Joan LaCosta Guilty May Win Clemency," *Commercial Appeal*, October 26, 1929, 15.

15. "Joan LaCosta Guilty May Win Clemency," 15.

16. "Girl Race Driver Collapses When Found Guilty of Attempted Robbery," *Montgomery Advertiser*, October 26, 1929, 1.

17. "Girl Race Driver Collapses When Found Guilty of Attempted Robbery," 1.

18. "Demand Prison Term for Woman," 3.

19. Owen L Scott, "Flapper Bandits in Chicago on Increase," *Times-Tribune*, November 1, 1929, 15.

20. "Girl Red Slicker Bandit Gets One Year to Life," *Austin American-Statesman*, November 1, 1929, 3.

21. "Woman Bandit Is on Trial," *Daily Republican-Register*, October 31, 1929, 2.

22. "Girl 'Slicker Bandit' Found Guilty by Jury," *Chicago Tribune*, November 1, 1929, 20.

23. "Girl 'Slicker Bandit' Found Guilty by Jury," 20.

24. "Girl 'Slicker Bandit' Found Guilty by Jury," 20.

25. "Grand Jury Says Crime Flagrant," *Chattanooga Daily Times*, November 9, 1929, 3.

26. "Girl Auto Race Driver Is Put on Probation," *Rock Island Argus*, November 8, 1929, 18.

27. "Girl Acquitted of Theft Charge Will Seek Plane Career," *Register*, November 10, 1929, 2.

28. "Joan LaCosta to Be Pilot for Air Line," *Democrat and Chronicle*, October 27, 1929, 6.

CHAPTER FIFTEEN

1. "Joan LaCosta, Racing Star, Is to Wed Salesman," *Chicago Tribune*, October 10, 1931, 3.

2. "Scorns 13 as Unlucky Number," *Tampa Daily Times*, January 25, 1934, 9.

3. Henry Vance, "The Coal Bin," *Birmingham News*, October 1, 1946, 11.

4. "Friends Pay Tribute to Woman Racer," *Birmingham Post-Herald*, September 26, 1934, 1.

5. "'Skip' Fordyce to Crash into Board Wall Riding a Fast 'Motorbike,'" *Birmingham News*, September 26, 1934, 2.

6. "Famous Dixie Pilot Dies in Holiday Race; Victory in His Grasp," *Johnson City Chronicle*, September 4, 1934, 1.

7. "Eye Witness to Doug Davis' Crash Relates How Flyer Went to Death," *Atlanta Constitution*, September 4, 1934, 8.

CHAPTER SIXTEEN

1. "Woman Auto Racer Takes Treatment for Nerve Trouble," *Tallahassee Democrat*, August 4, 1937, 8.

2. "Woman Auto Racer Takes Treatment for Nerve Trouble," 8.

3. "Woman Auto Racer Takes Treatment for Nerve Trouble," 8.

4. W. Kent Jenkins, "Daredevils for Profit, Thrill & Publicity," *Atlanta Constitution*, March 13, 1932, 53.

5. "Comets," *Paducah Sun*, January 27, 1910, 4.

Selected Bibliography

"1928 First Flying Club." Aviation Chicago. https://www.aviation-chicago.com/timeline
/excerpts/26-1928-first-flying-club (accessed March 10, 2024).

"5,000 Thrilled by Daring Pilots at Legion Races." *Sioux City Journal*, July 6, 1926.
Newspapers.com.

"Another Star Enters Races at Lakewood." *Atlanta Constitution*, May 6, 1926.
Newspapers.com.

"Artists and Models." *Chicago Tribune*, May 10, 1926. Newspapers.com.

"Auto Racer Quits Track for Clouds, Seeking a Career." *Clarion-Ledger*, April 22, 1928.
Newspapers.com.

"Auto Races Pull Overflow Crowd." *Lincoln Journal Star*, September 6, 1927.
Newspapers.com.

"Auto Racing Tomorrow." *Gazette*, August 22, 1925. Newspapers.com.

"Auto Speed Stars Ready for Trials at Fair Grounds." *Clarion-Ledger*, May 26, 1926.
Newspapers.com.

"Auto Speed Trials Draw Great Crowd, No Records Broken." *Clarion-Ledger*, May 27,
1926. Newspapers.com.

"Bandit Tells of Forced Marriage." *El Paso Times*, November 1, 1929. Newspapers.com.

"Big Crowd Is Pleased with Fair." *Quad-City Times*, August 16, 1927. Newspapers.com.

Bortle, John W. "The Great Daylight Comet of 1910," *Sky & Telescope*, January 13, 2010,
https://skyandtelescope.org/astronomy-news/the-great-daylight-comet-of1910
(accessed February 11, 2024).

"Car Burns; 'Will Drive Wheels Off,' Says Woman Racer." *Journal Times*, April 16, 1926.
Newspapers.com.

Carver, W. M. "New Marble Shop." Advertisement. *News Democrat*, December 27, 1901.
Newspapers.com.

"Champ Dirt Track Driver in Tri-State Fair Auto Races." *Commercial Appeal*, September
26, 1915. Newspapers.com.

Chevrolet, Arthur, and Louis Chevrolet. *Frontenac Cylinder Heads and Fronty Racing
Cars: Speed Specialties and Racing Units*. Indianapolis, IN: Chevrolet Bros. Mfg.
Co., April 1, 1925.

"The Chicago Beach." *National Hotel Reporter*, August 21, 1928. Newspapers.com.

"Cliff Woodbury Wins Auto Race at North Shore." *Chicago Tribune*, June 15, 1925.
Newspapers.com.

Cooper, Ben. "Atlanta's Airport." *Atlanta Constitution*, October 30, 1927. Newspapers.com.

Dalrymple, Dolly. "Mlle. Joan LaCosta, 'Meteor Maid,' Disappointingly Unlike Auto Racer." *Birmingham News*, May 28, 1926. Newspapers.com.

"Daredevil Drivers Here for Auto Meet." *Montreal Star*, August 21, 1925. Newspapers.com.

"Demand Prison Term for Woman." *Times*, October 25, 1929. Newspapers.com.

"Disbrow Arraigned in Federal Court on Liquor Charge." *Atlanta Constitution*, May 18, 1926. Newspapers.com.

"Disbrow in Montreal." *Gazette*, August 20, 1925. Newspapers.com.

"Disbrow Jealous, Is Reply of Girl Racing Driver." *Atlanta Constitution*, May 6, 1926. Newspapers.com.

"Disbrow Unwilling to Meet Woman Speed Champ in Local Racing Classic." *Montgomery Advertiser*, May 8, 1926. Newspapers.com.

"Disbrow-LaCosta Match Is Likely." *Clarion-Ledger*, May 21, 1926. Newspapers.com.

"Drivers Protest Woman in Race." *Ogden Standard-Examiner*, August 6, 1926. Newspapers.com.

"Dry Raids in Loop Area Net Agents 2 Trucks of Liquor." *Chicago Tribune*, November 30, 1929. Newspapers.com.

Edgewater Flying Club, Inc., "Fly with Us." Advertisement. *Aeronautics*, September 1929. Google Books.

"Exchangites Honor Ladies at Banquet." *Clarion-Ledger*, May 25, 1926. Newspapers.com.

"Eye Witness to Doug Davis' Crash Relates How Flyer Went to Death." *Atlanta Constitution*, September 4, 1934. Newspapers.com.

"Fair's Crowds above Average despite Rains." *Des Moines Register*, September 4, 1926. Newspapers.com.

"Famous Dixie Pilot Dies in Holiday Rrace; Victory in His Grasp." *Johnson City Chronicle*, September 4, 1934. Newspapers.com.

"Famous Veteran of Dirt Track Drivers to Match Skill against Lampkin." *Democrat and Chronicle*, August 30, 1925. Newspapers.com.

"Famous Woman Auto Racer to Drive in Wichita Races." *Wichita Beacon*, June 28, 1916. Newspapers.com.

"Find All Dead in Air Liner." *Chicago Tribune*, September 9, 1929. Newspapers.com.

Fitzpatrick, Rita. "Court to Rule on Review of Borins' Battle." *Chicago Tribune*, November 22, 1946. Newspapers.com.

"Flyer and Dancer on Jaycee Program." *Atlanta Constitution*, October 27, 1927. Newspapers.com.

Forman, Chandler. "Joan LaCosta Shatters World's Auto Mark at Hamline: Woman Driver Sets World's Mile Record." *Star Tribune*, June 20, 1926. Newspapers.com.

"Friends Go to Aid of Accused Race Driver." *Commercial Appeal*, October 18, 1929. Newspapers.com.

"Friends Pay Tribute to Woman Racer." *Birmingham Post-Herald*, September 26, 1934. Newspapers.com.

"Gas!." *Chicago Tribune*, May 18, 1924. Newspapers.com.

"Girl Acquitted of Theft Charge Will Seek Plane Career." *Register*, November 10, 1929. Newspapers.com.

"Girl Auto Pilot Flirts with Death When Mount Flashes through Fence." *Star Tribune*, July 5, 1924. Newspapers.com.

"Girl Auto Race Driver Arrested for Robbery." *Morning Call*, October 8, 1929. Newspapers.com.

"Girl Auto Race Driver Is Put on Probation." *Rock Island Argus*, November 8, 1929. Newspapers.com.

"Girl Auto Racer Smashes Record." *Morning Call*, October 4, 1926. Newspapers.com.

"Girl Auto Racer Willing to Attempt Paris Hop." *Minneapolis Star*, June 16, 1927. Newspapers.com.

"Girl Champion to Try for Records in Jackson." *Clarion-Ledger*, May 21, 1926. Newspapers.com.

"Girl Driver Is Proud of Her Title." *Marshall News Messenger*, November 5, 1926. Newspapers.com.

"Girl Race Driver Collapses When Found Guilty of Attempted Robbery." *Montgomery Advertiser*, October 26, 1929. Newspapers.com.

"Girl Racer under Arrest as Robber." *Kingsport Times*, October 6, 1929. Newspapers.com.

"Girl Red Slicker Bandit Gets One Year to Life." *Austin American-Statesman*, November 1, 1929. Newspapers.com.

"Girl 'Slicker Bandit' Found Guilty by Jury." *Chicago Tribune*, November 1, 1929. Newspapers.com.

"Grand Jury Says Crime Flagrant." *Chattanooga Daily Times*, November 9, 1929. Newspapers.com.

"Her Smile Robbers' Lure." *Chicago Tribune*, September 30, 1923. Newspapers.com.

Hillyer, Elinor. "Settling Down in the Air." *Atlanta Journal*, April 15, 1928. Newspapers.com.

"Historic Memphis Train Stations and the Memphis Street Railway." https://historic-memphis.com/memphis-historic/trainstations/trainstations.html (accessed February 11, 2024).

"Horey, Watters, Disbrow and Girl Driver Entered in Fair's Closing Events." *Atlanta Constitution*, October 17, 1925. Newspapers.com.

Illinois, Cook County Marriages, 1871–1968. Entry for Joseph S Maurer and Marion Joan Martins, October 3, 1931.

"J. Alex Sloan." Iowa Hall of Fame & Racing Museum, March 24, 2018. http://www.iowaracingmuseum.com/hall-of-fame/legendary-inductees (accessed February 18, 2024).

"J. Alex Sloan." National Sprint Car Hall of Fame & Museum, 1990. https://www.sprintcarhof.com/pages/hall-of-fame.aspx (accessed February 18, 2024).

Jenkins, W. Kent. "Daredevils for Profit, Thrill & Publicity." *Atlanta Constitution*, March 13, 1932. Newspapers.com.

"Joan Falls in Faint as She Leaves Stand." *Chicago Tribune*, October 24, 1929. Newspapers.com.

"Joan LaCosta Arrives Today for Big Races." *Atlanta Constitution*, October 6, 1926. Newspapers.com.

"Joan LaCosta Racing Star, Is Wed to Salesman." *Chicago Tribune*, October 10, 1931. Newspapers.com.

"Joan LaCosta Will Drive in Fair Races." *Commercial Appeal*, October 14, 1927. Newspapers.com.

"Joan LaCoste, Champion Woman Auto Speed Driver, Is Detained after Hearing in Theft Case." *Times*, October 8, 1929. Newspapers.com.

"Joan LaCoste, Famous Woman Auto Race Driver Who Appeared at Fair Here, Held in Chicago for Robbery." *Daily Times*, October 7, 1929. Newspapers.com.

"Joan LaCoste Goes On Stand before Court." *Daily Chronicle*, October 23, 1929. Newspapers.com.

"Joan LaCoste Guilty May Win Clemency." *Commercial Appeal*, October 26, 1929. Newspapers.com.

"Joan LaCoste to Be Pilot for Air Line." *Democrat and Chronicle*, October 27, 1929. Newspapers.com.

"Joan LaCoste to Use Duesenberg Racer." *Atlanta Constitution*, October 8, 1926. Newspapers.com.

Johnson, D. W., et al. "Periodical Cicadas in Kentucky." Lexington: University of Kentucky College of Agriculture, Food, and Environment, 2020.

"Judge in Good Humor as Joan's Trial Is Opened." *Messenger*, October 22, 1929. Newspapers.com.

Kemp, Bill. "Life of 1920s Bloomington Race Driver Filled with Mystery." *Pantagraph*, August 14, 2011. https://pantagraph.com/news/local/life-of-1920s-bloomington-race-driver-filled-with-mystery/article_f31687da-c613-11e0-8121-001cc4c002e0.html (accessed February 11, 2024).

Kentucky, Office of Vital Certificates. Marriage Certificate Record Book A-2, page 398. Entry for Walter Martins and Marion Huddleston, February 14, 1921.

"LaCosta Will Pit Her Skill against Green." *Birmingham News*, May 27, 1926. Newspapers.com.

"LaCosta Suffers Injured Ankle." *Atlanta Constitution*, May 8, 1926. Newspapers.com.

"LaCosta to Race Disbrow Saturday despite Illness." *Atlanta Constitution*, May 14, 1926. Newspapers.com.

"LaCosta-Disbrow Will Match Speed on Local Track." *Clarion-Ledger*, May 22, 1926. Newspapers.com.

"Lampkin Sets New Dirt Track Records in Auto Race Classic." *Montgomery Advertiser*, May 13, 1926. Newspapers.com.

"Lampkin Sets New Record in Montgomery Race." *Atlanta Constitution*, May 13, 1926. Newspapers.com.

Lawrence, Bob. "James Jim 'Jimmie' Costa, Jr." Bob Lawrence's Vintage Auto Racing Web Ring for Kansas Racing History, https://kansasracinghistory.com/tripod/Costa/Jimmie-Costa.htm (accessed February 25, 2924).

"Legion Adds Day Fireworks." *Sioux City Journal*, July 3, 1926. Newspapers.com.

"Les Allen Hits Fence in Auto Race at Aurora." *Chicago Tribune*, July 5, 1926. Newspapers.com.

"A Lesson in the Curriculum of World's Records." Skandinaviske Berliner Korrespondenz, April 14, 1926. Author's collection.

"Louis Disbrow 'Soak' Wife Says in Petition." *Tulsa World*, December 6, 1922. Newspapers.com.

"Louis Disbrow Refuses to Race against LaCosta." *Atlanta Constitution*, May 4, 1926. Newspapers.com.

Malnic, Eric. "Pilot Launched Atomic Age over Hiroshima." *Los Angeles Times*, November 2, 2007. https://www.latimes.com/archives/la-xpm-2007-nov-02-me-tibbets2-story.html (accessed March 10, 2024).

"Many Dodge Jury Duty in Trial of Girl, Ex-Auto Racer." *Chicago Tribune*, October 22, 1929. Newspapers.com.

"Marion Martin Challenges Lady Auto Racing Champion." *Calgary Herald*, July 8, 1925. Newspapers.com.

"Martins Wins Two at Roby Speedway." *Times*, May 23, 1927. Newspapers.com.

McCutcheon, John T. "Amending the Declaration of Independence." Cartoon. *Chicago Tribune*, July 5, 1926. Newspapers.com.

———. "Disaster Is a Stimulant to American Cities." Cartoon. *Miami Herald*, September 24, 1926. Newspapers.com.

———. "The Battle for the Front Page." Cartoon. *Chicago Tribune*, September 9, 1929. Newspapers.com.

———. "Taken for a Ride." Cartoon. *Chicago Tribune*, October 25, 1929. Newspapers.com.

McLaughlin, Kathleen. "Girl in Cell as Bandit Baffles Police Quizzers." *Chicago Tribune*, October 5, 1929. Newspapers.com.

"Memphis Will See Young Woman Racer." *Greenwood Commonwealth*, June 7, 1926. Newspapers.com.

"Mile a Minute Pace Made by Youthful Woman Pilot Great Crowd Cheers Racers." *Clarion-Ledger*, October 23, 1925. Newspapers.com.

"Miss Joan LaCosta, World's Champion Woman Racer, Makes Bid for Ocean Flight." *Rock Island Argus*, August 13, 1927. Newspapers.com.

"Mlle. LaCosta, Speed Queen, Accepts Louis Disbrow's Challenge for Match Race." *Atlanta Journal*, May 9, 1926. Newspapers.com.

"Mlle. LaCosta, 'Queen of Speed,' Turned from an Opera Career to the Thrills of Piloting Racing Autos." *Sioux City Journal*, July 5, 1926. Newspapers.com.

"Mlle. LaCosta Sets Two-Mile Auto Record of 2:18 4-5 on Fair Track; Boyer Air Act Off; Pilot Not Here." *Daily Times*, August 16, 1927. Newspapers.com.

"Mlle. Lacoste Enters Races at Lakewood." *Atlanta Constitution*, October 6, 1927. Newspapers.com.

"Montgomery to Have Auto Races on May 12th." *Weekly Herald*, May 6, 1926. Newspapers.com.

"A Mother's Love Never Dies; an Old, Old Story." *Chicago Tribune*, November 7, 1920. Newspapers.com.

"Mrs. J. Alex Sloan Succumbs to Burns." *Jackson Daily News*, April 18, 1919. Newspapers.com.

"Pilot Is Killed in Speed Trial at Roby Track." *Chicago Tribune*, June 8, 1925. Newspapers.com.

"Plane Brings St. Nick Here." *Pensacola News Journal*, December 23, 1928. Newspapers.com.

"The Pretty Girl Auto Racer Who Turned Burglar." *San Francisco Examiner*, December 8, 1929. Newspapers.com.

"Pretty Jean on Trial." *Daily Independent*, October 21, 1929. Newspapers.com.

"Race Board Declares LaCosta Is Eligible for Lakewood Events." *Atlanta Constitution*, May 8, 1926. Newspapers.com.

"Racer in Auto Drives in Sea at 225-Mile Pace." *Evening Journal*, February 23, 1928. Newspapers.com.

"Racer Killed at Fair Track." *Star Tribune*, June 19, 1927. Newspapers.com.

Radbruch, Don. *Dirt Track Auto Racing 1919–1941 A Pictorial History*. Jefferson, NC: McFarland, 2004.

Rasmussen, P. V., photographer. "A Lesson in the Curriculum of World's Records." Photograph. Skandinaviske Berliner Korrespondenz, April 14, 1926. Author's collection.

Redwine, Robert. "Charred Bodies Carried Down Mountainside." *Chicago Tribune*, September 9, 1929. Newspapers.com.

"Scorns 13 as Unlucky Number." *Tampa Times*, January 25, 1934. Newspapers.com.

Scott, Owen L. "Flapper Bandits in Chicago on Increase." *Times-Tribune*, November 1, 1929. Newspapers.com.

"Sig Haughdahl and Mlle. Martens, French Pilot, to Head Program of Events." *Democrat and Chronicle*, August 29, 1925. Newspapers.com.

"'Skip' Fordyce to Crash into Board Wall Riding a Fast 'Motorbike.'" *Birmingham News*, September 26, 1934. Newspapers.com.

South Dakota State Fair. Advertisement. *Daily Deadwood Pioneer-Times*, September 12, 1926. Newspapers.com.

"Speed Car Events Promise Exciting Races Wednesday." *Clarion-Ledger*, May 2, 1926. Newspapers.com.

"Speed Fans Howl Their Mightiest as Cars Roar around Exhibition Oval." *Edmonton Journal*, July 14, 1925. Newspapers.com.

"Speed Kings Say Palace Tracks in Excellent Racing Condition." *Waco News-Tribune*, October 25, 1926. Newspapers.com.

"Speed Much Safer Than Slow Driving, Says Champ Woman Auto Driver after Accident." *Des Moines Tribune*, August 28, 1926. Newspapers.com.

"Speed Queen Will Arrive Here Today." *Atlanta Constitution*, May 7, 1926. Newspapers.com.

Speedo. "New Marks Promised for Half-Mile Oval." *Birmingham News*, May 28, 1926. Newspapers.com.

"Sports." *Forest Park Review*, July 12, 1924. Newspapers.com.

"Survivors of Many Struggles Bring Back Grim Days of War." *Philadelphia Inquirer*, October 13, 1926. Newspapers.com.

"Sweepstakes to Feature Jubilee Auto Race Meet." *Calgary Albertan*, July 10, 1925. Newspapers.com.

Taylor, Sec. "Sittin' In with the Athletes." *Des Moines Register*, June 17, 1936. Newspapers.com.

"Tommy Milton Tells of His Racing Experiences." *Fort Wayne Sentinel*, March 6, 1920. Newspapers.com.

"Track Fit for 'Dust-Dogs' to Go Their Best." *Leader-Post*, July 2, 1925. Newspapers.com.

"Tragic Death of Doug Davis Closes Colorful Air Career." *Atlanta Constitution*, September 4, 1934. Newspapers.com.

"Two Foreign Stars to Appear in Auto Races Here May 12." *Montgomery Advertiser*, April 30, 1926. Newspapers.com.

U.S. Census Bureau, Cook County Illinois, 1910. https://data.census.gov.

———. 1920. https://data.census.gov.

———. 1930. https://data.census.gov.

"U.S. Lady Champ Loses to French Girl Race Driver." *Leader-Post*, July 3, 1925. Newspapers.com.

Vance, Henry. "The Coal Bin." *Birmingham News*, October 1, 1946. Newspapers.com.

"Veteran Auto Race Driver to Appear in Classic at Fair Grounds May 12." *Montgomery Advertiser*, May 4, 1926. Newspapers.com.

"Wages and Hours of Labor." *Monthly Labor Review* 28, no. 1 (1929): 128–41. http://www.jstor.org/stable/41813501 (accessed March 4, 2024).

Watson, Elmo Scott. "Bird Women." *Cuba Review*, September 8, 1927. Newspapers.com.

"Watters Here for Fair Races." *Atlanta Constitution*, October 7, 1925. Newspapers.com.

"What the Marble Shooters of Other Cities Are Doing." *Dispatch*, June 4, 1926. Newspapers.com.

Wheatley, Cliff. "Greyhounds Give Fans Big Thrill." *Atlanta Constitution*, October 9, 1927. Newspapers.com.

Williams, Gordon. "In the Realm of Sports." *Reading Times*, August 30, 1935. Newspapers.com.

"Woman Auto Racer Caught in Attempted Jewel Robbery." *Commercial Appeal*, October 6, 1929. Newspapers.com.

"Woman Auto Racer Takes Treatment for Nerve Trouble." *Tallahassee Democrat*, August 4, 1937. Newspapers.com.

"Woman Bandit Is on Trial." *Daily Republican-Register*, October 31, 1929. Newspapers.com.

"Woman Champion Turns Robber." *Reidsville Review*, October 7, 1929. Newspapers.com.

"Woman Champions" Montage. Photograph. *Popular Mechanics*, December 1926. https://archive.org/details/PopularMechanics1926/Popular_Mechanics_12_1926/page/n181/mode/2up (accessed March 9, 2024).

"Woman Daredevil Killed in Stunt. *Brooklyn Daily Eagle*, September 25, 1924. Newspapers.com.

"Woman Daredevil Wilts in Court." *Joplin Globe*, October 8, 1929. Newspapers.com.

"Woman Driver of Racing Car Has Test of Nerve." *Bridgeport Telegram*, April 30, 1926. Newspapers.com.

"Woman Driver Will Try to Break Dirt Track Records." *Clarion-Ledger*, October 22, 1925. Newspapers.com.

"Woman 'Speed King' Is Held for Holdup." *Miami Herald*, October 8, 1929. Newspapers.com.

"Women in Transportation History: Joan Newton Cuneo, Race Car Pioneer and Good Roads Advocate." *Women in Transportation History*, March 31, 2021. https://transportationhistory.org/2021/03/31/women-in-transportation-history-joan-newton-cuneo-race-car-pioneer-and-good-roads-advocate (accessed February 18, 2024).

Woodard, M. L. "On Automobile Row." *Lincoln Nebraska State Journal*, September 5, 1926. Newspapers.com.

"Wreck Reenacted as Cameras Click," April 15, 1926.

PERIODICALS

Abbeville Herald
Akron Beacon Journal
Albuquerque Journal
Argus-Leader
Arizona Republic
Arkansas Democrat
Asbury Park Press
Atlanta Constitution
Atlanta Journal
Atoka County Jeffersonian
Austin American-Statesman
Bakersfield Morning Echo
Belvidere Daily Republican
Benton Advocate
Berkshire County Eagle
Billings Gazette
Birmingham News
Birmingham Post-Herald
Blockton Enterprise
Boston Globe
Bradford Evening Star and Daily Record
Bridgeport Telegram
Brooklyn Citizen
Brooklyn Daily Eagle
Brownsville Herald
Buffalo Courier Express
Buffalo Times
Bureau County Tribune
Burlington Free Press
Calgary Albertan

Calgary Herald
Capital Times
Carbondale Free Press
Casper Star-Tribune
Central New Jersey Home News
Charleston Daily Mail
Charlotte Observer
Chattanooga Daily Times
Chattanooga News
Chicago Tribune
Chillicothe Constitution-Tribune
Cincinnati Enquirer
Clarion-Ledger
Commercial Appeal
Courier-Post
Coshocton Tribune
Courier
Courier-Journal
Cuba Review
Daily Advertiser
Daily Chronicle
Daily Deadwood Pioneer-Times
Daily Herald
Daily Independent
Daily News
Daily Oklahoman
Daily Press
Daily Record
Daily Register
Daily Republican-Register

Davis Reflex-Journal
Daily Sentinel
Daily Times
Dayton Daily News
Dayton Herald
Decatur Daily News
Decatur Herald
Democrat and Chronicle
Des Moines Register
Des Moines Tribune
Detroit Free Press
Dispatch
Edmonton Journal
Edwardsville Intelligencer
El Paso Herald
El Paso Times
Evansville Press
Evening Herald Courier
Evening Journal
Evening News
Forest Park Review
Fort Lauderdale News
Fort Wayne Sentinel
Fort Worth Record-Telegram
Fort Worth Star-Telegram
Freeport Journal-Standard
Fresno Morning Republican
Gazette
Grand Forks Herald
Great Falls Tribune
Green Bay Press-Gazette
Greenville News
Greenwood Commonwealth
Harrisburg Telegraph
Hartford Courant
Herald and Review
Herald-Press
Honolulu Advertiser
Honolulu Star-Bulletin
Hutchinson News
Indiana Gazette
Indianapolis News
Indianapolis Star
International Banker

Iowa City Press-Citizen
Jackson Daily News
Jefferson City Post-Tribune
Johnson City Chronicle
Johnson City Staff-News
Joplin Globe
Journal Gazette
Journal Times
Kansas City Star
Kansas Labor Weekly
Kentucky Post and Times-Star
Kingsport Times
Knoxville Journal
Knoxville News-Sentinel
La Crosse Tribune
Lansing State Journal
Latrobe Bulletin
Leader-Post
Lebanon Daily News
Lima Morning Star and Republican-Gazette
Lincoln Journal Star
Lincoln Nebraska State Journal
Lincoln Star
London Illustrated News
Los Angeles Evening Express
Los Angeles Evening Post-Record
Los Angeles Times
Macon News
Marshall News Messenger
Messenger
Miami Herald
Miami News
Miami Tribune
Minneapolis Journal
Minneapolis Star
Montgomery Advertiser
Montreal Star
Morning Call
Morning News
Muncie Evening Press
Muscatine Journal
Muskogee Daily Phoenix and Times-Democrat
Nashville Banner
National Hotel Reporter

New York Herald Tribune
News-Democrat
News Journal
News-Press
News-Record
Oakland Tribune
Ogden Standard-Examiner
Orlando Sentinel
Ottawa Citizen
Ottawa Journal
Owensboro Messenger
Pacific Transcript
Paducah Sun
Paducah Sun-Democrat
Palm Beach Post
Pensacola News Journal
Pentagraph
Philadelphia Inquirer
Pickens County Herald and West Alabamian
Pittsburgh Post-Gazette
Pittsburgh Sun-Telegraph
Post-Crescent
Quad-City Times
Rapid City Journal
Record
Reading Times
Register
Reidsville Review
Representative
Republican and Herald
Republican-Northwestern
Ridgewood Herald
Roanoke Times
Rock Island Argus
Rushville Republican
Rutland Daily Herald
Rutland News
Sacramento Bee
San Bernadino County Sun
San Francisco Examiner
Sand Mountain Banner
Santa Barbara News-Press
Santa Cruz Sentinel
Saskatoon Daily Star

Shreveport Journal
Sioux City Journal
Spokesman-Review
Springfield News-Leader
St. Joseph Gazette
St. Louis Globe-Democrat
St. Louis Post-Dispatch
Standard Union
Star Press
Star Tribune
Star-Gazette
Star-Phoenix
Sterling Daily Gazette
Stockton Independent
Suburbanite Economist
Sun Herald
Tampa Bay Times
Tampa Times
Tampa Tribune
Tallahassee Democrat
Tennessean
Terre Haute Star
Terre Haute Tribune
Times
Times-Democrat
Times-Tribune
Times Union
Toronto Star
Tribune
Tulsa Daily Register
Tulsa World
Valley Morning Star
Waco News-Tribune
Waco Times-Herald
Washington Gazette
Weekly Herald
Wetskiwin Times
Wichita Beacon
Wiregrass Farmer
Wisconsin State Journal
Women in Motorsport
Wood County Reporter
Yazoo Herald
Yonkers Statesman

Acknowledgments

This book would not exist without the efforts of Kate Piatt-Eckert. From the editing of the first draft to the compilation of the bibliography, she was instrumental in the shaping and polishing of this story. I thank her for making all of this possible.

Toni Cooksey (Joan's daughter) and her daughter Sarah Lawrence graciously invited me into their lives and their home. Their insights and direct connection to Joan LaCosta helped make her come alive to me as her biographer. My gratitude is immeasurable.

Thanks to my agent Najla Mamou, who advocated for Joan's story from her first read-through, and Brittany Stoner, whose guidance through the publishing process has been invaluable.

Fellow author Tim Hillegonds has been an inspiration both with his literary journey and with his kind advice, as has Karen Beattie, who gave me insightful feedback early in the process.

On a more personal level, there have been many supporters of my creative efforts, notably Terran McCanna, Ted Douglass, Deb "Kit" Gorman, Jason Rouse, Lori Ferraro, Emily Baxter, Sean McGrath, and Jim White and Margaret Piatt. Thank you for your perennial encouragement.

Index